NONPROFITS IN CRISIS

PHILANTHROPIC AND NONPROFIT STUDIES

Dwight F. Burlingame and David C. Hammack, *editors*

NONPROFITS in CRISIS

Economic Development, Risk,
and the Philanthropic Kuznets Curve

Nuno S. Themudo

Indiana University Press

Bloomington and Indianapolis

This book is a publication of

Indiana University Press
Office of Scholarly Publishing
Herman B Wells Library 350
1320 East 10th Street
Bloomington, Indiana 47405 USA

iupress.indiana.edu

Telephone orders   800–842–6796
Fax orders   812–855–7931

Themudo, Nuno S.
    Nonprofits in crisis : economic development, risk, and the
philanthropic Kuznets curve / Nuno S. Themudo.
        pages cm. — (Philanthropic and nonprofit studies)
    Includes bibliographical references and index.
    ISBN 978-0-253-00685-1 (cloth : alk. paper) — ISBN 978-0-253-
00695-0 (ebook) 1. Nonprofit organizations—Management—
Case studies.   2. Nonprofit organizations—Finance—Case studies.
I. Title.
    HD62.6.T525 2013
    338.7—dc23   2013016441

1 2 3 4 5   17 16 15 14 13

To my lovely family

Contents

Preface

Why do some countries have a strong nonprofit sector while others do not? This book offers a new answer to this question by focusing on a neglected puzzle: the fact that Mexico—a democratic, middle-income country—has the weakest nonprofit sector in the world. Cross-national analysis reveals that, far from being exceptional, Mexico fits into a broader pattern. Middle-income countries such as Mexico, Brazil, and India tend to have smaller nonprofit sectors than both rich and poor countries. Moreover, middle-income countries typically have the lowest levels of philanthropy, civic participation, and social capital. I label this puzzling nonlinear relationship between level of economic development and nonprofit sector strength the "philanthropic Kuznets curve" (PKC), because its U-shape resembles the famous Kuznets curve. The PKC challenges existing theories of the nonprofit sector, which predict a linear relationship with economic development. To explain the PKC, the study develops a new theoretical framework and tests it using advanced statistical methods for cross-national analysis as well as detailed qualitative and quantitative analysis of Mexico.

This book draws on economic and game theory to develop a new theoretical explanation of nonprofit sector strength based on the impact of economic risk. Middle-income countries are disproportionately exposed to macroeconomic crises and instability, which create risk for middle-income countries' citizens and organizations. The nonprofit sector is especially vulnerable to such systematic economic risk, because it has more limited opportunities to access capital and insurance markets than do government and business. The problem is compounded by the fact that in high-risk economies, donors are likely to heavily discount the future, being even less likely than in more stable economies to support the development of nonprofits' long-term capacity and capital base, which are essential for the sustainability of the sector. Consequently, both philanthropy and the nonprofit sector tend to be weaker in middle-income countries than in rich and poor countries.

This theoretical explanation also predicts that nonprofits in fields of activity with shorter-term impacts, such as emergency food assistance, are less likely to be adversely affected by macroeconomic risk than those in fields with longer-term impacts, such as environmental conservation. Moreover, nonprofits in high-risk environments will be more likely to be resource-dependent on commercial activities, because nonprofit income from philanthropy and government grants is likely to be more adversely affected by risk than income from commercial sales. Economic volatility and risk, therefore, is hypothesized to have a profound influence over the nature and strength of the nonprofit sector, helping to explain the puzzling PKC.

On the cusp of what has been termed the "Great Recession" (2008–2009), this book's focus on the impact of economic crises and risk on the nonprofit sector is timely. On March 9, 2009, the Dow Jones closed at 6,547, down from 14,164 on October 9, 2007. Although officially the recession ended in June of 2009 in the United States, the impact of this epochal decline will probably still be felt for many years. Indeed, five years later, the Dow Jones has still not recovered. Perceptions of risk relating to the stock market, and even traditionally safe investments such as housing, have fundamentally changed. Current political debates focus on the crisis's effects, such as unemployment and the high level of public debt that has resulted from government efforts to stimulate the economy. The Great Recession reminded everyone, even those in relatively stable economies, that the effects of economic shocks are often profound and persistent.

To test and refine its risk-based explanation of philanthropy and nonprofit sector strength, this book combines econometric examination of cross-national data with a detailed study of the effects on Mexican nonprofits of the so-called Tequila Crisis, which devastated the Mexican economy in the mid-1990s. As I wrote this book, I was struck by the similarities between the "Great Recession" and the "Tequila Crisis." Findings from organizational case studies, organizational registration data, and a random survey of Mexican nonprofit leaders before, during, and after the crisis coalesce around the profound impact of macroeconomic volatility and risk. Available data on the impacts of the Great Recession on the nonprofit sector in the United States are broadly consistent with the analysis of the Mexican nonprofit sector. Similarly, analysis of cross-national evidence lends strong support to the theorized relationship between level of economic development, macroeconomic risk, and nonprofit sector strength. The empirical analysis shows that high levels of economic risk can lead to a stubborn "risk trap" that undermines nonprofit sector development. In high-risk environments, nonprofits have a greater need for capital, liquidity, and reserves, but ironically stakeholders are less likely to support capital accumulation than in more stable ones. Constant organizational change in reaction to a short and intense macroeconomic cycle and the high death rate among local nonprofits in risky environments increases the mismatch between donor interests and organizational priorities (i.e., "philanthropic friction"), further undermining supporters' propensity to support nonprofits in the long term. This analysis helps to explain why economically unstable middle-income countries, such as Brazil, India, and Turkey, tend to have very weak nonprofit sectors and low levels of philanthropy, volunteerism, and civic participation. It also helps to explain why the nonprofit sector is stronger in more stable environments. If, as many commentators now warn, economic volatility is on the rise everywhere, then understanding how nonprofits cope with macroeconomic risk is particularly pressing.

During my field work in Mexico, I was struck by the silence in the media and academia about the impact of the Tequila Crisis on the nonprofit sector. As Mexican society obsessed about banks and the peso, the heroic struggles of nonprofits focusing on equally important issues, such as improving the life of poor, indigenous communities, and children with special needs, were sidelined. This book is also an effort to tell some of those stories. Like so many other books on the nonprofit sector, this book documents widespread heroism in the nonprofit sector. But it also highlights great fragility and vulnerability, as this research allowed me to witness the complex dynamics and many of the inescapable contradictions involved in nonprofits' efforts to generate social change in risky environments. I believe it is only by recognizing our weaknesses that we can address them. In this sense, this book is more than a study: it is a call to action. Many nonprofit entrepreneurs told me that they couldn't afford to think about economic risk and had instead to hope for the best. Risk remained an intangible concept, out of minds and balance sheets—until it materialized. Similarly, government officials systematically transferred risk to nonprofits, because they wrongly assumed that risk is better managed when it is privatized. Such attitudes endanger the effectiveness and sustainability of the nonprofit sector. Psychologists and behavioral economists have often demonstrated that our thinking about risk is not always sound. Nonprofit leaders and policy makers must, therefore, manage risk deliberately. This book makes several specific policy and management recommendations to this effect, the most notable of which is that international donor agencies should create a financial "liquidity facility" to aid the nonprofit sector in countries experiencing macroeconomic crises. We must recognize that while nonprofit organizations may not be "too big to fail," they are too important to fail. This is especially true during times of macroeconomic distress.

Many people have contributed to this project. I would like to especially thank the members of Mexican nonprofits—too many to name here—who generously gave their time, often when they had no time to give. Several colleagues offered insightful suggestions and invaluable critiques of drafts. In particular, I want to thank Lisa Alfredson, Helmut Anheier, Beate Antonich, Lord Ralf Dahrendorf, David Hammack, Sarabajaya Kumar, David Lewis, Danielle Loustau-Williams, Alejandro Natal, Hakan Seckinelgin, and the anonymous reviewers. I presented parts of this study at the conferences of the Association of Researchers on Nonprofit Organization and Voluntary Action, International Society for Third-Sector Research and International Studies Association, benefiting from thoughtful audience feedback. I can recall specific suggestions made by David Billis, Ramon Borges-Mendez, Alnoor Ebrahim, Mike Edwards, Femida Handy, Margaret Harris, Hagai Katz, and Jon Van Til, all of which I tried to incorporate in this study. I benefited greatly from classes with Professors Christopher Pissarides and Peter Abell at the London School of Economics, which opened my eyes to the importance of market frictions, risk, and the critical role of institutions. I would also like to thank several people at Indiana University Press, who patiently supported and guided this publishing venture, especially Dwight Burlingame, David Hammack, Robert Sloan, and Angela Burton. Carol Kennedy did a superb job copyediting the manuscript. At the University of Pittsburgh, I benefited from the trust and support of John Keeler, Kerry Ban, Paul Nelson, Kevin Kearns, and Lou Picard.

Funding for various stages of the research was generously provided by the European Union's Fourth Framework Program, Portugal's Fundação para a Ciência e Tecnologia (Praxis XXI/ BD/9581/96), Mexico's Consejo Nacional para la Ciencia y Tecnologia, London School of Economics, and the University of Pittsburgh's Graduate School of Public and International Affairs and Center for Latin American Studies. El Colegio Mexiquense provided gracious hospitality during my visiting professorship in 1998 and in various subsequent follow-up field trips.

My deepest thanks go to my lovely family. To my parents, Nuno and Maria Teresa Themudo, who always encouraged me to ask questions and take risks in the pursuit of what is important. To my Mexican family—Alejandro, (Tio) Rafael, and (Tia) Alma Martinez-Gonzalez—who taught me the generosity and cordiality of Mexican culture. This study would not have been possible without their support. To my wife, Lisa, who encouraged my research ever since we first met at the London School of Economics, listened patiently to my every latest "discovery," commented on endless drafts, and supported me when deadlines loomed. And to my daughters, Sofia and Maria, who have taught me that we often need to look at the world with "new eyes" to better understand its mysteries and that we don't always need to start with the corners in solving a puzzle. I owe my family much more than a debt of gratitude. (As of the summer of 2012, I owe three years of dishwashing, two years of vacuum cleaning, one year of dropping off and picking up the kids at school, one year of trips to the park and playground, and about one year of food shopping—though, in my defense, I did do most of the laundry and dog walking.) I dedicate this book to them.

NONPROFITS IN CRISIS

1 A Cross-National Philanthropic Puzzle

"SOMETIMES THINGS GET worse before they get better"—Doña Mica reflected during an interview.[1] She was apologetic about the fact that her new initiative, which focused on building the capacity of indigenous youth to develop microenterprises, was rapidly losing money. Yet she remained confident that Fovaso—a small nonprofit organization in Central Mexico—would soon be financially viable again. When Fovaso's financial woes began, the organization embarked on a major strategic reorientation, phasing out its philanthropic programs to focus on social enterprise. As she explained, the hope was that a commercial model based on lending and selling rather than giving to clients would offer a more financially sustainable and potentially more effective approach to fighting poverty. Her sanguine outlook, however, was hard to understand. Survival of small nonprofit organizations in Mexico is challenging in the best of times. But when I interviewed Doña Mica, Mexico was in the midst of the so-called Tequila Crisis, which "caused one of the worst recessions to hit an individual country since the 1930s" (Krugman 2008:32). The stock market had recently lost almost half of its value, unemployment was at record high levels, and Mexico's risk premium was the highest in the world.[2] At the time, no one knew how deep the crisis was going to be. Eventually the economy did improve, and Fovaso experienced some temporary financial relief. Over time, however, Fovaso's troubles returned. Ironically, the new social enterprise model alienated supporters of the previous model and failed to attract sufficient new support, leading to a reduction in social impact and financial decline. The fate of Fovaso was important because it was one of the few nonprofits in Mexico dedicated to the welfare and empowerment of two of its most vulnerable groups: rural indigenous women and children with special needs. To witness the decline of this valuable organization, which at its peak had employed more than forty people, was devastating for its clients, already hard hit by the crisis. Learning that Fovaso closed its doors in the early 2000s was also difficult for me, because I had previously volunteered a great number of hours to the organization. After almost a decade since its demise, no organization has stepped in to fill the vacuum in poverty alleviation work left by Fovaso's disappearance.

This book focuses both on the nonprofit sector in general and on specific cases studies of Mexican nonprofits like Fovaso, which tried to work and survive—not always successfully—in a risky environment. Study of these organizations' local vicissitudes generates broader lessons about philanthropy and the nonprofit sector, which perfectly complement wider cross-national statistical analysis. The main argument proposed here is that the apparently simple notion of risk helps explain the fundamental and contradictory influence of economic development on the nonprofit sector.

When economic development leads to increases in macroeconomic instability, nonprofits tend to face rising levels of economic risk, and nonprofit sector strength tends to decline. In contrast, the nonprofit sector tends to become stronger when economic development decreases macroeconomic instability and the risk nonprofits face. In other words, *risk resulting from the process of economic development is a major influence on nonprofit sector evolution.* Such risk is a powerful, yet largely neglected, influence on philanthropy and the sector.

The trajectory of nonprofits such as Fovaso over the past two decades provides a vivid example of the Mexican nonprofit sector's travails. Annually, Mexicans donate a smaller fraction of national income to the nonprofit sector than citizens in any other country, around half a billion purchasing power adjusted dollars. They also volunteer less than anyone else does.[3] Accordingly, Mexico has the weakest nonprofit sector in the world, employing only 0.4% of its labor force (Salamon et al. 2004). A different assessment ranked Mexico lowest globally in terms of nonprofit sector capacity and impact (Anheier and Salamon 2006). In sharp contrast, the nonprofit sector is burgeoning in the United States, where it is a significant part of the economy and culture. Most Americans are born in a nonprofit, and it is in nonprofits that they go through many of life's most critical moments: getting a degree, marrying, practicing their faith, recovering from sickness, and participating in the policy process. Consequently, 92% of the adult population belongs to at least one nonprofit and about 75% to more than one (Anheier 2005:76). It is not surprising, therefore, that Americans give over $300 billion annually (slightly over 2% of GDP) to the nonprofit sector, which employs close to 10% of the labor force in the United States, twenty-five times more than in Mexico even when adjusted for labor force size. Of course, the nonprofit sector is hardly an American phenomenon. The Netherlands and Sweden, for example, enjoy even higher levels of philanthropy, while Canada and Ireland have larger nonprofit sectors as a proportion of their labor force. Mexico's philanthropy and nonprofit sector are small when compared to such countries, but what is astounding is that they are smaller even than in poor countries such as Tanzania, Kenya, and the Philippines as well as ex-communist countries such as Romania and Hungary.

Why does Mexico have the weakest nonprofit sector in the world? Mexico's nonprofit sector anemia is surprising because current theory predicts that a country with intermediate levels of economic development and welfare spending, significant protection of civil liberties and political rights, and a favorable legal framework for nonprofit organizations should encourage significant philanthropy and a medium-sized nonprofit sector.[4] Why are Mexicans less generous than others? Why are they less likely to make donations and volunteer for social causes? More generally, why do some countries have a vibrant nonprofit sector and others do not? The experience of countries with weaker nonprofit sectors, such as Mexico, is very relevant to general questions about the sector in other countries (see Hammack 2002). It offers a valuable opportunity for the study of the causes of nonprofit sector weakness and an important contrast to most existing research, which has focused on the much more developed nonprofit sector in rich countries. Indeed, study of this apparent outlier generates new theoretical insights that can subsequently be tested against broader cross-national evidence, thus revealing more general explanations than are currently available.

While anchored in a detailed analysis of the Mexican nonprofit sector, this book has broader, comparative ambitions. Cross-national research has been essential in expanding our understanding of philanthropy (e.g., Ilchman, Katz, and Queen 1998; Thomas 2004; Musick and Wilson 2008; Hammack and Heydemann 2009) and the nonprofit sector (e.g., Salamon and Anheier 1998; Hammack 2001; Glasius, Lewis, and Seckinelgin 2004; Salamon et al. 2004; Themudo 2009). Yet, because of the frequently abstract nature of current work in the field (Anheier 2004:3), and because the necessary data have only recently become available, few studies have tested the predictive power of nonprofit theories against cross-national data. Additionally, most of the studies that have examined cross-national data have limited their analysis to rich, Western countries. This has weakened our confidence in generalizations of theoretical insights across different geographical contexts, particularly across the Global North/South divide (Lewis 1998). By examining both Northern and Southern data, this book presents a rare angle on philanthropy and the nonprofit sector, contributing to the emerging field of comparative nonprofit sector research. It will show that research on Mexico's philanthropic anemia helps us understand the broader causes and consequences of nonprofit sector weakness in Mexico and elsewhere.

At stake is much more than an embarrassing ranking for Mexico. Since a robust nonprofit sector is generally associated with the healthy functioning of democracy and the market, the country's philanthropic anemia is likely to have political and economic ramifications. For example, a weak nonprofit sector might limit the opportunities for underrepresented groups to have a say in Mexico's incipient democracy, contributing to the country's low levels of civic participation. Nonprofit sector weakness helps to explain the paradoxical and troubling finding that the majority of Mexicans were disappointed with democracy even as in the year 2000 the country held its first free presidential election in over seventy years.[5] Moreover, nonprofit sector weakness might contribute to low social trust and widespread corruption (Themudo 2013), which, in turn, is likely to hurt economic development and social stability (see Putnam 1993, 2000; Knack and Keefer 1997; Uslaner 2008). Consistent with this prediction, for the past two decades Mexico's economy has been relatively stagnant, while crime rates have exploded. The country's current social instability is a major threat to its citizens and even its neighbors, as the escalation of violence and crime along Mexico's northern border powerfully illustrates.

In this chapter, I begin by uncovering the puzzle that lies at the heart of this book and the Mexican experience. Then I demonstrate the challenge it poses to existing theory and introduce the basic tenets of a risk perspective on the nonprofit sector, all the while highlighting the important implications for policy and research. I finish by laying out the plan of the book.

An Enigma Wrapped in a Puzzle:
Mexico and the Philanthropic Kuznets Curve

Mexican researchers have hypothesized that the country's undersized nonprofit sector is primarily due to the uniqueness of its political history (e.g., Verduzco 2003; Terrazas 2006; Layton 2009). This is a plausible explanation. Between 1929 and 1997, Mexico was a de facto single-party democracy. Throughout the duration of its rule, the Partido Revolucionario Institucional (PRI) was effective in co-opting and neutralizing (often through repression) any dissenting views (McAdam, Tarrow, and Tilly 2001). Such a political context, the argument goes, hampered the emergence of an independent nonprofit sector. However, while it is impossible to deny the importance of Mexico's idiosyncratic political history, a comparative outlook suggests other key factors may be at play. Several other countries, such as Brazil, Hungary, and South Korea, which have very different political histories, also display a weak nonprofit sector. We must contrast, therefore, explanations based on Mexico's unique political history against more general explanations of nonprofit sector weakness to assess their relative explanatory power and generate a more complete explanation for our puzzle.

A cross-national outlook also offers fresh doubts about the explanatory power of nonprofit theory. As detailed below, current theories predict a linear relationship between nonprofit sector strength and the level of economic development. The Mexican case, however, points to the intriguing possibility that this relationship might in fact be nonlinear. Surprisingly, cross-national evidence supports this supposition.[6] Figure 1.1 plots the U-shaped relationship between philanthropy and level of economic development for countries included in the Johns Hopkins Comparative Nonprofit Sector Study. The predicted relationship is clearly nonlinear, with middle-income countries typically displaying the lowest levels of philanthropy.

Astonishingly, the U-shaped pattern can be found in every main operationalization of the nonprofit sector (such as nonprofit employment, expenditure, volunteering, and giving) and is also evident in every field of nonprofit sector activity for which we have comparative measures, namely culture, education, health, social services, environment, development, advocacy, foundations, international, professional associations, religion, and women's organizations.[7] To illustrate, Figure 1.2 depicts the relationship between prosperity and the two main measures of nonprofit sector size. It includes the scatter plot for the actual values of total nonprofit sector employment as well as predicted values for total nonprofit sector employment and expenditure.[8]

Using a different dataset with twice as many countries, Figure 1.3 depicts the same nonlinear pattern in the relationship between civic participation, social capital, and economic development across countries. While this book focuses on philanthropy and general nonprofit sector size rather than membership, civic participation or social capital, Figure 1.3 shows that this nonlinear pattern is not a figment of a particular dataset or indicator of the nonprofit sector. Other studies have missed this important pattern in

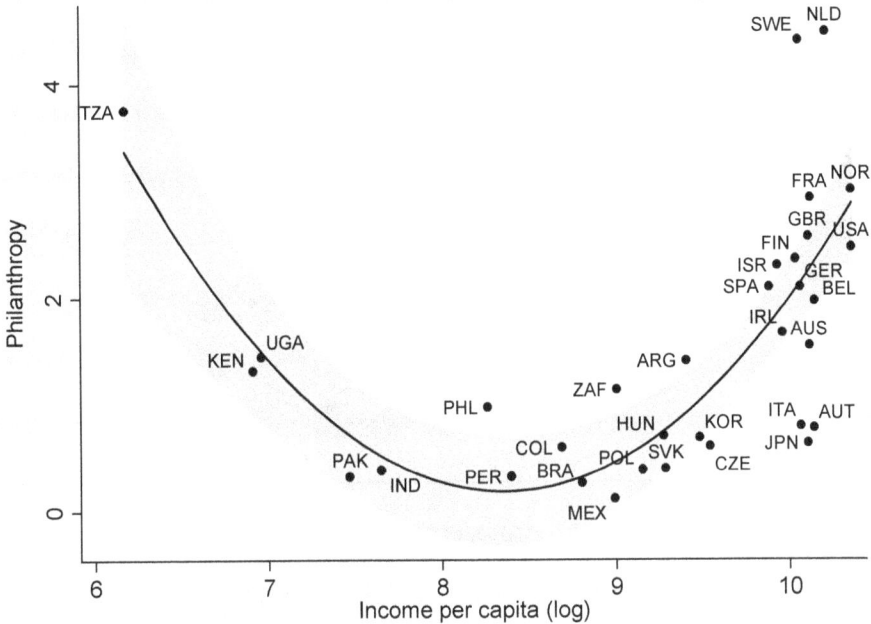

Figure 1.1. Philanthropy and economic development. Notes: Based on author's analysis of Johns Hopkins Comparative Nonprofit Sector data (ca. 1995–2000). The shaded area indicates the 95% confidence interval for predicted philanthropy. Philanthropy measured by giving and value of volunteering as a proportion (%) of GDP. Level of economic development is measured by the natural log of income per capita (in 1995) from the World Development Indicators dataset.

part because they have looked for a linear relationship or focused on the comparison of only two broad groups of countries: developed and developing. The profound differences between poor and middle-income countries, however, suggest the need for a more fine-grained portrait of the nonprofit sector globally, and especially of the "developing world," than has been generally undertaken in cross-national research of philanthropy and the nonprofit sector.

In this book, I label this nonlinear relationship between economic development and nonprofit sector strength the "philanthropic Kuznets curve" (PKC) because its U-shape resembles the "Kuznets curve." Half a century ago, Simon Kuznets argued that the relationship between social equality and economic development follows a U-shaped curve. He argued that at low levels, economic development leads to a decrease in economic equality, but at high levels, economic development contributes to an increase in economic equality (Kuznets 1955). More recently, researchers identified an analogous,

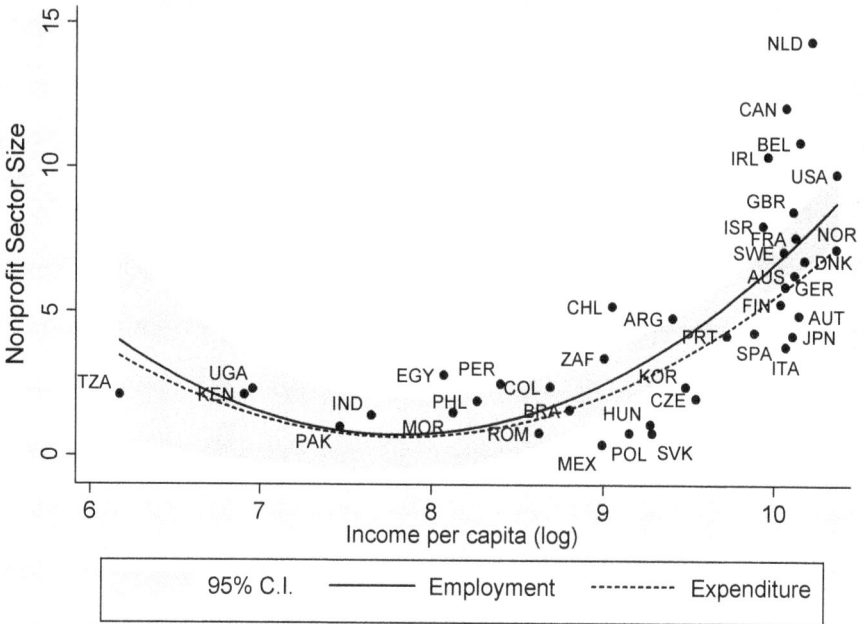

Figure 1.2. Nonprofit sector size and economic development. Notes: Author's analysis based on Johns Hopkins Comparative Nonprofit Sector data (ca. 1995–2000). Total employment includes both paid and full-time-equivalent volunteering as a proportion (%) of the labor force. The shaded area represents the 95% confidence interval for predicted total employment. Expenditure measured as a proportion (%) of GDP. Level of economic development is measured by the natural log of income per capita (in 1995) from the World Development Indicators dataset.

nonlinear relationship between environmental conservation and prosperity, whereby environmental conservation first falls as the level of economic development rises, reaches a turning point, and then increases as the level of economic development continues to rise. Like the original Kuznets curve, this "environmental Kuznets curve" has quickly become a major area of research in economics (e.g., Binder and Neumeyer 2005; Acemoglu 2009). The PKC has cross-sectional and longitudinal interpretations; that is, it describes a pattern of change in philanthropy and the nonprofit sector as countries develop economically over time, as well as a pattern of cross-sectional variation at any one time between countries at different levels of economic development.[9]

Evidence of a robust PKC is even more striking given the potential biases against the accurate measurement of nonprofit sector size in poor and non-Western countries. Civic groups in such countries are often dismissed as nonvoluntary manifestations of

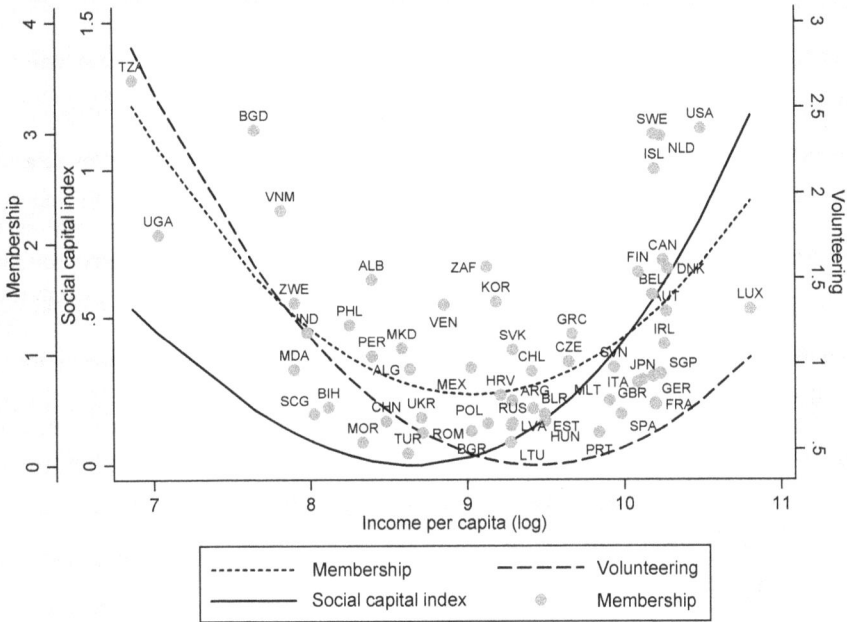

Figure 1.3. Civic participation, social capital, and economic development. Notes: Author's analysis based on World Values Survey, Fourth Wave (1999–2001). Membership reflects the national average number of organizations of which respondents were members. Volunteering reflects the national average number of organizations in which respondents volunteered. Social capital index is measured by multiplying membership, volunteering, social trust, and political participation. Economic development is measured by the natural log of income per capita (in 1998) from the World Development Indicators dataset.

kin and clan relationships. Moreover, civic groups in poor countries are less likely to formally incorporate than their counterparts in rich countries and, despite their important social contributions, tend not to be included in nonprofit sector measures (Anheier 2005:82). The comparative evidence presented here demonstrates that *the nonprofit sector can be as vibrant in poor countries as in rich ones,* even according to several indicators of the "real" (read "Western") nonprofit sector. Levels of nonprofit volunteering are much higher in Tanzania or Uganda than in some rich countries such as Portugal, Austria, or Japan and much higher than in middle-income countries such as Mexico, Brazil, or Poland. This fact is consistent with Musick and Wilson's (2008:343) finding that alongside the United States the highest levels of volunteering can be found in some of the poorest countries in the world, namely Bangladesh, Tanzania, Zimbabwe, and

Uganda.[10] Moreover, levels of nonprofit expenditure as a proportion of national income in Tanzania and Kenya are on par with those in Italy and Austria, and much higher than those in most middle-income countries. Comparative nonprofit sector data lend support, therefore, to the minority view that civil society in poor countries is much more vibrant than generally acknowledged by academics and policy makers, who tend to view such contexts as the prototypical realms of "amoral familism," dominated by relationships based on patronage and other forms of social coercion (Hann and Dunn 1996).

What accounts for the profound variation in philanthropy and nonprofit sector strength across countries manifested in the PKC? Why are Americans so generous and the Dutch and Swedes even more so? Why are Mexicans apparently so ungenerous? Why does growing national prosperity apparently hurt philanthropy and nonprofit sector at low levels of economic development? More basically, how does prosperity impact philanthropy and the nonprofit sector? What can policy makers do to encourage philanthropy and nonprofit sector growth beyond the obvious introduction of tax incentives and protection of civil liberties? Mexico's experience suggests that we cannot take the nonprofit sector for granted and that these questions deserve careful study. In this book, I offer some answers to these important questions.

The PKC and Nonprofit Sector Theory

Increasing recognition of the nonprofit sector's social and economic contributions has made its study an important topic in the social sciences. A significant body of research, therefore, has sought to explain the emergence and development of the nonprofit sector. Familiar to many, for example, are studies on the impact of social diversity (e.g., Olson 1965; Weisbrod 1988; Chang and Tuckman 1996), religious competition (e.g., James 1989; Burger and Veldheer 2001), trust and asymmetric information (e.g., Hansmann 1987; Ben-Ner and van Hoomissen 1991), expanded civil liberties and political opportunities from democratization (e.g., Tarrow 1994; Hammack 2001), legal and regulatory frameworks (e.g., Galaskiewicz and Bielefeld 1998; Anheier and Salamon 1998; Salamon and Toepler 2000; Hammack 2001), modernization (Durkheim 1984 [1893]; Putnam 2000; Putnam and Goss 2002), economic growth and development (e.g., Hirschman 1982; Hammack 2001), higher social welfare spending and tax benefits for nonprofits (e.g., Salamon 1987; Smith and Lispky 1993; Beito 2000; Steinberg 2003), nonmonetary values among entrepreneurs (e.g., Young 1983; James 1989; Rose-Ackerman 1996), globalization (e.g., Boli and Thomas1999; Clark 2003; Ebrahim 2003; Lewis 2007), and "social origins" (Salamon and Anheier 1998). This extensive body of work, however, is unable to explain the PKC. To demonstrate this, I begin by examining approaches that focus on the relationship between the nonprofit sector and economic development. Later, I examine alternative approaches that, despite not focusing directly on the relationship with economic development, might nevertheless help to explain cross-national variation in philanthropy and nonprofit sector size.

Economic Development and the Nonprofit Sector

Traditional approaches suggest that economic development has a detrimental effect on philanthropy and the nonprofit sector. They propose different mechanisms at both structural and individual levels for this effect, namely the rise of the welfare state, modernization, and increasing opportunity costs of labor that accompany economic development. Both government failure and welfare state approaches suggest that economic development typically leads to expansion of government social spending, which in turn weakens the demand for nonprofit sector provision (e.g., Weisbrod 1988; Salamon and Anheier 1998). Government failure theory proposes that the nonprofit sector is a response to failures of the state to provide the kinds of collective goods that people want but that the market is unable to provide. To the extent that the government increases its provision of such collective goods, reducing government failure, the need for nonprofit provision should decline. Like government failure theory, welfare state theory suggests that the emergence of the welfare state "crowds out" traditional welfare-related nonprofits, leading to an inverse relationship between the size of the nonprofit sector and the scale of governmental collective goods provision (Salamon and Anheier 1998; Skocpol 1992). Given that charitable organizations and welfare programs often seek to perform the same role, it is reasonable to suppose that, as welfare programs expand and their coverage becomes more universal, demand for nonprofit sector services should fall. A few scholars also believe that countries with strong welfare states not only have less need for volunteer services but also nurture a culture that stigmatizes volunteer work as charity (Ascoli and Cnaan 1997; Gaskin and Smith 1997). The decline of mutual-benefit societies and cooperatives since the 1940s (Beito 2000; Anheier 2004) would appear to lend support to this perspective.

An alternative approach, deriving from modernization theory and the earlier work of the illustrious sociologist Émile Durkheim (1984 [1893]), proposes that economic development leads to structural changes in the economy (such as division of labor, urbanization, and industrialization) that, in turn, weaken the social cohesion of traditional societies. Increasing division of labor and migration may undermine traditional social bonds, while the rise of the welfare state may contribute to the decline of traditional self-help associations as welfare state theory posits (Salamon and Anheier 1998). According to Putnam and Goss (2002:15–6): "Conventional accounts, of which modernization theory is the most relevant, have described a trajectory that begins with the industrial revolution and the technological innovations accompanying it. The mass movement of people from cohesive, rural areas to big, anonymous, atomistic cities translates into an overall decline in community and social capital." More recent analyses of the alleged decline of civic engagement in the United States point to technological change—a key element of modernization and economic development—in shaping social relationships. Famously, Putnam (2000) argues that the spread of television and the Internet is reducing face-to-face interactions, with detrimental consequences for philanthropy and the nonprofit sector. From a rational choice perspective, Olson (1965) argues that as the opportunity cost of participation increases, rational actors are less likely to participate in collective action (e.g., by volunteering). By increasing the opportunity cost of labor, then, economic development may reduce civic participation (see Acemoglu and Robinson 2006). In the same way, rising opportunity cost of labor can also weaken social entrepreneurship as the opportunity cost of the labor involved in starting a nonprofit rises. Therefore, we should expect that economic development would lead to a decrease in nonprofit entrepreneurship, volunteering, and other forms of collective action.[11]

A competing set of approaches, predicts a symbiotic, or direct, relationship between economic development and both philanthropy and nonprofit sector size. Research on giving and volunteering commonly suggests that higher levels of philanthropy tend to be associated with higher levels of financial, human, and social capital (e.g., Havens, O'Herlihy, and Schervish 2006), which, in turn, are directly associated with economic development. Higher national income should also lead to an expansion of other types of nonprofit revenue. Drawing lessons from a comparison of studies on the evolution of the nonprofit sector in the United States, Netherlands, France, and United Kingdom, David Hammack (2001:158–159) concludes that higher household income and wealth in those countries have, since the 1960s, enabled "many families to significantly increase their purchase of the educational, health care, cultural, and social services that nonprofits provide." The rapid expansion of the nonprofit sector in the United States has been partly due to the fact that, as service providers, nonprofits have benefited from the rapidly expanding share of services within the economy since the 1950s (see Hammack and Young 1993; Weisbrod 1998b; Hammack 2001). Another approach suggests that increases in social welfare spending, which typically accompany prosperity, may lead to nonprofit sector growth by increasing public funding for nonprofits (Anheier and Salamon 2006). Like social welfare theory, Salamon's (1987) "interdependence theory" argues that as national economies develop, citizens tend to demand more welfare provision. However, interdependence theory argues that the rise of states' welfare responsibilities actually encourages nonprofit sector development. The argument is that nonprofits can compensate for various types of government failure, while government can compensate for various types of "voluntary failure" inherent to the nonprofit sector. Both sectors can therefore establish partnerships to improve service provision. The high proportion of public funding as a percentage of total nonprofit revenues in rich countries is taken as evidence in support of interdependence arguments (Salamon 1987), as is the fact that governments in both sides of the North Atlantic have since the 1960s greatly increased their purchase of services provided by nonprofits (Hammack 2001:158–159). The welfare state, and especially universalistic systems, can also contribute to a reduction in social inequality and the strengthening of the social contract, which Uslaner (2002) and Rothstein (2005) argue is essential for social capital development. In turn, they argue, social capital promotes nonprofit sector expansion.

High levels of social inequality, therefore, should be a key factor contributing to both low levels of social capital and nonprofit sector weakness.

Mancur Olson (1982) offers an alternative explanation for a direct relationship between level of economic development and nonprofit sector strength. He argues that economic development and the concomitant rise of government power and resources increase the incentives for citizens and corporations to create nonprofit organizations to influence the policy process. Lastly, while most scholars believe that the cultural forces of modernization (e.g., rationalization, secularization, materialism, individualism) are eroding people's commitment to the public good, a few authors have suggested that modernization may promote nonprofit sector development by encouraging "post-material" values, such as environmental conservation and women's empowerment, which are directly associated with volunteering and broader participation (see Dekker and Van den Broek 1998; Themudo 2009). Ronald Inglehart (1997) argues that economic development is not necessarily conducive to decreasing rates of civic participation because although economic modernization means a shift from traditional to secular values that discourages volunteering in some nonprofit fields, the shift from survival to self-expression values encourages volunteering in all nonprofit fields.[12] Modernization, therefore, can have a positive impact on volunteering. Indeed, Pippa Norris (2003:157) found that purchasing power adjusted GDP per capita was positively associated with volunteering across forty-six countries. Various influential approaches, therefore, suggest a direct relationship between economic development and nonprofit sector strength.

The PKC contradicts both sides of this long-standing debate and offers an opportunity to break the stalemate. Welfare state, government failure, modernization, and collective action approaches predict that rich countries should have limited nonprofit sectors. The strength of the nonprofit sector in rich countries, however, denies their main prediction. In contrast, government-nonprofit interdependence, post-materialism, and human and social capital approaches predict that poor countries should have limited nonprofit sectors. The relative strength of the nonprofit sector in poor countries when compared to middle-income countries, however, contradicts their prediction. Moreover, while all approaches agree that the nonprofit sector in countries at intermediate levels of prosperity should be of intermediate size, the general weakness of the nonprofit sector in such contexts contradicts them. *By proposing that philanthropy and the nonprofit sector either always decline or always rise with economic development, available theories cannot account for the PKC.* Despite often being supported by statistically significant correlations, linear predictions fail to capture the complex relationship between economic development and the nonprofit sector. In addition, examinations focusing on the impact of other variables on the sector might have inadvertently dismissed an economic development effect by failing to control for its nonlinear effects.[13] Reliance on linear explanations has limited our ability to understand the nonprofit sector's nonlinear evolution.

Other Theories of the Nonprofit Sector

Having discussed the limitations of theoretical arguments that focus on the relationship between economic development and nonprofit sector strength, we must now examine predictions derived from other theories of the nonprofit sector, and consider their merit as explanations for the PKC. Nonprofit sector emergence and development are commonly explained by reference to government and market failure. Relating nonprofit sector development to government failure, Weisbrod (1975, 1988) argued that the higher the level of social heterogeneity the lower the ability of government to satisfy heterogeneous demands and the stronger the incentive for nonprofit sector development. Yet, social diversity cannot account for the PKC. Since social diversity is generally higher in poor countries (see, e.g., Knack and Keefer 1997; table 3.1 in this book), the theory would suggest that the nonprofit sector should be strongest in poor countries. The strength of the nonprofit sector in rich countries questions the theory's relevance as a main explanation for the PKC and for the cross-national variation of nonprofit sector strength in general. In addition, Mexico has a moderate level of social diversity, so social diversity cannot explain Mexican nonprofit sector frailty. Relating nonprofit sector development to market failure, Hansmann (1987) proposed that the nonprofit sector generates more trust than the business (for-profit) sector in fields where consumers are unable to evaluate the quality of service provision. In such environments, for-profits can exploit asymmetrical information to covertly lower service quality and maximize their profits. Nonprofits' nondistribution constraint reduces the pressure to generate profits for shareholders and, consequently, the pressure to lower service quality. All else being equal, therefore, consumers should generally prefer nonprofit providers in sectors characterized by asymmetrical information, such as health care, child and elderly care, and pure academic research. More generally, in cross-national perspective the nonprofit sector should be largest where trust in business is weakest (Anheier and Salamon 2006). However, while trust in business has a U-shaped relationship with national prosperity, it displays a direct relationship with nonprofit sector size—the opposite of what the theory predicted. Similarly, the moderate levels of trust in business in Mexico cannot account for its nonprofit sector weakness.

Another set of explanations emphasizes the influence of religion. For example, Estelle James (1989) argued that the degree of religious competition is a predictor of nonprofit sector size. The number and variety of churches in pluralistic religious systems sparks competition among them for members, which, in turn, leads to a proliferation of activities designed to keep members involved and committed (Woolley 2003:158). Indeed, religious competition tends to be lowest in middle-income countries, a fact that is broadly consistent with the PKC. However, religious competition is not a statistically significant predictor of variations in nonprofit sector size across nations, due to the large variance in religious competition at each level of economic development.[14] In addition, since Mexico has more religious competition than some countries with much larger nonprofit sectors, such as Ireland, Portugal, and Colombia, this hypothesis has a limited ability to explain the Mexican case. Intensity of religious values, that is, "religiousness" and "religiosity," is a different mechanism through which religion may influence the nonprofit sector. Based on their empirical investigation of volunteering at the cross-national level, Musick and Wilson (2008:359) claim that "in virtually all countries for which there are reliable data, frequency of church attendance is positively related to volunteering. The comparatively high rate of volunteering in the United States can be attributed to the religiosity of the American people." However, the United States is an exception among rich countries. Analysis of World Values Survey data shows that, generally, both religiousness and religiosity decline with economic development.[15] This explanation, then, cannot account for the PKC.

A different set of explanations focuses on political institutions. Many scholars have argued that the protection of civil liberties, such as freedom of association, expression, and worship, is a major determinant of civil society (Gutmann 1998; Inglehart 1997; Putnam 2000) and nonprofit sector strength (e.g., Wuthnow 1988; Hammack 2001; Brody 2006; Clemmens 2006). Similarly, a competitive democratic system provides political opportunities that facilitate social movement emergence and activity (e.g., McAdam 1982; Tarrow 1994). Democratic regimes, then, are more likely to foster a vibrant non-profit sector than autocracies, as the latter is typically inclined to limit freedom of association and to repress independent nongovernmental voices. Democratic governance can also contribute to nonprofit sector strength, because its traditional focus on majority interests encourages the emergence of the nonprofit sector to fulfill neglected needs of minority groups (Douglas 1987).

David Hammack (2001) argues that the increasing protection of civil liberties is a fundamental reason for the expansion of the nonprofit sector on both sides of the North Atlantic since the 1960s. He shows how, even in apparently strong democratic regimes such as the United States, minority groups have historically faced systematic restrictions to their civil liberties and considerable obstacles to creating nonprofit organizations. Restrictions on the civil liberties of minority groups should have a profound impact on philanthropy and nonprofit sector size, especially since the nonprofit sector commonly seeks to fulfill the unmet needs of such groups. On the other hand, however, the fact that democracy, civil liberties, and political rights have a direct, linear relationship with economic development questions their ability to independently explain the PKC or the Mexican puzzles. This apparent contradiction between the obvious importance of political regime and its inability to explain nonprofit sector weakness in middle-income countries suggests that the protection of civil liberties and political rights is a necessary but not sufficient condition for nonprofit sector development. This supposition is consistent with Helmut Anheier's (2004) argument that civil liberties provide a measure of civil society "space." Most middle-income countries are formal democracies with intermediate levels of civil liberties and political rights (e.g., Mexico, Romania, Slovakia, Brazil, and Hungary), which suggests that most middle-income countries have significant "space" for nonprofit sector development, but their nonprofit sectors have not grown to fill it.

By facilitating or hindering the creation and operation of nonprofit organizations, the legal framework is another main influence on nonprofit sector development (Salamon and Toepler 2000; Archambault 2001; Hammack 2001; Layton 2009). Unfortunately, research on legal frameworks in developing countries is sorely missing. Salamon and Toepler (2000) is one of the few exceptions. They generated the Johns Hopkins Nonprofit Law Index by examining the legal framework governing nonprofits in several countries. The index includes an evaluation of the general legal posture (right to associate, allowable general purposes, allowable political activities), establishment (unincorporated organizations permissible, membership requirements, capital requirements, government involvement on boards, government discretion in granting legal status, and appeal procedures) and financing of nonprofit organizations (broadness of organizational tax exemption, income tax exemption, real estate/property tax exemption, stamp and other duties exemption, indirect tax exemptions, permissibility and tax treatment of unrelated business activities, taxation of unrelated business income, organizational tax benefits for contributions, tax benefits for individual donors, tax benefits for corporate donors). Surprisingly, the authors find that Mexico is one of only four countries with a "high" index score (the other countries are the United States, the Netherlands, and Israel). This exceptionally favorable legal framework stands in stark contrast with Mexico's frail nonprofit sector. The only other middle-income country examined in Salamon and Toepler's (2000) study, Brazil, has a much less favorable legal framework, though it still was more favorable than Japan's framework and only slightly less favorable than Germany's. Thus, while it would be foolish to deny the importance of the legal framework, it seems unable to explain nonprofit sector weakness in middle-income countries. Reflecting on the apparent irrelevance of legal framework to explain the Mexican nonprofit sector, Michael Layton (2009) suggests that this may be because the legal framework might not be implemented in practice or because a permissive framework might be a necessary but not sufficient cause for nonprofit sector development.

A different approach focuses on the "social origins" of the nonprofit sector. Salamon and Anheier (1998) argued that the nonprofit sector is embedded in political and welfare regimes, which are a product of historical relationships between classes and social institutions. Political and welfare regimes reflect the balance of power between social classes as well as between state and society. "Choices about whether to rely on market, nonprofit, or state provision of key services are not simply made freely by consumers in an open market as advocates of the economic theories seem to assume. Rather, these choices are heavily constrained by prior patterns of historical development that significantly shape the range of options available at a given time and place" (226). Such patterns of historical development generate various "nonprofit regimes," which according to Salamon and Anheier can be classified as corporatist, liberal, social democrat, and statist depending on the strength of government and nonprofit sector. With relatively weaker nonprofit and government sectors, the vast majority of poor and middle-income countries would be classified under a "statist" regime (Anheier 2005:136). This classification, therefore, is unable to capture the variation represented by the PKC. Salamon et al. (1999) developed a potentially more useful scheme based on broader comparative data. They group the world into various regions, each with its own characteristic nonprofit sector. Such regions tend to be more determined by culture than geography. Thus, the Anglo-Saxon model is common to geographically distant countries sharing a common cultural heritage. It is unclear how the social origins framework or culture could account for the PKC. Firstly, the strong variation in nonprofit sector strength as a country develops economically would seem to question the typically very inertial evolution of political regimes and culture. Secondly, the countries with the weakest nonprofit sectors do not easily fit any political regime typology. Mexico, Brazil, Peru, and Argentina share Latin American roots, but what do they share in common with Slovakia, Poland, Romania, and South Korea? Likewise, cultural explanations seem unable to account for how seemingly similar cultures can accommodate wide disparities in nonprofit sector strength. For example, there are large nonprofit sector differences between Chile, Argentina, and Mexico and between the Netherlands, Germany, and Austria.

As a pervasive social trend, globalization presents a final set of key influences on nonprofit sector development (Edwards and Hulme 1995; Lindenberg and Bryant 2001; Clark 2003; Anheier and Themudo 2004; Lewis 2007). Because international donor agencies are key funders of nonprofit organizations in developing countries, they have a direct influence on nonprofit sector development in those countries (Fowler 2000). Donors may also contribute to the spread of democratic values and privatization policies through the spread of neoliberal ideology among states, both of which can indirectly contribute to nonprofit sector development (Edwards and Hulme 1995; Lewis 2007). At the private level, through the diffusion of communications technologies and cheap travel, globalization decreases the costs of nonprofit action across borders and increases public awareness about social needs abroad (Clark and Themudo 2004). Existing accounts, however, suggest that these mechanisms have a linear, direct influence on the nonprofit sector, and since globalization processes are typically direct correlates of economic development, they cannot account for the PKC or the Mexican case.

To be sure, while current theories cannot explain the PKC independently, they may still help to explain cross-national variation in nonprofit sector strength collectively. Thus, to better assess their influence, the cross-national statistical analysis included indicators for political regime, ethic fragmentation, religious diversity, modernization, globalization, legal framework, size of government, level of trust in business, and social inequality. On the other hand, to ensure that the empirical analysis identifies a causal effect of economic development and not one of its correlates—such as level of democracy, modernization, or globalization—in part of this study I opted to hold those influences constant. I did so by focusing on the impact of an economic shock—the "Tequila Crisis"—on the evolution of the Mexican nonprofit sector over a relatively short period. Important confounding influences, such as political regime, legal framework, social inequality, culture, and geography remained largely constant during the natural experiment, from mid to late 1990s. On the other hand, economic prosperity and stability varied widely, which permitted the systematic assessment of their influence on the sector.

Economic Instability, Risk, and the Nonprofit Sector

The PKC, then, provides a fundamental cross-national "stylized fact," which nonprofit sector research must seek to explain. This book develops an explanation for the PKC based on economic risk. Simply put, it argues that the nonprofit sector in middle-income countries faces an exceptionally high level of economic risk—understood as uncertainty or variation in the range of possible economic outcomes so that adverse outcomes are possible—which, in turn, generally depresses philanthropy and nonprofit sector size. Economic development, therefore, influences the level of economic risk nonprofits face and, consequently, nonprofit sector strength.

This study combines analysis of cross-national data on economic risk and the nonprofit sector with a detailed analysis of how the Tequila Crisis (1994–1995) influenced the Mexican nonprofit sector. Analysis of how nonprofits fared in this context is important not only from the perspective of those who, like me, have a passion for Mexico and its people. The Tequila Crisis provides an invaluable opportunity for an exploration of nonprofit leaders' preferences, tensions in the relationship between different stakeholders, and the mechanisms through which risk influences nonprofits—all of which become especially apparent in situations of resource scarcity and uncertainty about the future. As Peter Gourevitch (1986:17, in Williams 2001:6) put it, "Prosperity blurs a truth that hard times make clearer."

Economic crises offer a near ideal observation ground from which to examine the impact on the nonprofit sector of a sudden change in the level of risk within a relatively constant political, institutional, and social context. During crises, risk materializes in output losses, and new expectations about potential future losses are formed. Of course, risk does not affect the nonprofit sector only during economic crises. Thus, this study follows up several Mexican nonprofit case studies for over a decade and broader indicators of the nonprofit sector in Mexico since the 1980s.

On the cusp of the "Great Recession" (2008–2009), we are all painfully aware that economic crises have devastating social and economic costs. Aside from lost output, economic crises typically also entail large "rescue packages" for their resolution. Honohan and Klingebiel (2003) find, in a sample of forty banking crises, that governments spent an average of 6.2% of GDP on crisis resolution in developed countries and a whopping 14.7% of GDP in middle-income countries. The approximate resolution cost of the Tequila Crisis was between 20 and 24% of GDP (Halac and Schmukler 2004). Economics crises, then, have lasting impacts on economic agents' risk expectations. This is partly because resolution costs linger on after a crisis is officially over. "The government may finance these [resolution] costs through a combination of a rise in taxes (whether present or future), a fall in spending, and an increase in the inflation tax" (Halac and Schmukler 2004:5n14). Uncertainty about how governments will finance the costs of resolution and recovery as well as how the market will evolve more generally, then, increases economic risk long after the end of an economic crisis. That is partly why indicators of risk such as market volatility and the risk premium tend to be countercyclical, that is, they are highest during and immediately after downturns (e.g., Campbell and Cochrane 1999; Aydemir 2008).

Mexico's economy has had a turbulent history and, unfortunately, Mexico is not alone. At least since the 1970s, middle-income countries have faced higher levels of macroeconomic volatility than either rich or poor countries (Wolf 2005; Perry 2009). According to Eichengreen and Bordo (2001, table 7), the period between 1973 and 1997 registered more than forty-four crises in developed countries, with average GDP losses of 6.25%. Middle-income countries, in contrast, experienced ninety-five macroeconomic shocks, with average GDP losses of 9.21%. The list of the most severe macroeconomic crises in the past three decades includes a disproportionate number of middle-income countries: the debt crisis in the 1980s, which was most severe in Latin America, Turkey (1994), Venezuela (1994), Mexico (1994–1995), Thailand (1997), Malaysia (1997), Indonesia (1997), South Korea (1997), Russia (1998), Brazil (1998), Turkey (2001), and Argentina (2001–2002) (Perkins et al. 2006, ch. 14). Of note, recent data display a similar pattern. The global 2008–2009 crisis also affected middle-income countries the most. Between 1997 and 1999, average GDP in middle-income countries declined 6.91% compared to 5.3% in rich countries and 1.49% in poor countries (Canuto and Lin 2011:5, table 1.1).

We know surprisingly little about the causes of economic volatility. Several explanations have been proposed—from John Maynard Keynes's "animal spirits" to technology shocks, political cycles, and "rational panics"—but there is little agreement about their relative merit (Acemoglu 2009). Accordingly, researchers have suggested different explanations for middle-income countries' exceptional levels of macroeconomic volatility. One explanation focuses on structural transformations within the economy, which may increase volatility and risk (Davis and North 1971; North 1990; Acemoglu 2009). Research on the original Kuznets curve suggests that economic development entails profound economic and social transformations as society transitions from a traditional, rural society to a modern, urban society (Kuznets 1955). Developing countries are experiencing such transformations at an unprecedented pace. Changes that took place over centuries in Western Europe currently take only a few decades in developing countries (Kuznets 1973). That is especially true in middle-income countries, where rapid structural transformations have greatly contributed to their high levels of macroeconomic volatility (Agenor 2002; Lustig 1999). A second explanation focuses on the accelerated pace with which have middle-income countries liberalized their economies and opened up to international financial and trade flows (e.g., Krugman 2008; Perkins et al. 2006). As Lustig (1999:14) put it, even as the Tequila Crisis "was unfolding, Mexico was hailed as a 'model reformer' by policymakers and investors alike." "Model reforms" therefore may lead to imbalances and volatility (Lustig 1999). A third explanation focuses on political instability. The fact that most middle-income countries are young democracies contributes to their political instability, which, in turn, leads to economic instability (see Williams 2001; Acemoglu and Robinson 2006).

This book presents further empirical evidence that risk from macroeconomic instability, whether measured as volatility or inflation, does indeed peak in middle-income countries. Assuming, for the moment, economic volatility and risk have a negative impact on nonprofit sector strength, the inverted-U shaped relationship between level of economic development and macroeconomic risk is consistent with the puzzling U-shaped relationship between economic development and nonprofit sector strength. In other words, the PKC can be partly explained by the influence of economic development on risk and the influence of risk on the nonprofit sector. How does economic volatility, and associated risk, influence the nonprofit sector? Is it reasonable to assume that risk always has a negative impact on the sector? While it might appear obvious that macroeconomic volatility should depress the nonprofit sector, several factors may affect the relationship. On one hand, because philanthropic giving depends directly on private income (e.g., Havens, O'Herlihy, and Schervish 2006), falling private income during recessions should depress philanthropic giving. On the other hand, falling investment returns and wages during recessions should encourage giving and volunteering. Falling opportunity cost of labor (real wages) lowers the cost of participation in collective action (Acemoglu and Robinson2006), which should boost volunteering and civic participation. Also, falling opportunity cost of capital (i.e., investment returns) during recessions lowers the cost of giving, which should boost philanthropic giving. Moreover, in countries with a counter-cyclical fiscal policy, higher government spending during recessions could mean higher government funding to nonprofits. Also important is the fact that, while on balance recessions tend to depress nonprofit resource availability, macroeconomic volatility includes both good and bad years. On average, developing countries experience a downturn 22% of the time (Easterly, Islam, and Stiglitz 1999:18). While the causes for this pattern remain unclear, it means that they enjoy almost four years of growth for every downturn year. The upward side of volatility means that volatile economies typically also experience periods of strong growth. As Olsson (2002:xiii) argues, "Operating in [middle-income countries] is riskier than doing so in the developed world. This is largely because they are often characterized by greater economic and political instability. [T]his is, however, no reason to steer clear of these markets because there are higher levels of return on offer for those that understand and can manage risk effectively." Volatility, therefore, may also present significant opportunities for the nonprofit sector. If volatility weakens the nonprofit sector, why are nonprofits generally unable to take more advantage of the good years?

The influence of risk has received surprisingly little attention in the academic literature on nonprofits (Wedig 1994; Young 2006, 2007), perhaps because most research on the nonprofit sector emanates from environments with relatively low levels of risk. Thus, in my attempt to understand this influence I turn to broader social theory, particularly finance and game theory. By combining these different approaches to the study of risk, the argument developed here goes beyond depicting how risky environments present considerable obstacles to the nonprofit sector, to explain why some nonprofits are more affected than others and why the nonprofit sector develops in some countries and not others. It also specifies the key mechanisms through which economic risk influences the nonprofit sector and illuminates nonprofit adaptation strategies to economic volatility and risk.

To accomplish these tasks, the book develops an explanation for the variation in philanthropy and nonprofit sector size based on the influence of risk. The main argument is simple, yet powerful. Risk influences philanthropy and other contributions to the nonprofit sector because resource providers are generally risk-averse. As such, risk influences the rate with which supporters discount future benefits to society and to themselves from nonprofit sector activity in relation to the cost of contributions in the present. As risk rises, the net present value of future nonprofit sector impact declines, discouraging voluntary contributions to the sector. In stable, low-risk environments, discounting of future benefits is small and the nonprofit sector can thrive. However, in unstable, high-risk environments, discounting of future nonprofit benefits relative to present contributions discourages contributions to the nonprofit sector. As chapter 2 will further explain, rising risk levels typically attenuate most other incentives for philanthropy, such as reputation effects and long-term access to nonprofit services.

A key implication from this approach is that the impact of risk on different nonprofits depends on the riskiness of their programs. Because short-term impacts are less discounted than long-term ones, support in high-risk environments should privilege nonprofit organizations and programs focusing on the short term. This is important because long-term problems, such as global warming, do not disappear during high-risk periods and in fact may actually worsen. However, supporters' willingness to contribute to addressing long-term problems may change. On the other hand, as risk falls, and long-term impacts become more appealing, support should swing back to programs and organizations with a more long-term focus.

Despite the potential opportunities for nonprofits focusing on emergencies and other short-term causes in high-risk environments, overall risk should have a weakening impact on the nonprofit sector. This is due to several interrelated effects. First, even nonprofits focusing on the short term have to make long-term investments (e.g., on organizational development), but they will find few supporters willing to contribute to such investments in high-risk environments. Without such investments, these organizations will find it increasingly difficult to work effectively and survive. Second, reductions in risk level in the context of volatile economies may reduce support for organizations and programs focusing on the short term in favor of those focusing on the long term. Third, the fact that supporters' preferences may adjust much more rapidly to varying risk level than do nonprofit programs and capacity leads to increasing "philanthropic friction," that is, the mismatch between supporter preferences and nonprofit capacity. In an extreme case, a nonprofit may begin a process of change toward more short-term programs in response to changed supporter preferences following a sudden increase in risk—for example, an economic shock—but by the time that change is in effect, falling risk level may encourage supporters' preferences to shift back to long-term programs . . . ! Nonprofit leaders may also overadapt by radically transforming their programs and organizations in response to perceived changes in risk preferences that are not, in fact, real. Fourth, and finally, in some cases friction may lead to loss of confidence in nonprofits and even the sector in general. Eager to attract support during high-risk periods, nonprofit leaders may promise to focus on short-term impacts. Once they secure support, however, nonprofit leaders may be tempted to invest instead in starved long-term programs and organizational development. Nonprofit leaders generally discount future impacts of their organizations less than outside supporters do. Leaders commonly use a lower discount rate than supporters do, because leaders face lower risk with respect to nonprofit impacts: they have better information, more control over activities, and a higher investment in the organization. Some supporters may withhold contributions, weary that their support, primarily intended for short-term emergency work, will be saved or spent on long-term programs and organizational development. In addition, if nonprofits do not show immediate impact during times of generalized economic distress, they may lose supporter and even broader social trust in nonprofits as "caring" organizations. Another important implication from the risk theory is that risk will have a stronger impact on the contributions of non-core supporters.

Risk, and its impact on the nonprofit sector, also depends on nonprofits' level of resource vulnerability. Diversification into other types of support, such as commercial revenue and government funding, may mitigate declining philanthropic support. Nonprofits may also avoid insolvency and minimize disruptions to their capacity and programs by having low fixed costs and a reserve fund. High levels of risk, however, may limit support for organizational development and increase organizational vulnerability. Ultimately, therefore, the process of building up financial, physical, human, and social capital depends on the level of support for the nonprofit sector's long-term impacts and survival. This feedback effect between external risk and organizational vulnerability suggests that risk may lead to a trap in nonprofit sector development.

By reducing the present value of future nonprofit sector impact and by increasing philanthropic friction, risk reduces the value donors attribute to philanthropic contributions, undermining support for the nonprofit sector. Falling support, in turn, contributes to organizational vulnerability and endangers nonprofit sector sustainability. These predicted risk impacts combine to generate an understanding of the impact of economic shocks that is distinct from their simple impact due to changes in supporters' and other stakeholders' income. Procyclicality of household income and company profits clearly plays a key part in explaining the procyclicality of philanthropic giving. However, an explanation based on the impact of income cannot account for the increase in some types of giving during recessions, such as general giving to emergencies and short-term programs. An explanation based on risk helps to explain these apparent inconsistencies. It also provides a new explanation for the more general procyclicality of philanthropic giving. Moreover, the cross-national variation in philanthropy and nonprofit sector strength, which the PKC depicts, is inconsistent with predictions of a linear relationship between nonprofit sector strength and household income. Instead, much of the influence of cross-national variation in the level of economic development must be understood from the perspective of its impact on risk and the subsequent impact of risk on the nonprofit sector.

Implications

Research on the PKC and on the impact of risk on nonprofit sector strength offers new opportunities for theoretical development and new policy insights. A major motivation for systematically examining the links between economic development, risk, and the nonprofit sector is the search for development paths that enhance nonprofit sector development in the future. Given the sector's contributions to welfare, public goods, democratization, and economic development itself, much is at stake. In the case of poor and middle-income countries, the PKC provides a convenient framework to guide policy makers' current efforts to "build" civil society. According to the PKC, the early to middle stages of prosperity could be quite detrimental for the nonprofit sector. The extent to which decision makers ought to devote their limited time and resources to designing and implementing policies for nonprofit sector development depends on the extent to which the driving forces underlying the PKC are susceptible to such policies. In other words, if nonprofit sector decline is an inevitable consequence of rising prosperity, attempts to avoid such damage in the early stages of development might be futile. Understanding the mechanics of virtuous and vicious cycles enables us to find an intervention point. The risk mechanism, which the present study identifies, suggests that some interventions, such as reducing macroeconomic risk, are structural and therefore difficult to implement, while others, such as decreasing nonprofit organizations' vulnerability, are more specific and feasible. From a policy perspective, therefore, the PKC points to a historical tendency rather than a natural law. Indeed, the evidence in this book suggests a proactive approach, whereby policy makers could learn from experience and adopt nonprofit sector–friendly development strategies that would permit the nonprofit sector to "bridge across" the PKC (Figure 1.4).

Economic development could lead to the lower path ABC. The adoption of corrective policies that reduce nonprofit vulnerability, and thereby reduce nonprofit sector decline, leads to an evolution represented by the bridge ABD. Avoiding the path of greater nonprofit sector vulnerability would help to prevent the costly-to-reverse nonprofit sector decline and, with a "double dividend," boost future economic growth prospects. In other words, the bridge would enable developing countries to short-circuit more conventional development paths (such as ABCE in the figure). In general,

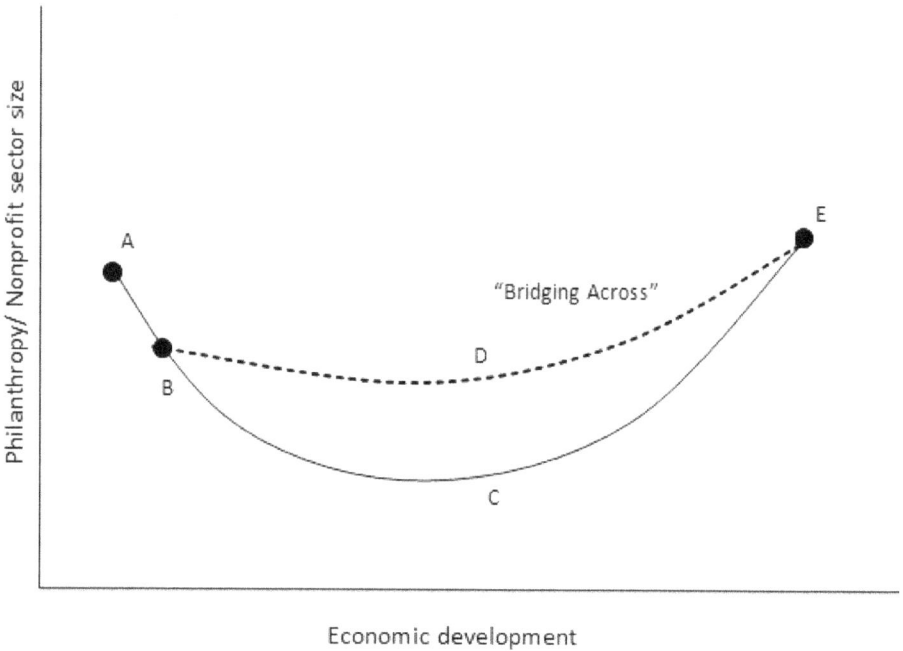

Figure 1.4. "Bridging across" the philanthropic Kuznets curve.

successful "bridging across" policy should be based on the awareness that, at early stages, economic development is accompanied by higher macroeconomic volatility and risk. Policy makers can monitor harmful impacts on the nonprofit sector and address them through complementary measures.

The analysis presented here offers fresh insights into public policy aimed at non-profit sector development in developing countries. Unfortunately, as this study shows, during crises government support for the nonprofit sector frequently gives way to other policy concerns such as rescuing the financial sector. Even during recovery periods, government support commonly shifts a disproportionate level of risk to the nonprofit sector through public-private contracting arrangements. International donor agencies, on the other hand, generally phase out their support to developing countries as their economies develop (Collier and Dehn 2001), without consideration of how the non-profit sector is impacted by both economic development and the withdrawal of international aid (Suwannarat 2003). Currently, international donors' phasing-out policy is at odds with their stated interest in helping to build civil society in developing countries. Nonprofit leaders and supporters can also pursue several steps to increase nonprofit resilience and effectiveness as detailed in the conclusion.

A systematic examination of the links between economic development, risk, and the nonprofit sector is also relevant to the nonprofit sector in rich countries. Risk is intrinsic to the human experience and a key motivation for the evolution of social institutions (e.g., Acemoglu 2009; Beck 1992; Giddens 1999; North 1990; Shiller 2003). Thus, risk is increasingly central to contemporary social debates. In *Risk Society,* Ulrich Beck (1992) maintains that society, which has been characterized primarily by mechanisms for the distribution of resources, capital, and income, is becoming characterized by mechanisms for the distribution of risk. For example, the welfare system can be seen less as a redistribution system designed to address poverty and more as a system to reduce risks. As Giddens (1999) observed, "the welfare state, whose development can be traced back to the Elizabethan poor laws in England, is essentially a risk management system. It is designed to protect against hazards that were once treated as at the disposition of the gods—sickness, disablement, job loss and old age." Accordingly, political contests increasingly center on reducing risks such as social vulnerability, economic crises, terrorism, and environmental disaster.

Even if we do not agree with Beck's argument, a risk perspective encourages reinterpretation and reassessment of critical social debates, such as those surrounding appropriate roles for the state and society. For example, the welfare system is being reformed everywhere. According to Nicholas Barr (2001:262), "under the old system, it was regarded as the duty of the state to look after people. A reformed system should encourage the idea that, though the state has an important role in promoting welfare, citizens—both individually and through various aspects of civil society—need to take responsibility." This reform is partly dictated by fiscal constraints and partly by arguments that the private sector can manage most types of risk more effectively than government (Barr 2001; OECD 2008). As the nonprofit sector takes on renewed roles in social risk management and protection, understanding the relationship between risk and the nonprofit sector is imperative. Consideration of risk has also led to new calls for state involvement in the welfare system and the economy as the insurer of last resort (Moss 2002). The unprecedented involvement of governments across the world in rescuing their economies during the recent economic crisis (2008–2009) is a manifest example of how risk forces a reassessment of appropriate roles for the state and the market.

As a permanent social fixture, risk always merits careful study. However, on the cusp of the worst crisis since the Great Depression, understanding the impact of economic risk on the nonprofit sector is also urgent. In the United States, philanthropic giving suffered the worst decline, in current-dollars terms, since accurate records began in the 1950s (Center on Philanthropy at Indiana University 2010). Reports of struggling nonprofits faced with a decline in revenue and a simultaneous increase in social need abounded in the media. Also several high-profile economists, including the editors of the *Economist* magazine and Paul Krugman, have repeatedly warned that the recovery will be long and hesitant in the best of scenarios. Worse still, the recent crisis may be just the beginning of a new wave of global crises that are fuelled by global financial market integration and the globalization of systemic risk (De Nicolo and Kwast 2002; Alexander, Dhumale, and Eatwell 2006) as well by the fact that G-7 sovereign debt levels as a proportion of GDP are nearing sixty-year highs (IMF 2010:3).[16] The Federal Reserve's current concerns about a possible "double dip" in GDP and decision to leave interest rates at record low levels until at least 2013 are clear signs of pessimism about the recovery prospects in the United States and Europe.

While the impact of economic volatility, and risk more generally, on markets and the state has received considerable academic and policy attention, systematic research on the impact of risk on the nonprofit sector is in its infancy (Young 2006). The International Monetary Fund alone produced over five hundred research reports on various dimensions of macroeconomic risk and volatility between 1995 and 2010, but none of them focused on the nonprofit sector.[17] This book seeks to contribute to a better understanding of this important relationship and to inform nonprofit sector theory and policy at a time of significant economic risk.

This book makes important headway in defining policy steps to help build nonprofit sector resilience. The risk explanation proposes that, by leading to profound changes in stakeholder preferences, the impact of economic crises goes far beyond a temporary reduction in disposable incomes. Risk has a particularly debilitating impact upon social support for capital formation and long-term investments within the nonprofit sector, reducing the opportunities for financial, physical, human, and social capital development. This fact opens the door for policy makers, nonprofit leaders, and donors to play a role in reducing nonprofit sector vulnerability and, consequently, the impact of potentially unavoidable macroeconomic volatility in the future. How can nonprofit leaders promote nonprofit resilience and social impact? Noteworthy lessons from the evidence presented in this book include the critical roles of volunteering, commercialization, and risk transfers between government and the nonprofit sector.

The stakes are high. Increased attention to the nonprofit sector has been partly fueled by growing doubts about the capacity of the state and the market to cope with today's challenges (see Anheier 2004; Clark 2003). Voluntary, nonprofit organizations have the knowledge, direct connections to society, flexibility, horizontal structures of decision-making, and expertise that the state lacks (Clark 1991; Hadenius and Uggla 1996; Hulme and Edwards 1997). Nonprofits, therefore, have become important actors in the provision of services that the state cannot or will not deliver as effectively. Even Mexico's small nonprofit sector is still a key player in public policy. Mexican nonprofit organizations employ an estimated 141,024 full-time equivalent staff (Verduzco 2000). This figure corresponds to an impressive 56.2% of local government or 10% of federal government employment in Mexico.[18] These figures tend to be considerably higher in other countries, since they have larger nonprofit sectors. Thus, nonprofit sector strength has critical implications for society's service delivery capacity and, consequently, welfare.

Increasing attention to the nonprofit sector has also been fueled by the recognition that the nonprofit sector is essential for civil society and social capital development

(Anheier 2004), which are often directly associated with democratization and effective running of government (e.g., Fisher 1993; Putnam 1993) as well as the smooth functioning of markets and economic development (e.g., Knack and Keefer 1997; Narayan 1999; Putnam 1993; Woolcock 2001). Civil society has also been associated with many other socially desirable goals, such as the nonviolent transition from dictatorships to democracy (Acemoglu and Robinson 2006), a cleaner environment (Binder and Neumayer 2005), and lower levels of government corruption (Themudo 2013). By influencing nonprofit sector strength, therefore, economic development and risk have profound—and often detrimental—social impacts.

Plan of the Book

Having identified the PKC as a robust empirical phenomenon lacking adequate explanation, the following chapters go on to determine what dynamic, interactive mechanisms are commonly responsible for this nonlinear pattern (see McAdam et al. 2001:312), and derive relevant theoretical and policy implications. Building upon finance and game theory, chapter 2 lays out a theoretical explanation of nonprofit sector strength based on the influence of economic risk. It analyzes different types of economic risk and their impacts upon support for the nonprofit sector and upon organizational vulnerability. Chapters 3 through 5 assess the consistency between the theory's predictions and both cross-national statistical evidence and longitudinal evidence on the Mexican nonprofit sector. They illuminate the mechanisms at play and generate insights about potential ways to counteract the negative impact of risk on the nonprofit sector. The cross-national nature of the PKC and the lack of clarity about how the proposed risk mechanism manifests itself in practice suggests that a combination of qualitative and quantitative research methods is appropriate. Using a "sequential mixed methods" research design (Creswell 2003) enabled triangulation between statistical analysis of individual survey and cross-national nonprofit sector data, a survey of nonprofit organizations, and qualitative fieldwork on organizational case studies. This combination enabled a more robust and nuanced analysis and testing of the theoretical hypotheses. Chapter 6 considers the broader implications of the PKC and the risk mechanism that explains it for welfare, democracy, and economic prosperity, in middle-income countries and elsewhere. The book ends by providing policy and management recommendations aimed at reducing nonprofit organization vulnerability and promoting nonprofit sector strength.

2 A Risk Perspective on the Nonprofit Sector

THIS CHAPTER PROPOSES a theoretical framework based on the influence of economic risk to explain variation in philanthropy and nonprofit sector size. In so doing, it will generate a hypothetical explanation for the PKC puzzle that is tested in subsequent chapters. Drawing on finance and game theory, it argues that risk fundamentally shapes the nature and extent of philanthropy and other contributions to the nonprofit sector. This framework extends insights from previous research on how risk influences the nonprofit sector. Research on nonprofit finance has highlighted the debilitating impact of financial vulnerability and risk on nonprofit organizations (e.g., Tuckman and Chang 1991; Keating et al. 2005; Young 2007). The impact of macroeconomic risk on the sector, however, is largely absent from past research, as is the impact of varying attitudes toward risk among organizational partners and individual supporters. This chapter employs theoretical analysis to help fill this gap.

The first part of this chapter introduces the primary outcome of interest for this study—nonprofit sector strength—and its hypothetical explanations: economic development, volatility, and risk. The second part then details how risk impacts individual motivations to support the nonprofit sector. In particular, economic theory explains why individuals are generally risk-averse. It also suggests that before contributing time and money to social causes, individuals estimate potential benefits and opportunity costs to themselves and to society. The key insight is that risk increases the discounting of future costs and benefits in relation to present costs and benefits. Game theory, on the other hand, models strategic interaction between individuals and establishes the conditions under which cooperation is likely and those under which it is not. One of game theory's most robust findings is that present cooperation is more likely when there is some possibility that players will meet again in the future. By reducing the probability of future meetings as well as the present value of future incentives for cooperation, risk reduces the incentives for many forms of voluntary cooperation, including support for the nonprofit sector. After examining individual motivations for philanthropic behavior, the third part of the chapter examines the impact of risk on other resources that nonprofit organizations can attract. Because the sector is comprised of organizations, the impact of risk on the sector depends to a large extent on the level of nonprofit organizations' vulnerability. Finance theory provides insights into the determinants of financial vulnerability in organizations, suggesting that it depends primarily on nonprofits' access to capital, "beta risk," resource diversification, and cost structure. The last section draws empirical implications from the risk framework and defines the conditions under which it can help explain the PKC.

Nonprofit Sector Strength

The primary outcome of interest in this study is nonprofit sector weakness, or alternatively strength, which consists of two related dimensions: philanthropy and sector size. Philanthropy captures individual participation in the sector through individual giving and volunteering in nonprofit organizations. Sector size includes philanthropy as well as other sources of support, such as commercial fees and government funding. To measure sector size, researchers commonly use statistics on total employment in the sector, including both paid and volunteer labor, as well as sector income and expenditures.

Following Salamon and Anheier's (1998) definition, the nonprofit sector is the set of organizations within a country that meet, in at least rough terms, the following set of standards: these entities should be (1) "Organized, i.e., institutionalized to some extent"; (2) "Private, i.e., institutionally separate from government"; (3) "Non-profit-distributing, i.e., not returning any profits generated to their owners or directors"; (4) "Self-governing, i.e., equipped to control their own activities"; and (5) "Voluntary, i.e., involving some meaningful degree of voluntary participation, either in the actual conduct of the agency's activities or in the management of its affairs" (33–34). This definition is consistent with a significant share of cross-national research on the nonprofit sector (e.g., Gidron, Barr, and Katz 2003; Brinkerhoff 2002; Franco 2005) and the main cross-national dataset used in this study: the Johns Hopkins Comparative Nonprofit Sector Project (CNP), conducted by Salamon, Anheier, and an international team of collaborators (e.g., Salamon et al. 1999, 2004).

Examining different indicators of both philanthropy and sector size is important because they reflect different dimensions of the nonprofit sector and they help to mitigate potential biases associated with cross-national indicators. By triangulating findings based on different measures and datasets, this study is able to increase confidence on consistent findings and suggest new lines of inquiry on inconsistent ones.

Economic Development, Volatility, and Risk

According to Amartya Sen (1999:1), development is "a process of expanding the real freedoms that people enjoy." Hence, "development requires the removal of major sources of unfreedom: poverty as well as tyranny, poor economic opportunities as well as systematic social deprivation, neglect of public facilities as well as intolerance or overactivity of repressive states." Economic development, then, refers to economic changes that lead to "the expansion of the real freedoms that people enjoy," such as increases in national output and average income per capita, education, health, technological innovation, industrialization, and urbanization (Kuznets 1973; Perkins et al. 2006). Economic volatility generally refers to the cyclical variation of macroeconomic output. According to the National Bureau of Economic Research (website), "a recession is a significant decline in economic activity spread across the economy, lasting more than a few months, normally visible in real GDP, real income, employment, industrial production, and wholesale-retail sales." A recession begins just after the economy reaches a peak of activity and ends as the economy reaches its trough. Between trough and peak, the economy is in an expansion. Overall, volatility can be measured by the standard deviation of economic growth for a given period (Easterly, Islam, and Stiglitz 1999).

Risk is commonly understood as the possibility of an undesired outcome, such as a car accident, illness, earthquake, or decline in asset values. To the extent that such undesired outcomes are possible, I face risk in the present. According to this view, the higher the probability that those events will take place in the future, the higher the risk I face now. Probability assessment of risky events is often personal and subjective because risk is related to the level of control over future events and future projections based on learning from past events (Chavas 2004). Many types of risk, however, are much more objective, estimated from a data-rich historical record or scientific theories. The risks of being in an airplane crash, developing cancer, and losing money in a casino would fall into this category.

In economics and finance, risk is associated with uncertainty over outcomes. Uncertainty exists when more than one outcome is possible, and the outcome is unknown in advance: the greater the potential variation in outcomes, the greater is the risk.[1] Our inability to predict the future, then, creates risk (Doherty 2000:17).[2] According to this view, risk is not the same as hazard or danger. Risk does not refer to the adverse quality of some outcomes (e.g., accidents, financial losses), but rather to the lack of knowledge about which of several outcomes may prevail. Thus, risk also entails potential gains from a positive embrace of risk. That is why risk-taking is the very source of wealth and innovation in a modern economy (Kuznets 1973; Giddens 1999). It is this second meaning of risk that is commonly associated with a direct relationship between risk and reward, so that riskier investments also have higher potential returns. Absolute risk reduction, therefore, is not an optimum strategy because it also eliminates the potential gains from taking risks. "Risk management can help you seize opportunity, not just avoid danger" (Borge 2001:3).

In a world of perfect certainty, there would be no risk. The expected return on an investment would always be equal to the actual return. Risk reflects the possibility that the actual return on an investment may be very different from the expected return. When we can estimate a probability distribution of possible returns—including negative returns—the mean provides a simple measure of the central tendency for returns. Variance measures the expected dispersion of likely returns around the mean. Thus, a popular measure of risk is the variance (or standard deviation) of the distribution of potential returns or outcomes. For example, in Modern Portfolio Theory and the Capital Asset Pricing Model, the risk of an investment is the variance of its returns (Borge 2001). Since this study focuses largely on nonprofit finance and other resources, finance theory plays a central role in the framework developed here, and standard deviation of the distribution of potential outcomes is one of its principal measures of risk.

When economists say that individuals are typically risk-averse, they mean that individuals faced with a certain outcome and an uncertain alternative with the same expected value will generally choose the certain outcome, that is, the outcome with lower expected variance (see Borge 2001; Young 2006). A risk-neutral agent, on the other hand, will be indifferent between a certain outcome and an uncertain alternative with the same expected value. Individuals, then, tend to forgo opportunities for exceptionally high returns because threats of equally significant losses typically accompany those opportunities. Risk-aversion stems directly from the "law of diminishing marginal utility" (see Varian 2004). To understand why this is the case, consider an individual facing a risky situation in which she has an equal probability of winning $1,000 or losing $1,000. Because the utility curve becomes flatter as wealth increases, the loss of utility from a fall in wealth ($1,000 in this case) exceeds the increase in utility from an equal gain in wealth. Risk, then, generates an expected net utility loss. An individual is worse off in this risky situation than in a riskless situation in which she can neither win nor lose $1,000. A risk-averse individual, therefore, must be compensated for taking risks by receiving a "risk premium," that is, the excess expected return of a risky alternative that an individual requires to be indifferent between the risky alternative and a riskless one. Alternatively, since individuals tend to prefer more certain outcomes, they will *discount* the expected value of a risky alternative according to its level of risk and their degree of risk-aversion. Discounting alternative outcomes based on their levels of risk produces risk-adjusted or "certainty equivalent" expected values, which individuals can compare with riskless alternatives before making an informed choice (Borge 2001; Varian 2004).

The future inevitably involves uncertainty and risk. Thus, risk-averse agents must discount the value of future, risky outcomes when comparing them to present outcomes. To be sure, risk is not the only reason why agents discount the future. Other reasons may include the "time value of money," impatience, and inflation. If given a choice between receiving $500 today or $500 in one year, most individuals would choose to receive the money today. Conversely, if instead the choice was between paying $500 today or $500 in one year, most individuals would choose to pay in one year—today's $500 can be invested, generating $500 plus the annual interest rate (r) in one year. Assuming the interest rate is positive, $\$500*(1+r)$ is larger than $500. Moreover, impatient agents may prefer money now even if the alternative includes compensation for the time value of money because society's interest rate may be lower than the rate needed to make an impatient individual indifferent about waiting. Inflation provides another reason why we should discount the nominal value of future financial outcomes.

Because the value of future outcomes depends on how far into the future they will take place, decisions in the present involving streams of costs of benefits at different points in time require conversion to a common unit, typically present values. Discounting of future costs and benefits involves converting the value of future costs and benefits into their equivalent value in the present. The less is known about a future outcome, the greater the variance of potential outcomes (i.e., the riskier it is) and the more it should be discounted. Furthermore, the more distant into the future, the more uncertain an outcome typically is and, consequently, the more it should be discounted. Risk discounting can be implemented by adding a risk discount rate to the opportunity cost discount rate or, preferably, by converting each future outcome into its certainty-equivalent value so that risk discounting can vary for different outcomes and different periods. Risk-aversion and the opportunity cost of invested resources, therefore, lead individuals and other risk-averse agents to discount the present value of future consequences from delaying consumption and investing in the present.

Different individuals may discount the same risky outcomes differently because people may have different attitudes toward risk. Degree of risk-aversion may relate to personality (i.e., cautious, adventurous) and economic circumstances such as wealth. Considerable controversy, however, remains over whether as wealth increases risk-aversion increases, decreases, or stays constant (Doherty 2000:17).

Risk-aversion also varies during the macroeconomic cycle. Several researchers have pointed out that risk, measured as market and output volatility, varies countercyclically, that is, rises during recessions and declines during economic booms (e.g., Schwert 1989; Campbell and Cochrane 1999; Aydemir 2008). Indeed, different measures of the price of risk, such as the expected equity premium, the volatility of the premium, and the Sharpe ratio (the ratio of expected premium to its volatility), are also countercyclical. The fact that risk rises during recessions is partly intuitive. During recessions, the risk that some firms will default on their creditors and inflict losses on investors rises significantly. But why does the risk premium rise even in the case of financially stable, low-risk securities? There is considerable academic debate over why this is the case.

One influential explanation for why risk premiums rise when the economy contracts suggests that risk-aversion is countercyclical (Campbell and Cochrane 1999). Asset-pricing models that allow risk-aversion to increase in recessions and decrease in expansions are capable of generating equilibrium asset returns that resolve the equity premium puzzle. If investors become more risk-averse when the economy declines, the risk premium rises. Moreover, higher risk-aversion during recessions reduces the demand for risky assets such as shares and further depresses their price. To the extent that agents respond strongly to public news, their actions might become highly correlated, increasing market volatility. Indeed, market correlations also vary countercyclically (Aydemir 2008).

Macroeconomic contractions, therefore, bring about both higher risk-aversion and higher risk, measured as higher output volatility and countercyclical market correlations. As a result, private investment declines sharply, despite the fact that the opportunity cost of capital typically falls during recessions. Investment decline is typically sharper than output and considerably sharper than nondurables consumption (see Krugman 2008). Attitudes toward risk, then, are fundamental to understanding the impact of risk.

In examining the relationship between risk and the nonprofit sector, we must also consider attitudes toward risk in organizations. At the organizational level, for-profits are typically assumed to be risk-neutral agents (Wedig 1994; Young 2006). Thus, they do not require a risk premium to take on risky projects. For-profits should focus on maximizing the expected value of investments and, consequently, profit. The reason why for-profits can be risk-neutral, when the shareholders owning them are risk-averse, is that shareholders can minimize their risk by holding a well-diversified investment portfolio. Within the portfolio, losses in one company should generally be offset by gains in another so shareholders face no idiosyncratic risk (though they still face systematic risk, discussed below). Similarly, government is often assumed to be a risk-neutral agent (Samuelson 1964; Vickrey 1964; Arrow and Lind 1970), although considerable debate remains in this area. In contrast, Wedig (1994) argues that, due to their incentive structure, nonprofits typically behave more like a risk-averse individual than a risk-neutral for-profit or government agency. Unfortunately, empirical research on attitudes toward risk within nonprofits is still very limited (Young 2006). The consequences, however, are profound. If nonprofits do indeed behave in a risk-averse manner, then they will reject projects that are "too risky" despite the fact that their expected impact may be welfare maximizing. Nonprofit risk-aversion would also have implications for public-private contracting between government and nonprofits. Within a partnership, risk should be allocated to the party that can most efficiently reduce or bear the risk. Unavoidable risk is most efficiently borne by the least risk-averse actor. In the cases of partnerships between government and for-profits, this will commonly mean that most risk should be allocated to for-profits because they are risk-neutral, are the parties with the best information about the project as agents responsible for project implementation, and can directly capture the rewards of bearing risk (e.g., OECD 2008). While government is often assumed to also be risk-neutral, significant research indicates that government agencies behave in a risk-averse manner, generally transferring as much risk as possible to private agents. In the case of government partnerships with nonprofits, however, this practice may lead to the allocation of risk to the most risk-averse partner: the nonprofit. Such misallocation should have significant welfare implications. I return to the topic of risk sharing within public-private partnerships below.

A second key component to understanding the impact of risk on the nonprofit sector is the distinction between idiosyncratic and systematic risk. From an organizational perspective, *idiosyncratic risk* refers to the potential shocks to which the organization is exposed that would typically have no impact on other organizations. For example, a member of the board of directors withholding contributions to the organization would impact organizational finances, but it would not affect other nonprofits. Thus, it is an idiosyncratic risk to the organization. *Systematic risk,* on the other hand, refers to potential shocks due to system-wide trends to which all agents in an economy (or system) are exposed. Donors may alter their organizational contributions in response to shocks such as war or economic crises, which constitute the most visible forms of systematic risk, or in response to economic cycles more generally, as factors such as level of output, inflation, and the interest rate continuously affect the whole economy (Doherty 2000).

Aside from having different origins, systematic and idiosyncratic risks are also distinct in that they require different management approaches. For example, diversification is effective in reducing idiosyncratic risk, but not in reducing systematic risk. The reason for this is that impact on an organization depends on how different risks relate to each other. For instance, many cash flows can be volatile. However, the combined risk from all these cash flows is not simply the sum of risks from each cash flow. An organization's exposure to other risks determines the ability of a nonprofit to tolerate any one risk. Even if risks are independent of each other, they combine to impose less total risk than the sum of their parts. Extensive research has shown that diversification is key to reducing idiosyncratic risk in settings such as business finance (Borge 2001; Doherty 2000:12), rotating credit associations, and farmers' livelihoods in Africa (Maluccio, Haddad and May 2000). In nonprofit finance, several studies have found resource concentration to be a main indicator of nonprofit financial vulnerability (e.g., Greenlee and Tuckman 2007; Tuckman and Chang 1991; Zietlow et al. 2007). Tuckman and Chang (1991) calculate the Revenue Concentration Index using the Herfindahl-Hirschman Index (Herfindahl index), a typical measure of market concentration. To measure nonprofit revenue concentration, the Herfindahl index can be calculated by squaring the relative proportion of each revenue type and then summing the resulting values. That is, it is calculated according to the formula: $RCI = \Sigma \, (revenue_i \, / \, total \, revenue)^2$ where $revenue_i$ is the revenue from one of three types: donations, earned income, and government funding. An RCI value of 1.0 corresponds to all revenue deriving from one source, that is, perfect concentration. The closer the RCI is to zero, the less concentrated a revenue portfolio is. The more equally divided their share of revenues from each source is, the less vulnerable the organization is believed to be.

While diversification is effective in dealing with idiosyncratic risk, it is ineffective in reducing systematic risk (Kearns 2007). To illustrate, an organization dependent on state government funding is exposed to the idiosyncratic risk that a new governor may not be sympathetic to the organization's work. By diversifying its resource mobilization portfolio to also include philanthropic giving, a nonprofit reduces the potential impact (i.e., risk) of an idiosyncratic cut in government funding. Philanthropic giving does not, however, protect against the systematic risk resulting from an economic crisis because, as the economy contracts, state government funding and philanthropy are likely to decline simultaneously. Systematic risk cannot be diversified away because it is the result of influences affecting all resource opportunities within the economy. As a result, resource opportunities are strongly correlated (i.e., rise together or fall together). Moreover, the systematic nature of macroeconomic volatility typically means that agents cannot avoid it or get protection by buying third-party insurance. Insurance rests on the principle of risk pooling, a form of diversification. Insurance is possible only when a particular type of adverse events affects only a small number of agents within a large pool. Insurers compensate the losses of the few affected agents using the premiums from the much larger number of agents who did not suffer any loss. This type of insurance is not possible when all or most agents suffer losses and make claims at the same time, as is the case in the aftermath of a systematic shock (Doherty 2000). Individuals and organizations, therefore, must find alternative strategies to deal with systematic risk. Most commonly, economic agents can reduce their vulnerability in the face of systematic shocks through self-insurance, that is, by building reserves that can be mobilized to meet future contingencies in a context of high uncertainty about the future. When building reserves is impossible or is itself risky due to limited opportunities for safe asset storage, economic agents must typically cut spending in line with declining income during economic shocks to minimize asset erosion (Carter and Maluccio 2003). Thus, to say that systematic risk cannot be diversified, avoided, or insured does not mean that all nonprofits are equally vulnerable to it. As explained below, nonprofits can reduce systematic risk by self-insuring, spending procyclically, and hedging.

Risk and Philanthropy

The preceding discussion on types and characteristics of risks and their potential impacts on individual and organizational behavior provides a background against which we can consider the more specific questions pertinent to this study. We begin with the question: how does economic risk influence philanthropy? This apparently simple question exposes a complex set of relationships between risk, collective action, social capital, and philanthropy, which have profound implications for nonprofit sector strength. While philanthropy is not the dominant form of nonprofit funding in any country (Salamon et al. 2004), its contribution to nonprofit sector strength greatly exceeds its relative weight in nonprofit finance. For example, in the United States alone, an estimated 10 million individuals serve as volunteers in board positions (Ilchman and Burlingame 1999:200). In fact, nonprofits could not exist without philanthropy. At early stages of existence, nonprofits depend primarily on the philanthropic contributions of their founders. Later, at a minimum nonprofits depend on the philanthropy of their board members in terms of volunteer labor and, typically, giving. Also, nonprofits capable of mobilizing philanthropic resources are generally preferred when government makes funding decisions (Bryce 2005) and are better able to avoid dangers from commercialization, such as shifting attention to sales and buyers instead of mission and beneficiaries (see Young and Salamon 2002).

Incentives, Collective Action, and Philanthropy

Collective action, that is, voluntary action for the common good, is critical for nonprofit creation and sustainability. Collective action has also been widely researched in the context of social movements (Tarrow 1994) and community mobilization (Ostrom 1990). Research on collective action is commonly concerned with identifying solutions to the collective action problem, which emerges in group settings where all individuals can benefit from a collective good but can avoid making individual contributions. In such settings, individuals will commonly free-ride the efforts of others (Olson 1965). Vilfredo Pareto (1935, vol. 3, sect. 1496:946–947) explains: "If all individuals refrained from doing

A, every individual as a member of the community would derive a certain advantage. But now if all individuals less one continue refraining from doing A, the community loss is very slight, whereas the one individual doing A makes a personal gain far greater than the loss that he incurs as a member of the community."

However, when all individuals withhold their contributions, collective action fails, and all are worse off. Individuals all act in their own material self-interest, and voluntary cooperation alone does not lead to production of public goods. Thus, collective action represents a social dilemma, where what is rational at the individual level, in the narrow economic sense, is irrational for the group.

Game theory offers important insights into social dilemmas. In particular, the Prisoner's Dilemma (PD) game aptly represents the incentives individuals face in social dilemma situations. In a PD game, the dilemma faced by the players is that each is better off by confessing to the authorities (and getting a lighter sentence as a result) than by keeping silence. But the outcome obtained when both confess is worse for each than the outcome if both keep silence (they both go free as the authorities have no confession of the crime).[3] Authorities are able to exploit the conflict between prisoners' individual and collective rationality in order to get voluntary confessions.

Such collective action dilemmas abound in the nonprofit sector. To the extent that philanthropy represents private provision for the public good, it is hindered by the collective action problem (Salamon 1987; Steinberg 2006). For example, an individual might be tempted not to give to nonprofit organizations such as public television because they can enjoy their programs independently of contributing. However, if no one contributes to these organizations, they will fail to provide services to causes that everyone values.

Nevertheless, the fact that philanthropy and the nonprofit sector exist represents a triumph over free-riding and the collective action problem. That is, the nonprofit sector embodies solutions to the social dilemma of voluntary public goods provision. How do they accomplish this? That is, how do nonprofit organizations sustain participation (see Jenkins 2006)? Mancur Olson (1965) proposed one possible answer, arguing that "selective incentives" are essential for a sustained solution to free riding. Selective incentives are essentially "side" private benefits (or sanctions) not directly related to the collective good for which contributions are sought, which groups can dispense to encourage contributions to collective efforts. To the extent that free-riders can be identified, the group can apply incentives selectively to encourage their voluntary participation. According to James Q. Wilson (1995), selective incentives can be material, solidary (i.e., arising from relationships with other people), and moral (i.e., doing the right thing).

Research on the nonprofit sector suggests that "consumption incentives" frequently motivate philanthropy, as in the cases of "contributions to churches, schools, cultural institutions, and professional organizations, from which givers and their families directly benefit" (Ostrander and Schervish 2004:804–805). In such cases, nonprofits can avoid free-riding by selecting who can access side material benefits and restricting noncontributors' access to them. Two problems, however, plague material selective incentives as a universal solution to free-riding. First, the more material benefits groups dispense, the less resources nonprofits will have available for the production of collective goods. This problem is exacerbated when groups are resource-starved to begin with, as is common at early stages of the group's life when only entrepreneurs and a few sympathetic supporters provide all resources. Second, if groups can provide a private benefit with sufficient profit to finance collective good production, they may attract competition by for-profits and other nonprofits. The result of such competition may be to strongly reduce, or even eliminate, any profits and consequently any leftover resources for collective good production. For example, one Mexican nonprofit organization created an environmental magazine that it distributed to its donors. The magazine acted as a selective incentive for donor contributions. Within a couple of years, however, three similar magazines emerged in the marketplace, one created by a competing nonprofit and two created by for-profits. If donors had been contributing primarily because they got the magazine in return, now they could get similar magazines more cheaply since they did not include a substantial donation in the price.

Solidary incentives constitute a second type of selective incentives that can be used to reduce free-riding (Wilson 1995). According to Ostrander and Schervish (2004:804–805) "the need to fulfill a social obligation that reproduces the bonds in a social network of friends and associates" motivates some types of philanthropy. In this case, philanthropy and participation may result from social pressure and the possibility of future retaliation against free-riders (e.g., Jenkins 2006; Musick and Wilson 2008). Within a stable social group, "it is possible for contributors to threaten potential noncontributors with punishments that are large enough that individuals prefer to contribute despite their short-run incentive to free-ride" (Vesterlund 2006:577). Moreover, costly signaling theories argue that prosocial behavior can generate important reputational benefits because it reliably indicates desirable and generally hidden traits of the signaler (Frank 1988; Zahavi and Zahavi 1997; Roberts 1998). Contributions to group efforts serve as signals of the contributor's commitment to the group; such signals are reliable because they are expensive to fake. Commitment to the group, on the other hand, is a valued characteristic that earns the signaler status and a variety of material rewards (Willer 2009). The fact that nonprofits make significant efforts to recognize their most active members and donors is consistent with the argument that donors may benefit from reputation effects.

The previous discussion eschews the possibility that contributions to the provision of collective goods are at least partly independent from any personal benefits donors may receive (Ostrander and Schervish 2004), that is, that they may be due to generosity and altruism. How good is the assumption that individuals always act in a way that maximizes their personal gains? According to Sen (1977:332): "I doubt that in general it is very good. ('Where is the railway station?' he asks me. 'There,' I say, pointing at the post office, 'and would you please post this letter for me on the way?' 'Yes,' he says, determined to open the envelope and check whether it contains something valuable.)

John Q. Wilson (1995) partly acknowledges the possibility of other-regarding behavior by claiming that moral or purposive incentives are the third and last main type of "selective incentives." These incentives correspond to the internal feeling of doing the right thing. Amartya Sen (1977:326) argues that we must distinguish between two different motivations for other-regarding behavior: sympathy and commitment:

> The former corresponds to the case in which the concern for others directly affects one's own welfare. If the knowledge of torture of others makes you sick, it is a case of sympathy; if it does not make you feel personally worse off, but you think it is wrong and you are ready to do something to stop it, it is a case of commitment. . . . It can be argued that behavior based on sympathy is in an important sense egoistic, for one is oneself pleased at others' pleasure and pained at others' pain, and the pursuit of one's own utility may thus be helped by sympathetic action. It is action based on commitment rather than sympathy which would be non-egoistic in this sense.

Arguably, however, moral and purposive incentives are not "selective"—at least in Olson's (1965) original formulation of the concept—since a group cannot control (or "select") who receives them in its effort to promote participation. Rather than selective, "Purposive incentives are inherently collective, based on commitment to a moral vision" (Jenkins 2006:319). Nevertheless, even though groups may have limited influence on collective morality and its individual interpretations, they may still benefit from the power of social norms and moral values in encouraging unselfish behavior (see Vesterlund 2006). Group members generally like to feel that they are doing their share (Sen 1977), and the very act of giving may generate what James Andreoni (1990) referred to as "warm glow"—the positive feelings that typically accompany acts of generosity. While nonprofits cannot control the extent to which a donor experiences "warm glow," the widespread practice of nonprofits sending costly "Thank you" notes to donors suggests that certain practices may contribute to it.

Individuals may also contribute to the collective effort because they value its purpose and the values for which it stands. According to Dwight Burlingame (2004:18), "virtue theories, which dominated philosophy up to the Enlightenment, dwelled on the importance of being charitable and concerned about others. [And for] humanists, relieving the suffering of others can provide meaning to the giver and contribute to the common good." In purposive philanthropy, contributions represent an investment in the hope of future social returns, such as less poverty or a better environment. A genuine concern for the welfare of others can fundamentally alter the free-riding calculus. As Roger Lohmann (1992:102) puts it, "To the extent that sharing of resources and purposes, mutuality and fairness that are the defining characteristics [of the "commons"] hold sway, one would expect the impact of free-riding to be minimal."

The fact that extensive philanthropy and a vibrant nonprofit sector exist in some contexts suggest that free-riding tendencies can be greatly attenuated. But how, then, can we account for philanthropic anemia and nonprofit sector weakness in other contexts? In theory, nonprofits can use selective incentives anywhere in the world. Strong social norms promoting prosocial behavior exist in all cultures, and donors probably experience as much, if not more, "warm glow" after they act in a generous manner in Mexico as they do in the United States. Yet, even after adjusting for the different size of their respective economies, Mexicans contribute thirty-two times less than Americans do in terms of philanthropy (including both giving and volunteering).[4] Given what is at stake, we urgently need more research that specifies more precisely the conditions under which free-riding behavior is more or less likely to occur (Lohmann 1992:122; Jenkins 2006). This study seeks to fill this gap by analyzing the powerful, yet still largely ignored, impact of risk on philanthropy.

Philanthropy, Risk, and the "Shadow of the Future"

Game theory suggests that most solutions to free-riding depend on the future being sufficiently important relative to the present.[5] Robert Axelrod referred to this relative importance of the future as the "shadow of the future."[6] Indeed, one of the most robust findings in experimental research on the two-person Iterated Prisoner's Dilemma is that cooperation in the present is probable only when players (a) are likely to meet again in the future and (b) do not apply a high discount rate to future benefits from cooperation (Feinberg and Husted 1993; Dal Bó 2005). As Robert Axelrod's (1984:174) seminal work in this area shows, "for cooperation to prove stable, the future must have a sufficiently large shadow. This means that the importance of the next encounter between the same two individuals must be great enough to make defection an unprofitable strategy. . . . It requires that the players have a large enough chance of meeting again and that they do not discount the significance of their next meeting too greatly."

Expectations about future cooperation are also critical in the context of philanthropy. Lise Vesterlund (2006:577) argues that

> donating to charity is rarely a onetime event; rather, people typically contribute to the same charity year after year. Whether repeated interaction affects the predictions of the classical model depends on the time horizon of the interaction. If donors believe that they may always contribute to the charity then the contribution game is one of infinite repetition, and the predictions of the classical model are quite different. In particular, the extreme free-riding result need not hold. With infinite repetition it is possible for contributors to threaten potential noncontributors with punishments that are large enough that individuals prefer to contribute despite their short-run incentive to free-ride. For example, if donors choose to punish free-riders by withholding all future contributions, the long-term cost of free-riding may exceed the short-term benefit, and it will be possible to sustain cooperation. However, if everyone recognizes that these interactions will eventually end, then such a strategy is not sufficient.

An implicit threat of retaliation against free-riders, therefore, will be effective only if the interaction will last long enough to make free-riding, and the losses from ensuing retaliation, more costly than contributing to the collective good.

Even when individuals have little chance of meeting again, however, research has also shown that the emergence of "indirect reciprocity" can elicit cooperation (e.g., Panchanathan and Boyd 2004). Whereas reciprocity describes the tendency of individuals to return favors directly to others who have helped them in the past, indirect reciprocity occurs when an individual is rewarded for being generous to someone else in the past. An individual might help another because he or she might one day need help as well and is fairly confident that even if the helped individual is not available to reciprocate, someone else in the community will. The emergence of indirect reciprocity is intimately linked to the ability of group members to share information about each player's behavior in the past. Even when there is a very small chance that the same two players may meet each other again, then, reputation effects can lead to cooperation. Indeed, indirect reciprocity has been widely demonstrated empirically (Wedekind and Milinski 2000; Barclay 2004).

The second requirement for cooperation under the "shadow of the future" is that individuals do not excessively discount future benefits from cooperation. This requirement is much harder to circumvent than the first one. As discussed above, the future may be less valuable than the present because of agent impatience and risk-aversion. In the future, costs and benefits are uncertain and relationships may end. One of the players may die, go bankrupt, or move away. Because agents cannot predict these factors with certainty, the next move is not as important as the current one. There may be no next move (Axelrod 1984:126–127).

By encouraging individuals to discount future outcomes, risk weakens the present value of selective incentives and the social impact from nonprofit activity; thus it generally contributes to a decline in philanthropy. For example, risk from uncertainty about group composition in the future attenuates social pressure incentives. Such risk can reduce the present value of future group retaliation against free-riders, making free-riding more appealing in the present. Similarly, as this type of risk rises, the present value of reputational capital from costly signaling contributions to the group is more heavily discounted, reducing the incentives for further contributions to the group. Risk from uncertainty about future consumption patterns contributes to higher discounting of future private consumption benefits. For example, I may not know whether I will be able to regularly go to concerts or play tennis in the future, which lowers the value of a subscription to the philharmonic or membership in a sports club. In the case of philanthropic contributions as an investment in public goods, risk from uncertainty about others' willingness and capacity to contribute might also attenuate generosity by increasing pessimism about the probability that collective action will succeed. As shown below, risk from uncertainty about others' contributions may lead to a self-fulfilling prophecy. An individual fearing that others will not contribute sufficiently may decide to withhold his or her own contributions. If this fear is widespread, most contributions will be withheld, leading to the confirmation of the original fear. Even when individuals are generous and willing to contribute to the public good independently of whether others also contribute, they may choose to withhold contributions due to pessimism about the impacts of collective action (see Walsh and Warland 1983; Jenkins 2006). By encouraging risk-averse individuals to discount the value of future public and private benefits in relation to the cost of present contributions, *risk boosts the incentives for free-riding*. In stable, low-risk environments, discounting of future benefits is small, and philanthropy is much more likely. But in unstable, high-risk environments, discounting of future nonprofit benefits relative to present contributions discourages collective action, philanthropy, and other contributions to the nonprofit sector.

In middle-income countries, economic transition and the macroeconomic instability it entails greatly contribute to high levels of all of the previously mentioned forms of risk. Labor migration and structural transition contribute to uncertainty about group composition in communities and nonprofit organizations, future consumption patterns, and the ability and willingness of others to contribute to collective goods. Risk from uncertainty about future economic prosperity may also lead agents to increase savings and reduce consumption in the present (Davis and North 1971), which would probably include consumption-motivated philanthropic contributions. Indeed, based on data from the Independent Sector's Giving and Volunteering in the United States, Havens, O'Herlihy, and Schervish (2006:554) found that households that report being worried about financial security give on average only about half the amount contributed by households who are not worried about financial security.[7]

To be sure, at times economic risk can help strengthen philanthropy and the nonprofit sector, as research on mutual aid associations has documented (see Beito 2000; Quiggin 2007). By pooling their individual risks, individuals in a community or mutual aid association may greatly reduce individual risk exposure. At the same time, two factors limit the effectiveness of mutual aid and community-level approaches to economic risk management in the long term. First, state provision of risk insurance has greatly weakened the role of mutual aid in risk protection (Beito 2000). The state has a natural advantage in risk management due to its ability through taxation and borrowing to spread risk (i.e., diversify) across a much larger pool of individuals than is available to communities or private associations (Samuelson 1964; Vickrey 1964; Arrow and Lind 1970). Second, like diversification, risk sharing is effective only against unrelated, idiosyncratic risks. It offers little protection against covariate risk because all members are impacted at the same time. Frequent macroeconomic shocks, then, should weaken risk-sharing mutual-aid associations. Evidence of the debilitating impact of economic risk on mutual aid associations during the Great Depression lends support to this argument (see Cohen 1990; Hammack 2003; Skocpol 1992). Due to its ability to spread risks across generations, the state is much better able to protect individuals against system-wide risks such as macroeconomic crises (Moss 2002; Hacker 2006).

Risk, therefore, may have a contradictory impact on different parts of the nonprofit sector, discouraging certain types of support and activity and encouraging others. The overall impact of economic risk will depend on the nature of risk as well as the extent of the risk that society faces. For instance, risk discounting implies that, in high-risk environments, social support will tend to focus on lower-risk, short-term impacts rather than higher-risk, long-term capacity development and impact. In the short term, risk may even increase available support for nonprofits focusing on emergency roles, as a higher discount rate impacts present emergencies minimally and contributions are likely to increase due to compassion toward dire needs or pressing collective duress. In the long term, however, even short-term-oriented nonprofits will experience declining support in high-risk environments because they, too, have to make some long-term investments, such as organizational capacity development. Long-term investments attract few supporters in high-risk environments. During good times, moreover, it should be harder than in bad times to find support for short-term-oriented programs and organizations.

Similarly, some types of selective and other incentives for philanthropy might be immune to risk discounting and, consequently, should be evolutionarily superior in high-risk environments. In theory, when benefits and costs occur simultaneously, discounting has no influence on agents' decision making. In most instances, however, discounting will penalize benefits more intensely than costs for two reasons. First, in many cases social benefits are likely to be more uncertain due to the higher ambiguity associated with measuring social benefits than with private costs. Second, from a donor's perspective costs generally precede social, and private, benefits. Individuals typically do not contribute to a public good after they have enjoyed it. Benefits, therefore, are likely to be to be more heavily discounted, because they entail more risk than costs do. Nevertheless, risk should have little effect on present benefits from philanthropy, such as material selective incentives consumed in the present, immediate social impact, socializing, and "warm glow." While risk affects both philanthropic giving and volunteering forms of philanthropy, volunteering should be more resilient to risk discounting because many of its benefits accrue to the contributor in the present. Overall, however, risk should still discourage volunteering since many motivations for volunteering are future benefits (e.g., long-term social impact, networking, and skill development).

"Philanthropic Friction"

Risk, especially in the context of a volatile economy, should greatly contribute to an increase in the mismatch between donor preferences and nonprofit goals, that is, between supply and demand for philanthropy. Adapting the notion of "labor friction" from economics—whose development earned Peter Diamond, Dale Mortensen, and Christopher Pissarides the 2010 Nobel Prize—we can refer to this mismatch as "philanthropic friction." Like its labor counterpart, philanthropic friction results from changes in demand and supply in a context of costly adaptation and inconsistent or incomplete information. Philanthropic friction exists at all times. For example, a nonprofit may lack the resources or efficiency for finding all the donors willing to support it. Alternatively, donors may abstain from giving because they cannot find the nonprofits they might have supported. As a result, philanthropy is lower than it could be in the context of complete information and no transaction costs.

Risk greatly contributes to philanthropic friction. In the context of risk from macroeconomic volatility, risk may lead to higher friction by encouraging rapid change in donor preferences, which nonprofits are unable to accompany. For example, the risk of further fatalities in the aftermath of a natural disaster can lead to an overnight change in donor preferences toward helping the victims. On the other hand, nonprofits commonly need significantly more time to be able to adjust their programs to address this emergency. Because supporters' preferences may adjust much more rapidly to variations in risk level than nonprofit capacity can, risk aggravates the mismatch between supporter preferences and nonprofit capacity, creating philanthropic friction. While recessions encourage short-term programs by leading to an increase in the rate with which supporters discount the future, booms should have the reverse effect. The lowering of risk expectations common to economic booms increases the present value of future benefits, encouraging a more long-term investment horizon. In volatile economies, this radical change in donor preferences can take place several times in a decade, leading to an almost continuous mismatch between donor preferences and organizational programs. To illustrate, donors can often put more or less emphasis on immediate versus future benefits, but education nonprofits are limited in their ability to shift their focus to fighting hunger or, more likely, retraining of laid-off workers in bad times. In addition, as the economy improves, they would have to switch back to long-term programs! As donor preferences change again, economic risk from macroeconomic volatility should increase the mismatch between donor preferences and organizational programs, which, in turn, tends to increase free-riding and reduce philanthropy.

Common responses to revenue declines during recessionary periods may further alienate supporters. Procyclical spending, for example, which involves spending cuts during recessions, when such spending is most needed, may reduce the relevance of nonprofits in the community's eyes. The common effort to stabilize resource mobilization by increasing fees can be another source of "friction." Higher service fees during recessions reduce the ability of some of the poorest community members to access the services at a time of worsening poverty. Following James and Young's (2007) "product portfolio map," which classifies different nonprofit services according to a dual bottom-line framework, as revenue drops in bad times, nonprofits may become increasingly drawn to "cash cow" programs (low social impact, high revenue) at the expense of "saint" (high social impact, low revenue) or even "star" (high social impact, high revenue) programs. To the extent that nonprofits are seen as having resources but are unwilling to seek immediate social impact during times of generalized economic distress, they may lose supporter and even broader social trust as they are increasingly seen as "uncaring" organizations.

To make matters worse, in some cases risk and the philanthropic friction it encourages may lead to a loss of confidence in nonprofits and even the sector in general. In theory, nonprofit leaders should generally discount their organizations' future impacts using a lower discount rate than the one outside supporters use. This could be because leaders may be more committed than other stakeholders to long-term program and organizational survival or because they face lower risk (less uncertainty) with respect to nonprofit impacts, as they have better information about impacts and more control over organizational activities. Eager to attract support during high-risk periods, nonprofit leaders may promise to focus on short-term impacts in line with donors' wishes. Once they secure support, however, nonprofit leaders may be tempted to save part of it or invest in resource-starved, long-term programs and organizational development. Consequently, some supporters may withhold contributions, weary that their support that is intended for short-term impact activities will be saved or used toward long-term programs. This problem could be alleviated if leaders were able to make a credible commitment to spend philanthropic contributions in line with donors' preferences. However, in the context of costly monitoring of nonprofit activities, such credible commitments are difficult to make. The wider the gap between leaders and donors' priorities, therefore, the more probable it is that trust in nonprofits and their leaders will decline. An implication of this argument is that when members, who control the nonprofit, are also its main donors, philanthropy and collective action should be less hindered by risk. The relative vitality of farmer, labor, and neighborhood associations in Mexico (Fox 1997), which tend to be member-controlled, is consistent with this implication.

Of note, a precise calculation of how risk affects future costs and benefits is not necessary for the argument that risk influences philanthropy and support for the nonprofit sector. Theoretical models often overplay individuals' calculative rationality. As Roger Lohmann (1992:15) admonishes, "The calculus of costs and benefits has become a universal index to what is rational." This is a significant problem since much of what the nonprofit sector works toward cannot be quantified. Yet, even if nonprofits and their supporters cannot or do not want to calculate the costs and benefits associated with their efforts and contributions, I would argue that risk aversion among donors is sufficient for risk to influence support for the nonprofit sector. Even if nonprofit leaders and supporters do not formally discount future options in high-risk environments, as long as they are risk-averse, increases in the risk associated with future outcomes should lead to a focus on the present as well as less appetite for embarking on and supporting long-term programs. Indeed, people generally respond to crises by focusing on immediate impacts at the expense of long-term ones.

The complex impact of economic risk on philanthropy presents considerable challenges for nonprofits. Of course, to understand the impact of risk on the broader nonprofit sector, we need to examine how risk affects the full gamut of nonprofit resources as well as the level of vulnerability to risk among nonprofit organizations (e.g., revenue diversification, access to reserve fund).

Risk, Non-philanthropic Revenue, and Organizational Vulnerability

A focus on the impact of risk uncovers the possibility that risk-aversion among funders of nonprofit organizations could depress their support to the sector in risky environments. Risk-averse funders may also try to transfer some of their risk onto nonprofits. Because this book focuses on economic risk resulting from macroeconomic volatility, the discussion below on the impact of risk on non-philanthropic revenue and nonprofit organizations emphasizes this type of risk.

Research has found that market volatility influences commercial consumption of social services as, during bad times, households consume less and postpone non-essential spending (see Agénor 2002). The impact on service fees will depend on the income elasticity of demand, that is, the percentage change in quantity demanded for a 1% change in household income. A few nonprofit fields focusing on essential services, such as health, may not face significant decline in revenues, and even fewer fields, such as education, may actually experience an increase in revenues as the declining opportunity cost of labor encourages workers to go back to school. The risk framework developed here suggests that risk should have a weaker depressing effect on service fees and other commercial revenue than it does on philanthropic giving, because fees and sales commonly generate immediate consumption impacts that are only minimally affected by risk. Moreover, fees for services are less dependent than philanthropy on supporter trust, which the risk framework suggests will tend to decline with risk. To be sure, risk can have a strong impact on commercial transactions with long-term impacts, such as the purchase of homes, cars, and other durables, whose benefits will span several years. Investment income is also likely to be partly dependent on the level of risk in the economy as the return on investment assets, such as company shares and government bonds, depends on macroeconomic performance. Nevertheless, commercial income resulting from sale of goods and services with an immediate, non-superfluous impact is likely to be significantly more resilient than philanthropy to changes in systematic risk.

Government and international donor funding may contribute to organizational resilience by offering an opportunity for diversification away from an exclusive focus on private support. However, the effect of this type of funding on resource vulnerability is much more complex, being partly determined by the terms of the funding contracts between nonprofits and the government agencies. Attitude toward risk among government agencies is a key influence on the nature of contracts celebrated between government and private contractors. Considerable debate remains over whether the government is generally risk-averse or risk-neutral. Arrow and Lind (1970) argue that government can spread the risk of public investment across all taxpayers so that each taxpayer faces a very small risk from government investment. Government, therefore, can act in a risk-neutral manner. Moreover, government is able to minimize risk by spreading it across a very large portfolio of public investments (Samuelson 1964; Vickrey 1964). However, this view has been widely challenged. As with other agents, the capacity of government to diversify its risk is limited by systematic risk. In developing countries, government's ability to spread risk is further limited by the small number of taxpayers and public investments (Kreimer, Arnold, and Carlin 2003). In addition, while government can in theory spread risk across all taxpayers, many risks are localized and may thus affect disproportionately some groups, who may oppose them and try to influence government to not undertake certain investments (e.g., Kreimer, Arnold, and Carlin 2003). Government agencies and officials, therefore, may often act in a risk-averse manner. In so doing, they may routinely transfer risk to the nonprofit sector through the contracting process. According to Bryce (2005:119), "When the government contracts with a nonprofit it is simultaneously transferring all or some significant portion of a risk to it." Government follows an extensive list of procedures to minimize its risk in the contracting process, regularly shifting risk to nonprofit organizations (Bryce 2005:54–55).

One example of how government transfers risk to the nonprofit sector is the ubiquitous practice of grant "leveraging." In this context, leverage—also referred to as "cost sharing"—refers to government being able to mobilize private resources to pursue the government's goals, decreasing government's true cost of program results (see Bryce 2005:105). Leveraging is a main reason why donors may get more benefits from a social investment through a nonprofit than through a for-profit. Leveraging is also very attractive from the perspective of individual government officials. There is some evidence that government officials tend to be more risk-averse than private sector employees (Bellante and Link 1981; Buurman, Dur, and Van den Bossche 2009). Moreover, government officials commonly face a disincentive to take risks: they are not rewarded for taking risks and may be sanctioned when risk materializes in failed projects (Acemoglu, Kremer, and Mian 2007). By supporting only recipients who are already supported by other donors, government officials reduce their risk of supporting an unworthy recipient. In a field where performance measurement is so challenging, the risk of being accused of negligence is much smaller if other agencies and donors—preferably distinguished members of the community—also support the same organization, which sends a signal of trustworthiness and low risk.

Researchers frequently caution nonprofits that such leveraged grants may divert them from their original purpose, that is, lead to co-optation (e.g., Clark 1991; Smith and Lipsky 1993; Najam 2000). What is absent, however, is a discussion of the implications of leveraging for the size and nature of the risks nonprofits face. Even in the absence of co-optation pressures, leverage can increase the economic risk nonprofits face. Since leveraged grants cannot be used to boost self-insurance (by helping to, for example, build financial reserves), by tying together funding streams that could have been uncorrelated, leverage decreases funding diversification and potentially even consumes nonprofit reserves when nonprofits must scramble to fulfill their share of the cost in a volatile environment. Finally, leverage may encourage governments to support financially conservative, risk-averse organizations with solid finances to ensure their ability to fulfill their private-match responsibilities. The process of risk shifting and leveraging creates systematic risk, negatively affecting all. In the end, standard government contracts typically allocate a disproportionate share of the economic risk to nonprofit organizations (Bryce 2005).

Another example of how government shifts risk to the nonprofit sector is through unilateral changes to contracted funding terms, especially during recessions. While governments in rich countries tend to spend countercyclically, in most countries governments tend to spend procyclically in line with a risk-averse attitude, implementing deep budget cuts during economic crises (Alesina and Tabellini 2005). In such environments, elected officials may want to maximize political impact of dwindling taxation resources by spending or giving the money directly to citizens, rather than disbursing it through a nonprofit intermediary. Even in countries with countercyclical public spending, volatility risk is likely to influence the relationship between nonprofits and government agencies. To the extent that voter preferences change over the economic cycle, government agencies may focus their spending during recessions on high-profile emergencies rather than fund long-term nonprofit programs. As a result, nonprofits often have to commit extra private resources to make up for unexpected income shortfall or cost overrun during recessions.

Research has long shown that the public sector commonly fails to fulfill its contractual obligations to make payments to nonprofits in a timely manner (e.g., Fowler 2000; Grønbjerg 1993; Smith and Lipsky 1993). In contracting relationships with for-profits, government typically has to pay compensation for delayed payments (OECD 2008) but, in a context of asymmetric power, government is able to make promises to nonprofits and then break them at no cost (Fowler 2000). In so doing, government reduces its own risk of running out of money in a given period by adding uncertainty and risk to nonprofits' already risky resource environment. Nonprofits must pay staff, buy equipment, pay rent. They must honor the contracts they sign. By delaying payment, government adds another layer of risk to nonprofits' environment. When faced with a payment delay, a nonprofit can use its own resources to make up for the temporary shortfall, thus effectively financing government, or delay the start of a new program or scale down an ongoing program until it receives the agreed payment, potentially undermining its social impact and relationship with supporters and clients. Such payment delays result from the power imbalance between contracting "partners" and constitute a de facto transfer of risk to nonprofits. Worse still, often government does not take its own errors into account when evaluating nonprofits, penalizing a nonprofit for delivering "subpar" outputs when this is partly due to government's contribution of "subpar" inputs (see Fowler 2000).

Government attitudes toward risk are critical in determining nonprofit sector vulnerability in a context of widespread government-nonprofit contracting. A risk-averse government will tend to adopt a procyclical fiscal policy and use the contracting process to shift risk to the nonprofit sector. Government funding and associated contracts are an important influence on nonprofit vulnerability and, consequently, the risk non-profits face.

To the extent that the different nonprofit revenue sources are correlated, nonprofits face systematic risk. Organizational sensitivity to systematic risk is typically referred to as *beta risk,* which is one of the fundamental pillars of corporate finance (Doherty 2000). Specifically, beta risk measures the responsiveness of a financial flow to changes in the economy.[8] The denomination *beta* derives from its calculation as the beta coefficient in a simple regression of portfolio returns on market returns. According to the Capital Asset Pricing Model, the expected returns on securities are linearly related to their beta risk. Beta risk is therefore an essential determinant of investment decisions and its value for most securities are readily available online.[9]

In the case of the nonprofit sector, beta risk values for different types of resource provider are not available and—as far as I know—have never been calculated.[10] For our purposes, a calculation of the responsiveness of case studies' income flows to changes in national economic output would be most useful. Since there are no financial markets transacting nonprofit securities, beta risk cannot be calculated by comparing organizational and market returns. An alternative method is the accounting method. This method is often used in corporate finance to estimate betas for large projects or organizational divisions, which are also not traded in the market. Rather than looking for variations in price level of a security, the accounting method examines the variation in a particular accounting variable of interest within the accounts of an organization or group of organizations. For example, we might be interested in examining the beta risk of government funding to the nonprofit sector. We can estimate the responsiveness of government funding (to an organization or to the whole sector) in response to changes in the national economy. A positive beta risk means that a resource is positively associated with the economy, rising when the economy grows and falling when it declines. A negative beta means that the resource and the economy move in opposite directions. A beta risk higher than 1.0 means that the resource is more volatile, and thus riskier, than the economy. For example, if government funding has a beta risk of 4.0, a 1% rise in GDP is associated with an average 4% increase in government funding to the nonprofit sector. On the other hand, a 1% contraction in GDP is associated with an average 4% decline in government funding to nonprofits. A beta risk between 0.0 and 1.0 means that the resource is less volatile (i.e., risky) than the economy. The impact of risk on the discounting of future nonprofit impacts suggests that support for long-term programs and organizational development will be highly procyclical, while support for emergency and short-term programs will tend to be mildly procyclical or even countercyclical. In theory, and as discussed above, commercial revenue and volunteering should have a lower beta risk than philanthropic giving and possibly government funding. Greater dependence on commercial revenue and volunteering, therefore, should reduce nonprofit vulnerability to systematic risk from macroeconomic volatility.

Once the beta risk of different income sources is calculated, the beta risk to which a nonprofit is exposed is the weighted average of all its resource betas, with the weight of each resource's beta equal to its proportion in the portfolio. To reduce its beta risk, therefore, a nonprofit must reduce its dependence on highly procyclical resources in favor of less procyclical ones. Ideally, it should move toward acyclical resources or combine procyclical and countercyclical resources. Of note, beta risk hedging is different from diversification since hedging also reduces returns—smaller revenue declines during crises correspond to smaller revenue increases during booms. Diversification, by contrast, leads to a reduction in portfolio risk without compromising its returns (Doherty 2000).

While beta risk may be a good predictor of revenue distress during downturns, it may not be a good predictor of organizational and programmatic distress because different organizations facing the same beta risk may have different level of organizational vulnerability. One organization, for example, may have a rainy day fund that can be mobilized when revenue declines during downturns so that the organization and its programs experience minimum distress. The impact of changes in different types of revenue, therefore, also depends on the level of organizational vulnerability.

In the face of beta risk (i.e., procyclical resource availability), nonprofits can reduce vulnerability to macroeconomic volatility through self-insuring, borrowing, reducing fixed costs, spending procyclically, and, in rare instances, hedging (i.e., taking on one risk to offset a second risk; this strategy reduces risk because the two risks are inversely correlated).[11] In line with general risk management research, nonprofit finance research suggests that self-insurance in the form of reserves, especially liquid and unrestricted net assets, is a fundamental strategy to reduce vulnerability to macroeconomic risk. Organizations can reduce the impact of revenue distress by accumulating capital to smooth spending across good and bad years. Woods Bowman (2007) and Kevin Kearns (2007), for example, advocate that nonprofits need to create contingency funds during times of plenty to survive and maintain their activity levels during recessions. By helping to smooth the variation of spending over time, a contingency fund enables organizations to meet their fixed expenses, such as salaries and rent. When organizations are unable to pay for their fixed expenses out of financial reserves, they have to downsize their staff and physical capital, with significant losses to organizational capacity. Financial capital, therefore, helps to protect organizations' physical, human, and social capital during bad economic times. Indeed, if we assume diminishing marginal returns to nonprofit spending, saving part of income during years of plenty and spending it during years of scarcity increases nonprofit impact. Procyclical spending, therefore, stands in opposition to efficiency principles. Smooth spending also makes sense from the perspective of protecting capacity investments in the long term, as discussed below. In theory, nonprofits could borrow during economic crises to meet sudden declines in revenue, but many nonprofits have limited access to borrowing, especially when declining revenue coincides with falling asset values, limiting their usefulness as collateral. Large fixed costs can also turn into a major liability during economic downturns (Young 2007). By lowering fixed costs, then, nonprofits should also reduce financial vulnerability to systematic risk. An emphasis on variable costs permits rapid cost cutting in line with sudden falls in revenues and reduces the probability that the organization will become insolvent. Procyclical spending, then, is an important risk management strategy when resource availability is also procyclical.

Nonprofit finance research has identified several other determinants of financial vulnerability. In their pioneering study of nonprofit finance, Tuckman and Chang's (1991) research identified two other indicators of financial vulnerability: low administrative expenses and low operating margins. Theoretically, a higher ratio of administrative to total costs can provide a financial margin to protect program spending during difficult times by offering the option of cutting (administrative) costs instead. An organization with low administrative costs does not have such a margin. Thus, high administrative costs can be an important element of organizational resilience to financial shocks (e.g., Tuckman and Chang 1991). Negative operating margin is a strong predictor of financial distress during the crisis. However, the contribution of positive operating margins to reducing financial risk must be balanced by the fact that, in mission-related activities, high margins may conflict with mission accomplishment. High margins increase the price of the service and therefore reduce the ability of beneficiaries, especially the poorest, to access it. Lastly, Keating et al. (2005) argue that a high proportion of income from investment and commercial sources is associated with low financial distress. Thus, a low proportion of income from investment sources and a low proportion of commercial income are also important indicators of financial vulnerability.

The ability of nonprofits to pursue different risk-reduction strategies is contingent on the nature of service they provide, and in particular their degree of "publicness" and their resource environment (Fischer, Wilsker, and Young 2007). Endowed nonprofits such as foundations have financial reserves, which greatly reduce their vulnerability to revenue declines in recessions. Nonprofits financed primarily through sales of private goods (e.g., hospitals and universities) can use their surpluses to build reserves, especially given the fact that they typically have tax benefits on income from activities that are related to their social mission. While such organizations must also use their surpluses to cross-subsidize public service activities, stakeholder pressure on these organizations to spend their surpluses is relatively low because clients already received the service they paid for and the government generally tolerates financial reserves. Nonprofits financed primarily through philanthropy and government grants and contracts for public goods provision have the least scope to build reserves. Government typically pays for services at below-cost rates, so that these organizations are encouraged to mobilize supplemental private funding (Bryce 2005). Philanthropic donations offer more opportunities for reserve building since donors are often unable to monitor a nonprofit to make sure that donations have been spent in service provision, but philanthropic donations are generally needed to supplement government funding that is insufficient to cover programmatic expenses. The ability to attract volunteers is probably highest in public-good-providing nonprofits. This might be due to volunteers deriving satisfaction from participation in the provision of public goods (see Hirschman 1982) as well as the fact that foundations and nonprofits that focus on private goods can afford to pay for the labor they need.

This discussion illuminates the vast range of nonprofit sector orientations and resources, and shows that different types of nonprofits may face different opportunities and challenges in their effort to reduce vulnerability to economic risk. It also suggests that shifts in a nonprofit's degree of public orientation have fundamental impacts on its resource environment and ability to deal with economic risk.

Empirical Implications

The risk framework has several testable implications for philanthropy and the nonprofit sector more generally. This section spells out those implications and the conditions under which the risk perspective should help explain the PKC.

The framework's broadest implication is that changes in the level of risk should influence philanthropy and the nonprofit sector over time and across nations. Specifically, *as risk increases over time, the nonprofit sector should weaken* and, therefore, *countries facing higher levels of economic risk should have a weaker nonprofit sector.* The depressing impact of economic risk, such as macroeconomic volatility, upon the nonprofit sector may seem intuitive, but there are strong reasons why we should expect the opposite impact to occur. Theoretically, the lower opportunity cost of labor and capital during recessions should bolster volunteering and donations. Both opportunity costs fall because the productivity of labor (i.e., real wages) and capital (i.e., interest rate) tends to decline during recessions. Moreover, economic downturns are only one side of economic volatility. On average, developing countries experience a downturn year for every four growth years (Easterly, Islam, and Stiglitz 1999). At the end of most economic cycles, therefore, national and household incomes are higher than at the start. Such an absolute increase in income should encourage philanthropy, assuming the commonly proposed direct relationship between household income and philanthropy (e.g., Havens, O'Herlihy, and Schervish 2006).

The risk framework suggests that risk impacts the nonprofit sector in both short and long terms. In the short term, countercyclical volatility and risk-aversion, which lead to countercyclical risk premiums and discounting (i.e., they increase during downturns), combine with procyclical incomes to produce a *general procyclical resource availability to the nonprofit sector.* Rising risk during a recession will increase the rate with which nonprofit supporters discount future nonprofit sector benefits and increase philanthropic friction, leading to a decline in support. Falling risk during boom periods should have the opposite effect, although risk expectations can remain high during a significant part of the recovery period, because high-risk expectations often persist following a shock (see Verschuur et al. 2007).

Because discounting of future benefits is proportional to how far in the future they are expected to occur, *in the short term, increases in macroeconomic risk should lead to falling support to most nonprofits, but may potentially lead to an increase in support to emergency nonprofits.* The rise in risk expectations and discount rate leads to a shift in donor preferences toward short-term programs with immediate returns. Emergency relief programs such as soup kitchens, food banks, and union activities designed to defend wages can receive greater support, while long-term programs such as those focusing on environmental conservation, preventative health care, and primary education are likely to attract less support. This rationale might be equally relevant for institutional donors, who must also include risk calculations in their financial support decisions. As the economy recovers, risk expectations eventually decline, leading to *a reversal in donor preferences away from short-term programs and back to long-term ones.* Predictions based on the impact of risk, therefore, differ from predictions based on the impact of household income in that risk predicts that nonprofits focusing on long-term impacts should be more negatively impacted than those focusing on short-term impacts. There is no obvious reason why predictions based on changes in household income should make a distinction between short-and long-term nonprofits and programs.

The risk framework also has implications for how risk influences different types of nonprofit resources. In contrast with for-profits and government, which are commonly assumed to be risk-neutral, individuals tend to behave in a risk-averse fashion. Thus, *individual philanthropy should be the type of resource that is most susceptible to risk.* Within philanthropy, individual giving is likely to be more impacted than volunteering. Of note, this impact can be either procyclical or countercyclical, depending on whether support is for long-term or short-term programs, respectively. *Risk is likely to have the lowest impact on commercial revenue* because costs and benefits from sales are more likely to coincide in time so that discounting has a minimal impact on this type of resource mobilization strategy. Consequently, resource dependence on commercial income is likely to be higher in riskier countries. The impact on government funding is less clear as there is considerable debate over whether government behaves in a risk-neutral or risk-averse manner. Hypothetically, *government agencies and officials are more likely to act in a risk-averse manner in high-risk-aversion cultures.* In such cases, risk is also likely to have a strong depressing effect on government funding to nonprofits. Government's ability to transfer risk to nonprofits, on the other hand, *should discourage resource dependence on government funding in high-risk environments.*

The risk framework also highlights the importance of organizational vulnerability, which is determined by the extent to which an organization lacks access to reserve assets, capital markets, a diversified supporter base, and a cost structure characterized by low fixed costs. High external risk levels should be more detrimental to more vulnerable organizations. Sustained high-risk levels over time, or one major shock, should lead to *vulnerable organizations becoming increasingly vulnerable and, in the worst-case scenario, perishing.* In the long term, repeated economic shocks may encourage risk expectations to remain high for a long period, which should generally weaken non-profits. This is because sustained high levels of risk will reduce social support for long-term investments, such as organizational capacity, capital, and building a diversified donor base, which nonprofits must undertake to survive and grow in the long term. On the other hand, by sustaining higher levels of organizational capacity through high-risk periods, resilient organizations may benefit from reduced competition when risk eventually declines and general demand for nonprofit services increases again. The fact that older and larger organizations tend to be more resilient encourages a "top-heavy sector" (see Lecy 2010). The higher the level of risk, the more top-heavy the sector is likely to become. The nonprofit sector in high-risk environments, therefore, should be characterized by *relatively few and relatively large organizations within a weak sector.* In a context of low social support for long-term investment, nonprofits must increase resilience by accessing resources that are less affected by risk, such as commercial revenue, an endowment, and international funding from lower-risk countries. In high-risk environments, then, the sector should include *a significant number of nonprofits with a strong commercial orientation,* as it greatly enhances nonprofit resilience and survival in such environments.

The monotonic, inverse relationship between risk and nonprofit sector strength, which the risk framework predicts, would help explain the PKC, if middle-income countries *commonly faced higher economic risk than either low or high-income countries.* The different impact upon different types of resources should lead to the nonprofit sector in middle-income countries having higher levels of resource concentration (lower diversification), and consequently facing higher levels of idiosyncratic risk, than in either rich or poor countries. The susceptibility of philanthropy and, potentially, government funding to macroeconomic risk mean that nonprofits must focus on the less susceptible commercial income. The relative erosion of some types of funding should increase concentration in the remaining types. Higher resource concentration, on the other hand, may increase nonprofit vulnerability to idiosyncratic shocks, especially among small organizations. Last of all, *variation in average citizen risk-aversion across countries should be directly linked to actual levels of macroeconomic risk in the long term.* Otherwise, risk may not have a significant impact on the nonprofit sector since higher macroeconomic risk in a country could be offset by its population's lower degree of risk-aversion. This hypothesis is consistent with research on risk perception, which suggests that shocks have a persistent effect on individuals' perception of risk level. However, empirical support for this hypothesis would be surprising as it departs from traditional conceptualizations of risk-aversion as constant, always rising or always falling with wealth (see, e.g., Kreps 1990).

A risk explanation for the PKC suggests that *risk significantly mediates the impact of economic development on nonprofit sector strength.* Even if analysis of the evidence lends support to the hypothesis that level of economic development determines risk and that risk determines nonprofit sector strength, risk may not be a valid mechanism for the influence of economic development on nonprofit sector strength. Rigorous mediation analysis must show that a measurable indirect (i.e., mediated by risk) effect of economic development on nonprofit sector strength is statistically significant and distinct from a direct (i.e., nonmediated) effect, all the while controlling for main confounding influences, namely level of democracy, social diversity, religious competition, social origins, and modernization. In other words, to support the claim that risk mediates the relationship, the indirect effect must be a significant component of the total effect. Evidence of a mediation impact means that economic development can undermine nonprofit sector strength by increasing risk, while simultaneously promoting it by increasing resource availability at the national level. To the extent that some countries experience more volatility than others in their economic development process, more volatile and riskier countries will have weaker nonprofit sectors for the same prosperity level. The implication, therefore, is that *within income groups (e.g., rich, medium and poor), countries that have been exposed to higher risk should have a weaker nonprofit sector.*

Empirical support for these hypotheses would lend great credibility to an explanation of nonprofit sector strength based on the role of economic development and risk. The next three chapters examine the consistency between these theoretical predictions and empirical evidence on both how nonprofit sector strength varies across nations (chapter 3) and how the Mexican nonprofit sector evolved over time, especially before, during, and after the Tequila Crisis (chapters 4 and 5). In so doing they illuminate and explain how the nonprofit sector copes with the reality of risk.

3 Economic Development, Risk, and the Nonprofit Sector in Cross-National Perspective

CHAPTER 1 PRESENTED a robust cross-national puzzle: the philanthropic Kuznets curve (PKC). Whether measured by giving, volunteering, civic participation, nonprofit sector employment, expenditure, or other correlates such as social trust and social tolerance, nonprofit sector strength invariably displays a U-shaped relationship with respect to the level of economic development across countries. Chapter 2 proposed that risk plays an important role in explaining this surprising nonlinear relationship. A major component of the way in which economic development impacts the nonprofit sector is by influencing the level of economic risk faced by nonprofit organizations and their supporters.

The risk explanation proposed offers insights into how risk influences philanthropy and the nonprofit sector. It captures the incentives driving individuals' and other potential supporters' choices that lead to nonprofit weakness, and points to some of the conditions under which the nonprofit sector should, or should not, flourish. To what extent are its predictions consistent with nonprofit sector evidence, and particularly the PKC?

This chapter examines cross-national data. The first section examines the impact of economic development on philanthropy and nonprofit sector size. After disentangling cause-effect relationships, analysis of cross-national data provides compelling support for the claim that economic development is a main cause of nonprofit sector strength; that the effect is nonlinear; and, in turn, nonprofit sector strength is also an important cause of economic development. The second section shows that risk, whether indicated by macroeconomic instability, nonprofit sector vulnerability, or risk-aversion, has an inverted U-shaped relationship with economic development. Systematic mediation analysis further demonstrates that economic risk and nonprofit sector exposure to it are determined by economic development and determine nonprofit sector strength. After careful control for potentially confounding influences, analysis estimates that risk is responsible for a significant share of the impact of economic development on philanthropy and nonprofit sector size. This chapter provides, therefore, compelling evidence in support of the PKC as a causal relationship and its risk explanation. The appendix describes variables operationalization, the cross-national dataset, and methods of analysis.

Examining the Effects of Economic Development on Nonprofit Sector Strength

As discussed in chapter 1, current theories of the nonprofit sector predict a linear relationship between nonprofit sector strength and the level of economic development. While some approaches, such as modernization, predict an inverse relationship between the two variables, other approaches such, as social welfare and voluntary failure, predict a direct relationship. These theories, however, have rarely been subject to systematic testing based on cross-national evidence and, especially, appropriate controls for reverse causation. Is social welfare spending a cause of nonprofit sector development or its effect? Carefully constructed historical analyses are invaluable in helping to disentangle causes and effects, but may lack wider generalizability. This section presents statistical analysis of cross-national evidence on the nonprofit sector that seeks to help fill these gaps. The appendix to this chapter describes the data and methods used.

Table 3.1 presents zero-order correlations between the main variables employed in the study. The linear Pearson's correlation between income per capita and nonprofit sector size, measured as total nonprofit sector employment, is remarkable ($r = 0.669$, $p < 0.001$). With such a strong direct linear correlation, it is not surprising that previous analyses have failed to identify the nonlinear nature of the relationship. The even higher Spearman's correlation (rho $= 0.778$, $p < 0.001$), however, indicates that the relationship may in fact be nonlinear. Pearson's correlation is strongly influenced by outliers, unequal variances, non-normality, and nonlinearity. The Spearman's rank correlation coefficient, on the other hand, focuses on the order (i.e., rank) of the data rather than the actual data values themselves to examine whether the relationship between two variables is monotonic. In so doing, it avoids many of the distortions that plague the Pearson correlation in nonlinear settings (see, e.g., Greene 2002). The linear correlation between income per capita and nonprofit expenditure is also high ($r = 0.570$) but modest with philanthropy ($r = 0.400$). Again, a significantly larger Spearman's correlation between philanthropy and economic development (rho $= 0.5634$) suggests that nonlinearity may be attenuating the linear correlation. Among the typical explanations for the nonprofit sector, and aside from economic development, only level of democracy ($r = 0.396$), government spending as a proportion of GDP ($r = 0.466$), and trade as a proportion of GDP ($r = 0.551$), which is a proxy for globalization, have statistically significant and direct linear correlations with nonprofit sector employment (at $p < 0.10$). Contrary to theoretical predictions, the proportion of the population living in urban areas, which is a proxy for modernization, displays a direct and statistically significant correlation with nonprofit sector employment ($r = 0.527$). This portrait is almost identical in the case of philanthropy, except for the fact that the correlation with democracy level does not reach statistical significance. The three indicators of nonprofit sector exposure to risk—the risk index, macroeconomic volatility, and the Herfindahl index—are all strongly and inversely correlated with both philanthropy nonprofit sector employment and economic development.

Table 3.1. Zero-order correlations between the variables

	Phi.	Emp.	Exp.	Income	Polity	Ethnic	Relig.	Busin.	Gini	Govt.	Trade	Anglo	Urban	Risk	Volat.
Phil, % GDP	1.000														
Np employment, % labor	.759*	1.000													
Np expenditure, % GDP	.657*	.859*	1.000												
Ln(GDP per capita)	.400*	.669*	.570*	1.000											
Polity IV index	.166	.396*	.346*	.394*	1.000										
Ethnic fragmentation	-.215	-.230	-.271*	-.438*	-.287*	1.000									
Religious diversity	.234	.176	.190	-.047	-.116	.145*	1.000								
Trust in business, % pop.	.090	.068	-.138	-.158	-.323*	.138	.018	1.000							
Gini	-.245	-.204	-.224	-.349*	-.284*	.504*	.006	.226	1.000						
Govt. spending, % GDP	.365*	.466*	.453*	.581*	.394*	-.266*	.003	.095	-.429*	1.000					
Ln(Trade, % GDP)	.319*	.551*	.442*	.401*	.321*	-.212*	.029	.190	-.314*	.344*	1.000				
Anglo-Saxon dummy	.170	.187	.167	-.018	-.097	.024	.345*	.474*	.243	-.127	-.112	1.000			
Urban, % population	.348*	.527*	.531*	.739*	.198*	-.234*	-.094	-.192	-.165	.453*	.576*	-.162*	1.000		
Risk index	-.669*	-.587*	-.361*	-.473*	-.334*	.222	-.241	-.223	.315*	-.463*	-.344*	-.071	-.195	1.000	
Economic volatility	-.619*	-.604*	-.378*	-.296*	-.379*	.162*	.099	-.176	.291*	-.381*	-.291*	-.066	-.062	.859*	1.000
Nonprofit Herfindahl	-.548*	-.413*	-.260	-.409*	-.262	.235	-.265	-.004	.253	-.398*	-.164	.080	-.168	.859*	.478*

Notes: Star denotes statistical confidence at 90% level.

Table 3.2 presents ordinary least squares (OLS) regression results examining the hypothetical quadratic relationship between economic development and the nonprofit sector. Philanthropy is the outcome variable in models 1–4, and nonprofit sector size (i.e., total employment) is the outcome variable in models 5–8. All models include both linear and quadratic income per capita terms as well as controls for level of democracy, ethnic fragmentation, and religious diversity. Models 1 and 5 are the basic models. Models 2 and 6 include the basic model and add controls for government spending, trade, and a dummy variable to indicate Anglo-Saxon legal code. To avoid bias from multicollinearity, these models exclude urbanization and Gini coefficient due to their significant correlation with government spending and trade. Models 3 and 7 include the basic model and add a control for urbanization. Model 7 also includes the Anglo-Saxon dummy because it reached statistical significance in model 6. Lastly, models 4 and 8 include controls for level of trust in business and social inequality.[1] As indicated by the adjusted-R^2 measure, the models explain most of the variation in both philanthropy and nonprofit sector size within the sample.

After controlling for probable confounding influences, the results are highly consistent with the PKC: average income per capita has the expected nonlinear relationship with both philanthropy and nonprofit sector size across nations. Thus, both philanthropy and nonprofit sector size first fall and then rise as economic development increases even after controlling for a wide range of competing explanations and confounding influences. Both linear and quadratic income per capita coefficients are significant from statistical and substantive perspectives. The magnitude of these effects is discussed below since they increase when the analysis controls for potential endogeneity between economic development and nonprofit sector strength (see table 3.3).

At the same time, consistent with most cross-national research on the nonprofit sector, the Polity IV index—the indicator of level of democracy as measured by a spectrum of governing authority—is directly linked to both philanthropy and nonprofit sector size, reaching statistical significance in all sector size models and one philanthropy model. Anglo-Saxon legal code is directly associated with both philanthropy and nonprofit sector size, though the association is statistically significant only in the nonprofit sector size model. These results suggest that both political regime and legal framework are important determinants of nonprofit sector size. On the other hand, contrary to modernization approaches, urbanization is directly associated with both philanthropy and nonprofit sector size, reaching statistical significance in both philanthropy and sector size models. Contrary to social heterogeneity (government failure) theory, ethnic fragmentation is inversely associated with philanthropy, but the relationship reaches statistical significance only in model 3. Ethnic fragmentation is directly associated with nonprofit sector size, although the relationship is statistically significant in only one of the models. Religious diversity is directly linked to both philanthropy and nonprofit sector size in most models, though the relationship is statistically significant in only two models. Government spending, trade, and trust in business do not reach statistical significance in any model. Lastly, social inequality is surprisingly linked directly with both philanthropy and nonprofit sector size, though the relationship is statistically weak.

One weakness of the previous analysis is that it does not control for the potential reverse causality between nonprofit sector strength and economic development. To address this potential source of bias, the analysis employs 2SLS and 3SLS regression estimations. Based on the results presented on table 2, measures of the different models' goodness of fit—Akaike information criterion, Bayesian information criterion, and R^2—indicate that the models focusing on traditional nonprofit sector explanations, such as democracy, ethnic fragmentation, religious diversity, and modernization (i.e., models 3 and 7 in table 2), have the highest explanatory power among full sample models and, consequently, are used in 2SLS and 3SLS models.[2]

Table 3.3 presents both 2SLS and 3SLS regression results. Models 1 and 2 focus on philanthropy as the dependent variable, while models 3 and 4 focus on nonprofit sector size. Consistent with the PKC, after controlling for potential endogeneity between economic development and nonprofit sector strength, economic development has a strong and statistically significant relationship with both philanthropy and nonprofit sector size. Both linear and quadratic terms of income per capita reach statistical significance in all models, which supports the claim that nonprofit sector strength first decreases and then increases as the level of economic development increases. Consistency between 2SLS and 3SLS results suggests the models were appropriately identified. Moreover, the linear and quadratic coefficients obtained after controlling for reverse causation indicate slightly stronger effects than were obtained using OLS. This fact means that the U-shaped curve is more pronounced (i.e., has higher slopes) after we control for the effect of nonprofit sector strength on economic development. This attenuation bias in OLS estimates is consistent with the direct reverse effect of nonprofit sector strength on economic development, which 3SLS identifies.

The analysis also shows that, in substantive terms, economic development has a powerful effect on nonprofit sector strength. In a quadratic (e.g., U-shaped) relationship, the effect of the explanatory variable varies at different levels of the outcome variable, which means that the magnitude of the effect must be estimated at different points. The change in the outcome variable (i.e., nonprofit sector strength) produced by a change in the linear and quadratic terms of the explanatory variable (i.e., economic development) is determined by the equation $dY/dX = b_1 + 2*b_2X$. In the case of philanthropy, and based on 2SLS estimates, the effect of economic development is equal to $-7.998 + 2*0.467X$. Hence, in a country with a natural log of income per capita of 8.86 such as Mexico, 1% rise in income per capita is associated with a 0.277% increase in philanthropy. In the case of nonprofit sector size, the corresponding effect of economic development is 0.602% increase in nonprofit sector size, that is, total employment as a proportion of the labor force. Alternatively, in a richer country such as the United States, which has a natural log of income per capita equal to 10.35, a 1% rise in income

Table 3.2. OLS regression results

Dependent variable	1 Philanthropy	2 Philanthropy	3 Philanthropy	4 Philanthropy (smaller N)	5 Sector size	6 Sector size	7 Sector size	8 Sector size (smaller N)
Ln(GDP per capita)	-4.929*** (1.009)	-4.624*** (1.388)	-6.354*** (1.105)	-4.643** (2.006)	-4.064*** (.868)	-3.184*** (.832)	-3.756*** (.961)	-7.939*** (2.385)
[Ln(GDP per capita)]^2	.294*** (.055)	.275*** (.077)	.363*** (.059)	.280** (.109)	.268*** (.050)	.218*** (.046)	.244*** (.053)	.481*** (.132)
Democracy index	.006 (.024)	.001 (.030)	.032# (.020)	-.012 (.035)	.030* (.016)	.035* (.016)	.033* (.016)	.045*** (.008)
Ethnic fragmentation	-.042 (.217)	-.138 (.224)	-.255# (.158)	-.204 (.280)	.415 (.292)	.195 (.332)	.309# (.203)	.099 (.391)
Religious diversity	.225* (.107)	.098 (.235)	.149 (.245)	.176 (.242)	-.021 (.264)	-.165 (.332)	.264# (.187)	.026 (.317)
Govt spending, % GDP		.012 (.012)				.005 (.014)		
Ln(Trade, % GDP)		-.001 (.063)				-.004 (.076)		

	(1)	(2)	(3)	(4)	(5)	(6)	(7)
Anglo-Saxon legal code dummy	.068 (.134)				.307** (.138)	.379*** (.138)	
Urban, % population		.010** (.004)				.007* (.004)	
Trust in business, % population			.220 (.514)				.297 (.366)
Gini			.006 (.012)				.014# (.009)
Intercept	20.970*** (4.513)	27.385*** (4.954)	18.917* (9.653)	16.053*** (3.790)	12.269*** (3.442)	14.889*** (4.257)	32.518*** (11.000)
Adjusted-R^2	.553	.611	.508	.704	.708	.739	.730
N.	36	36	31	40	40	40	34
Akaike IC	24.089	19.852	26.517	33.760	35.465	30.378	28.597
Bayesian IC	33.590	30.936	37.989	43.893	50.665	43.889	40.808

Notes: Robust standard errors reported between parentheses under unstandardized coefficients. Philanthropy is measured by the natural log of giving and volunteering as a percentage of GDP. Sector size is measured by the natural log of total nonprofit sector employment as a percentage of the labor force. ***$p < .01$; **$p < .05$; *$p < .10$; #$p < .15$ (two-tailed).

Table 3.3. Effects of economic development on philanthropy and nonprofit sector size

	1	2	3	4
Method	*2SLS*	*3SLS*	*2SLS*	*3SLS*
Dependent Variable	*Philanthropy*	*Philanthropy*	*Sector size*	*Sector size*
Ln(GDP per capita)	−7.998***	−7.772***	−5.813***	−6.346***
	(2.370)	(2.018)	(1.704)	(2.445)
[Ln(GDP per capita)]^2	.467***	.442***	.362***	.388***
	(.140)	(.108)	(.100)	(.134)
Democracy index	.007	.052	.028	.021
	(.033)	(.038)	(.032)	(.021)
Ethnic fragmentation	.057	.112	.195	.041
	(.525)	(.221)	(.389)	(.302)
Religious diversity	−.156	−.268	−.376	−.461#
	(.360)	(.221)	(.303)	(.296)
Urban, % population	.008	.011**	.008	.009*
	(.007)	(.004)	(.007)	(.005)
Anglo-Saxon legal code, dummy			.267#	.219
			(.165)	(.187)
Intercept	33.957***	33.485***	23.768***	26.384**
	(9.794)	(8.902)	(7.290)	(1.844)
Adjusted-R2	.481	.649	.707	.772

Dependent Variable		*ln(GDP per capita)*		*ln(GDP per capita)*
Philanthropy		1.960***		
		(.481)		
Sector size				.989***
				(.264)
Illiteracy, % pop.		−.003		.021***
		(.013)		(.006)
Ln(Trade, % GDP)		.024		.264***
		(.100)		(.063)
Property rights		−.010		−.011
		(.008)		(.009)
Age dependency		−5.277***		−4.071***
		(1.429)		(.695)
Intercept		11.247***		3.610***
		(2.485)		(.587)
Adjusted-R2		.549		.830
N.	36	36	40	40

Notes: Robust standard errors reported between parentheses under unstandardized coefficients. Philanthropy is measured by the natural log of giving and volunteering as a percentage of GDP. Sector size is measured by the natural log of total nonprofit sector employment as a percentage of the labor force. The instruments used in the first-stage regression were ln population, age dependency ratio, Muslims as percentage of population in 1980, and the other control variables. ***p < .01; **p < .05; *p < .10; #p < .15 (two-tailed).

per capita is associated with a 1.669% increase in philanthropy and a 1.680% increase in nonprofit sector employment. By contrast, in a country such as Pakistan, with a natural log of income per capita of 7.8, a 1% increase in income per capita is associated with a −0.713% change in philanthropy and a −0.166% change in nonprofit sector employment. Consistent with U-shaped relationships, in countries with an income per capita lower than the estimated turning point of $5,235 per capita (i.e., natural log = 8.563) for philanthropy, economic development leads to a decrease in philanthropy. On the other hand, the turning point for nonprofit sector employment is at a much lower level of annual income per capita—$3,068 (natural log = 8.029)—which means that between the turning point for philanthropy and the turning point for nonprofit sector size, economic development can have a positive impact on nonprofit sector employment but a negative impact on philanthropy. These findings lend strong support to the PKC as well as to the argument that philanthropy is more susceptible to economic risk than other nonprofit sector resources such as commercial revenue. This static (i.e., "snapshot") analysis suggests that non-philanthropic resources initially lead nonprofit sector recovery after the nonprofit sector employment turning point. At the same time, urbanization has a direct association with both philanthropy and nonprofit sector size, reaching statistical significance in 3SLS models. As expected, ethnic fragmentation and the Polity IV index are also positively linked with the two outcome variables, though without reaching statistical significance in any of the models. Contrary to theoretical expectations, religious diversity has an inverse effect on philanthropy and sector size, reaching statistical significance in the nonprofit sector size 3SLS model (model 4). As in the OLS analysis, an Anglo-Saxon legal system is positively associated with the outcome variables, reaching statistical significance in the 2SLS model.

The simultaneous estimation of cause-effect relationships in both directions enabled an assessment of how philanthropy and nonprofit sector size can help determine a country's level of economic development. The analysis presented here shows that nonprofit sector strength has a positive and statistically significant effect on income per capita. While such a result might perhaps be surprising to some, it is fully consistent with social capital theory and Putnam's (1993) findings on the long-term effects of variation in civic engagement across Italian regions on their respective economic development performance in the twentieth century. Briefly, he argues that by helping to promote social cooperation norms and build collaborative networks, nonprofits can help to develop social trust upon which political and economic systems in large, anonymous societies depend. Every business transaction and every contract involves an element of trust, without which markets cannot function (Arrow 1999). Likewise, social trust and networks reduce the immense challenges involved in collective action, which is critical for citizens to hold elected officials accountable and improving government functioning (Putnam 1993, 2000). Previously, this hypothesis had been supported in analyses of social capital (e.g., Knack and Keefer 1997). Social capital, however, remains a highly elusive policy target. The evidence presented here affirms the nonprofit sector's role in promoting economic development, providing a much more concrete option for policy makers interested in promoting economic development by strengthening philanthropic values in society: fostering philanthropic giving, volunteering, and nonprofit sector employment should encourage broader economic development. I return to this important lesson in the concluding chapter.

Testing the Mediating Impact of Risk as an Explanation of the PKC

Having demonstrated through various methods and indicators that variation in economic development leads to a nonlinear variation in nonprofit sector strength, this section examines the causes of this surprising relationship. Why does economic development at low levels undermine nonprofit sector strength and at high levels promote it? That is, why does nonprofit sector strength adopt a U-shape curve relationship with economic development?

The risk perspective advanced in chapter 2 laid the ground for an explanation of the PKC, combining economic, finance, and game theory insights to understand the impact of risk on collective action, philanthropy, and the nonprofit sector. As risk increases, philanthropy and nonprofit sector size should decrease, other things held constant: high risk, low philanthropy (and weak sector). On the other hand, the process of economic development will commonly increase risk at first and decrease risk at later stages so that middle-income countries are frequently the countries facing the highest levels of economic risk. The combination of an inverted U-shaped relationship between risk and economic development and an inverse relationship between nonprofit sector strength and risk should produce the PKC pattern, whereby nonprofit sector strength is lowest at intermediate levels of economic development. This section examines these three claims and systematically assesses the hypothesis that risk actually mediates the relationship between economic development and nonprofit sector strength, rather than simply being spuriously correlated to it.

Starting with a visual examination of the relevant relationships, figure 3.1 depicts the relationship between risk and economic development. It shows a remarkable association between different dimensions of risk, namely (1) macroeconomic volatility, measured by the standard deviation of economic growth between 1960 and 2000; (2) mean annual inflation rate also between 1960 and 2000; (3) subjective risk-aversion attitudes as estimated by Hofstede's cross-cultural research; and (4) the risk index. All variables display the predicted relationship with economic development. In the riskier middle-income countries, economic instability manifested in economic volatility and inflation overlaps with high risk-aversion in the population. By contrast, in the less risky poor and rich countries, economies are more stable and people are less risk-averse. Of note, higher risk-aversion in middle-income countries is quite surprising since previous research at the individual level has failed to find a consistent relationship between risk-aversion and level of wealth (Kreps 1990). This nonlinear relationship between risk-aversion and economic development, nevertheless, is consistent with the PKC. Also,

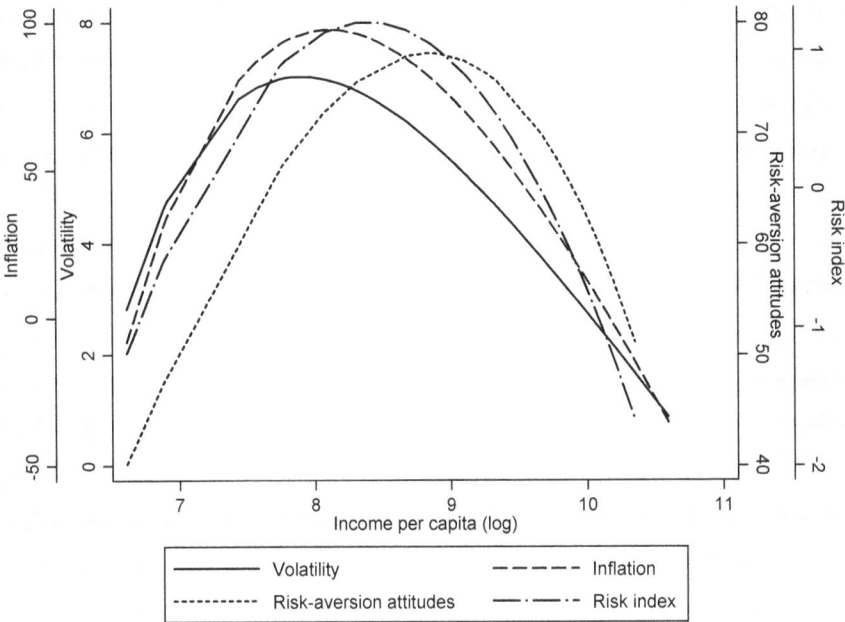

Figure 3.1. Economic development and different measures of risk. Notes: Based on the author's analysis of nonprofit sector data from the Johns Hopkins CNP (N=40), risk-aversion attitudes from Hofstede (2001), and economic data from the World Bank's World Development Indicators dataset. Inflation is the average inflation rate between 1960 and 2000. Volatility is the standard deviation of annual GDP growth between 1960 and 2000. The curves represent predicted values from estimation of a fractional polynomial regression.

macroeconomic instability appears to peak at a lower level of income per capita than risk aversion, suggesting that risk-aversion attitudes may persist even after the economy has become more stable.

An important hypothesis derived from the risk framework is that risk affects all resources, but different resources are affected differently. What is the evidence on how different nonprofit resources evolve with economic development? Figure 3.2 displays the relationship between economic development and the three main types of nonprofit resources for which we have cross-national data—commercial fees, government funding, and philanthropy (including both giving and volunteering) as a percentage of GDP. All resources first decline and then rise with economic development. As expected, philanthropy displays the most pronounced U-curve, bottoming out in middle-income countries. Government funding also declines with economic development but begins to recover at a lower level of economic development than philanthropy does. In line with our theoretical prediction that commercial revenue is the most resilient type of nonprofit resource, revenue from commercial fees displays the lowest level of responsiveness to changes in economic development (and consequently risk as well). It is surprising, however, that commercial fees are directly associated with economic development and level of income per capita only in rich countries. In terms of resource dependence, commercial income accounts for the largest proportion of nonprofit resources in middle-income countries. Middle-income countries commonly have high dependence on commercial fees. Receiving 85% of its income from commercial fees, the nonprofit sector in Mexico has the highest level of dependence on commercial fees in the world. To illustrate, commercial revenue accounts for 74% of total revenue in Brazil, 73% in Argentina, and 70% in Colombia. This compares with a global average of 49% (Salamon et al. 1999). On the other hand, largely due to the contribution of volunteering, philanthropy is the dominant resource in poor countries. Government funding tops the list in rich countries. The close relationship between resource dependence on government funding and risk-aversion is consistent with the argument that government's level of risk-aversion is directly related to the level of risk-aversion in the population, and that government funding will be a more attractive and reliable type of funding in countries where government agencies are less risk-averse. In countries where government agencies are highly risk-averse they are more likely to systematically shift risk to the nonprofit sector, which might lead to recipient organizations' fragility and even extinction. It is also possible that government agencies are less willing to fund nonprofits due to some of the risks involved in contracting out service provision. The next chapters help to clarify the complex relationship between government and nonprofits by examining the case of Mexico. Figure 3.2 also displays the evolution of resource concentration, measured by the Herfindahl index. The sharp declines in philanthropy and government funding between poor and middle-income countries lead to a strong rise in resource concentration on commercial revenue.

Figure 3.3 demonstrates that nonprofit risk exposure is closely associated with non-profit sector weakness. It depicts the remarkable relationship between nonprofit sector exposure to systematic risk (macroeconomic volatility) and idiosyncratic risk (nonprofit sector resource concentration), philanthropy, nonprofit sector size, and economic development. As risk increases, nonprofit sector strength declines. At higher levels of economic development, as risk decreases nonprofit sector strength increases. The way in which variation in nonprofit sector strength almost perfectly mirrors changes in risk exposure is consistent with the risk approach to explaining the PKC developed in the previous chapter. The inverted U-shaped relationships between both resource concentration in the nonprofit sector and macroeconomic volatility with economic development, on one hand, and the "mirroring" U-shaped relationships between both philanthropy and nonprofit sector employment with economic development, on the other, are highly consistent with the PKC and the risk explanation.

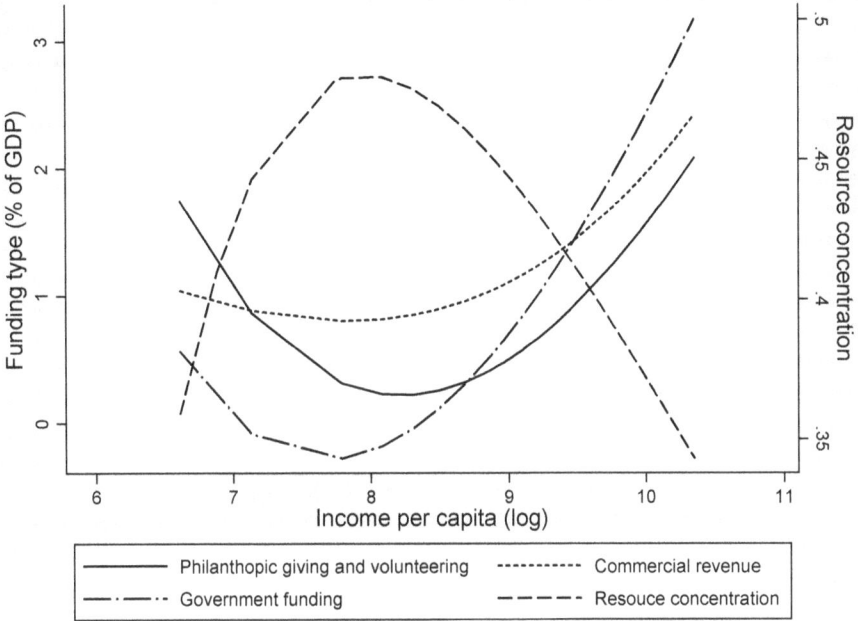

Figure 3.2. Nonprofit resources, resource concentration, and economic development. Notes: Based on author's analysis of Johns Hopkins CNP data. Resource concentration is measured by the Herfindahl index. The curves represent predicted values from estimation of a fractional polynomial regression.

The graphs in this section clearly show that the challenges nonprofits face at different economic development levels are very different. When the economy goes into a recession in a middle-income country—which is likely to be a frequent event—nonprofits are likely to experience a dramatic reduction in support for long-term programs as their highly risk-averse supporters discount the value of future investments and guard against possible income losses. The persistence of expectations of high risk limits organizational resources long after the economy has recovered, having a durable depressing impact upon supporter appetite for investments in long-term organizational development and capitalization. Those nonprofits are also likely to be dependent on a small number of similar supporters, so that organizational survival remains under threat, vulnerable to idiosyncratic shocks, even as the economy recovers. When the economy goes into a recession in rich or poor countries, nonprofits typically face smaller reductions in support and are more resilient to such reductions. Nonprofit

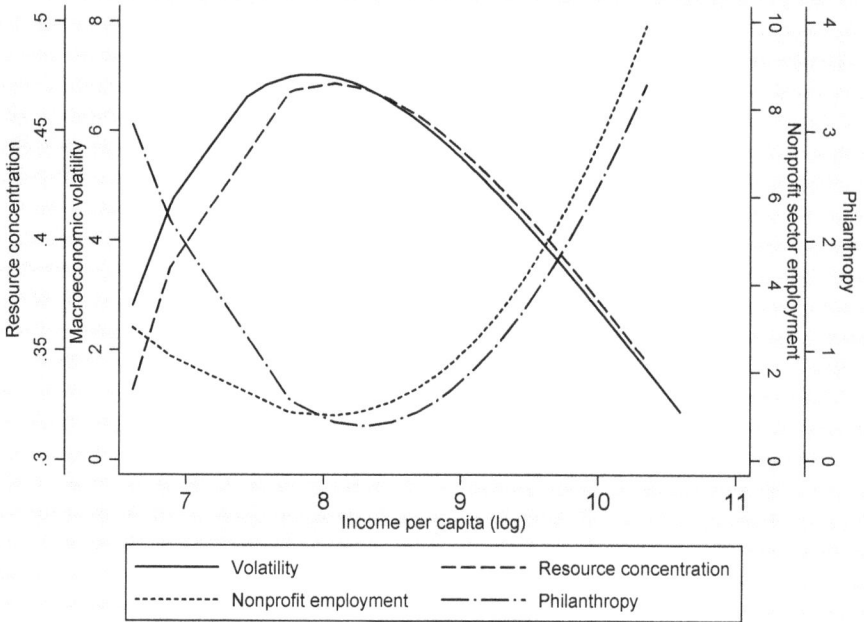

Figure 3.3. Risk, nonprofit sector strength and economic development. Notes: Based on author's analysis of nonprofit sector data from the Johns Hopkins CNP (N=40) and economic data from the World Bank's World Development Indicators. Resource concentration is measured by the Herfindahl index. The curves represent predicted values from estimation of a fractional polynomial regression.

friction due to changing supporter preferences and organizational long-term commitments is also likely to be limited in lower-risk countries.

The strong association between risk and nonprofit sector strength is illustrated in figure 3.4, which depicts the relationship between philanthropy, nonprofit sector size, and the risk index. It shows a remarkable consistency between the relationships of the two dimensions of nonprofit sector strength and risk. This consistency can be seen in both predicted (i.e., fitted) relationship and actual observations for each country. Moreover, the parabolic relationship between nonprofit sector size and nonprofit sector exposure to risk is surprising and indicates a potential "risk trap" in the relationship between risk and nonprofit sector strength. Though risk reductions are associated with nonprofit sector growth, risk has to fall sharply before the nonprofit sector in a high-risk country can grow significantly. This parabolic relationship might be caused by mutually reinforcing feedback effects between different dimensions of risk exposure.

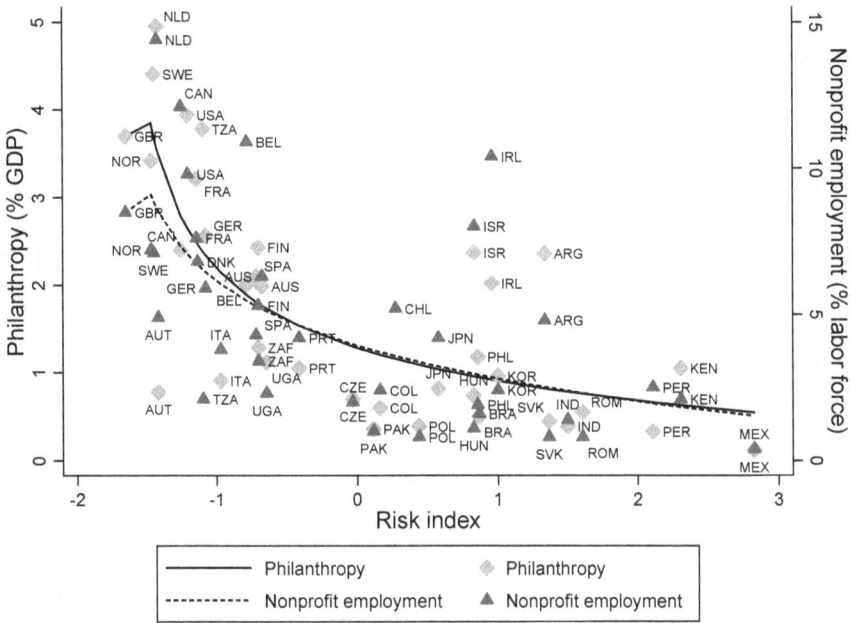

Figure 3.4. Risk index, philanthropy, and nonprofit sector size. Notes: Based on author's analysis of nonprofit sector data from the Johns Hopkins Comparative Nonprofit Sector Project and economic volatility data from the World Bank (1960–2005). The curves represent predicted values from estimation of a fractional polynomial regression.

For example, volatility risk might increase nonprofit sector resource concentration, which, in turn, might increase exposure to idiosyncratic risk. Volatility risk may also lead to an increase in risk-aversion, which may lead to discount rates remaining high long after volatility risk has fallen. Since discount rates undermine support for the sector, nonprofit sector size may continue to decline long after volatility risk has fallen. The Mexican study permits the observation of such hypothetical feedback effects over time. Chapters 4 and 5 will provide evidence and new hypotheses for this intriguing, and policy-relevant, risk trap.

The high degree of consistency between graphical evidence and the risk perspective is remarkable, especially considering the methodological difficulties in the measurement of risk and nonprofit sector strength. As compelling as this evidence may be, however, the claim that risk mediates the relationship between economic development and nonprofit sector strength must be systematically evaluated using mediation analysis, which examines both direct and indirect (mediated) impacts of economic development while controlling for potential confounding variables.

Mediation analysis permits testing of the three main hypotheses involved in explaining the PKC. The first hypothesis, which "Path C" in figure 3.5 illustrates, is that nonprofit sector strength, represented by philanthropy and nonprofit sector size, has a nonlinear (U-shaped) and statistically significant relationship with economic development (i.e., the PKC). The second hypothesis, which "Path A" illustrates, is that economic development has a nonlinear (inverted U-shaped) and statistically significant impact on the level of risk faced by the nonprofit sector, which is measured by the risk index. The third hypothesis, which "Path B" illustrates, is that risk partly undermines nonprofit sector strength even when the analysis controls for the direct impact of economic development on nonprofit sector strength. A significant indirect effect of economic development on nonprofit sector strength through risk is evidence that risk is indeed a mechanism through which economic development impacts nonprofit sector strength. Moreover, if economic development does not fully determine risk and risk helps to determine nonprofit sector strength, this analysis establishes that risk may also have an independent impact. That is, risk may have an impact on nonprofit sector strength even when economic development is constant.

Table 3.4 presents results from mediation analysis. Based on OLS regression, models 1 and 4 examine the total impact of economic development on nonprofit philanthropy and nonprofit sector size, respectively. Economic development has a nonlinear (U-shaped) and statistically significant relationship with philanthropy and nonprofit sector size. Models 2 and 5 examine the impact of economic development on the risk index. Economic development also has a nonlinear (inverted U-shaped) and statistically significant association with risk. Models 3 and 6 examine the impact of risk and the direct impact of economic development (after controlling for risk, which represents the indirect or mediated impact) on philanthropy and nonprofit sector size, respectively.

Following the multiplication method (MacKinnon et al. 2002), the indirect, or mediated, effect is determined by multiplying the effect of economic development on risk (Path A in figure 3.5) by the effect of risk on philanthropy or nonprofit sector size (Path B). By subtracting this indirect effect from the total effect of economic development on philanthropy or nonprofit sector size (Path C), we can estimate the direct, or nonmediated, effect. Sobel-Goodman mediation tests confirm the statistical significance of the risk index as a mediating variable ($p < 0.05$).

Because the relationship between economic development and nonprofit sector strength is nonlinear, total, mediated, and direct effects vary at different levels of economic development. These effects must, therefore, be calculated at different levels of interest. As shown on table 3.4, in a country like Mexico with a natural log of income per capita of 8.86, a 1% increase in income per capita produces a 0.059% increase in philanthropy through its impact on risk as well as a direct increase of 0.019%. Direct and

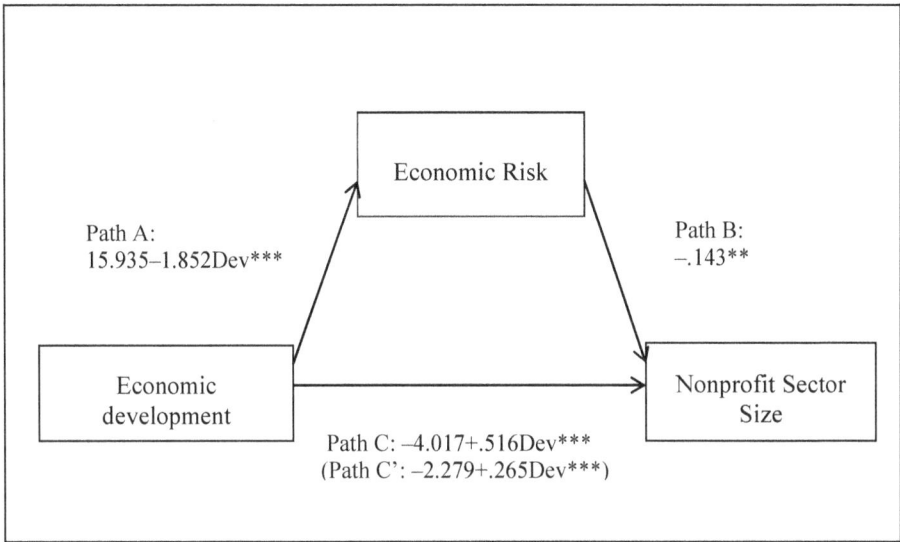

Figure 3.5. Mediation analysis. Notes: Unstandardized regression coefficients reported. Following the multiplication method, the indirect, or mediated, effect is equal to the effect of economic development on risk multiplied by the effect of risk on nonprofit sector size after controlling for the impact of economic development on nonprofit sector size. The indirect effect is in parentheses. Path C is the total effect of economic development on nonprofit sector size. Path C' is the indirect effect of economic development on nonprofit sector size through economic risk. As shown in Table 4, all regressions controlled for potential covariates, namely democracy level, ethnic fragmentation, religious diversity, Anglo-Saxon legal framework, and Urbanization. ***p<.01; **p<.05 (two-tailed).

indirect effects combine in a 0.078% increase in philanthropy for every percent increase in income per capita. In this case, the mediated effect accounts for 75.6% of the total effect. In the case of nonprofit sector size, 1% increase in income per capita leads to a 0.069% increase in nonprofit sector size due to the indirect effect on risk. This mediated effect represents 12.4% of the total impact of increases in income per capita on nonprofit sector size.

In the case of a rich country such as the United States, economic development has very different effects (table 3.4). The indirect effect through risk accounts for 29.4% of the total effect of increases in income per capita on philanthropy and 35.0% on nonprofit sector size. In the case of a poor country such as Pakistan, economic development has a negative impact on both philanthropy and nonprofit sector size. The indirect impact through risk accounts for 20.4% of the total impact in the case of philanthropy and is as large as the direct effect but in the opposite direction in the case of nonprofit sector size, greatly attenuating the total impact (table 3.4).

Table 3.4. Mediation analysis

	1	2	3	4	5	6
Path	C	A	B	C	A	B
Dependent Variable	Philanthropy	Risk	Philanthropy	Sector size	Risk	Sector size
Ln(GDP per capita)	-6.354*** (1.105)	13.925*** (2.936)	-4.745*** (1.387)	-4.017*** (1.378)	15.935*** (2.920)	-1.745 (1.555)
[Ln(GDP per capita)]^2	.363*** (.059)	-.814*** (.155)	.268*** (.078)	.258*** (.074)	-.926*** (.156)	.126 (.087)
Risk index			-.116* (.067)			-.143** (.082)
Democracy index	.032# (.020)	-.181* (.102)	.011 (.022)	-.026 (.030)	-.214** (.093)	-.056# (.033)
Ethnic fragmentation	-.055 (.258)	-.657 (.623)	-.131 (.218)	.197 (.289)	-1.143# (.742)	.034 (.332)
Religious diversity	.049 (.245)	-.416 (.706)	.001 (.218)	-.313 (.300)	-.784 (.696)	-.425# (.274)
Urban, % population	.010** (.004)	.004 (.011)	.010** (.004)	.008* (.004)	.006 (.010)	.009** (.004)
Anglo-Saxon legal code dummy				.369** (.144)	.703# (.424)	.470** (.173)
Intercept	27.385*** (4.954)	-56.786*** (13.200)	20.822*** (5.916)	15.994** (6.087)	-65.514*** (13.012)	6.653 (6.600)

Adjusted-R2	.611	.553	.640	.741	.586	.763
N.	36	36	36	38	38	38

Economic development effects

Total effect, Mexico	.078			.555		
Direct effect, Mexico	.019			.486		
Indirect effect, Mexico			.059			.069
Indirect/Total, Mexico			.756			.124
Total effect, U.S.	1.160			1.323		
Direct effect, U.S.	.819			.856		
Indirect effect, U.S.			.341			.464
Indirect/Total, U.S.			.294			.350
Total effect, Pakistan	-.691			-.008		
Direct effect, Pakistan	-.550			.212		
Indirect effect, Pakistan			-.141			-.220
Indirect/Total, Pakistan			.204			27.178

Notes: Bootstrapped standard errors reported between parentheses under unstandardized coefficients. Bootstrapping is explained in the methodology appendix to this chapter. Philanthropy is measured by the natural log of giving and volunteering as a percentage of GDP. Sector size is measured by the natural log of total nonprofit sector employment as a percentage of the labor force. ***p < .01; **p < .05; *p < .10; # p < .15 (two-tailed).

The differences in how economic development impacts philanthropy and nonprofit sector size are largely due to how economic development impacts non-philanthropic sources of support for the nonprofit sector. The total impact of economic development on the nonprofit sector is positive before its indirect impact is positive, which suggests that economic development promotes non-philanthropic resource development (e.g., fees) even as philanthropy continues to contract. Philanthropy's high susceptibility to economic risk is also manifest in the almost perfect overlap between the turning points of the indirect and total effects on philanthropy. This is consistent with the risk explanation, which predicts that philanthropy is more susceptible to risk than the other main types of nonprofit resources, government funding and commercial fees. To the extent that nonprofits can reduce their vulnerability by combining philanthropy with less susceptible sources, risk should impact nonprofit sector size less than philanthropy.

Assessing Cross-National Evidence on the PKC and its Risk-Based Explanation

This chapter is the first of three chapters assessing the empirical relationship between economic development, risk, and nonprofit sector strength. Analysis of cross-national statistical data presented in this chapter lends compelling support to the philanthropic Kuznets curve as a causal relationship between economic development and nonprofit sector strength as well as its theoretical explanation based on the mediating influence of risk.

The chapter began by employing various statistical methods to analyze the relationship between economic development, philanthropy, and nonprofit sector size, based on national accounts data from the Johns Hopkins CNP research and survey data from the World Values Survey. The results of this analysis show a remarkably robust relationship that is consistent with the PKC. Economic development has a nonlinear, quadratic effect on both philanthropy and nonprofit sector size. Moreover, the analysis lends support to the hypothesis of mutual causation between economic development and nonprofit sector strength. These results have significant theoretical and policy implications as discussed in the conclusion.

The second part of this chapter tested the joint hypotheses that economic development helps to determine the variation in economic risk across nations and, in turn, that economic risk helps to determine nonprofit sector strength. Numerous indicators show that economic risk has a nonlinear relationship with economic development. Compared to both rich and poor countries, middle-income countries generally display higher levels of macroeconomic instability, as indicated by higher levels of macroeconomic volatility, mean inflation, risk-aversion, and short-termism in the population as well as higher levels of resource concentration and dependence on commercial income in the nonprofit sector. This unlikely agreement among such diverse risk indicators, and their close association with nonprofit sector indicators, is astounding and lends preliminary support to the theoretical explanation developed in chapter 2. To fully understand the relationship between economic development, economic risk, and the nonprofit sector, the analysis also examined the relationship between risk and the nonprofit sector while controlling for potentially confounding influences. Systematic statistical analysis of mediation effects affirmed the hypothesis that economic development has an indirect effect on nonprofit sector strength through its effect on risk. Thus, analysis of cross-national statistical data suggests that risk is a main mechanism for the PKC and provides a robust explanation for the geographical variation in philanthropy and nonprofit sector size.

Limitations in available cross-national data suggest the need for additional analysis before conclusions about the impact of risk over time can be established. In particular, longitudinal evidence would greatly increase confidence that the confounding effect of all possible omitted variables is controlled for. Furthermore, aggregate data mask significant local variation, which is an essential part of the story: economic development and risk influence the nonprofit sector because they influence individual and organizational support for nonprofits. To ensure that analysis of the risk mechanism rests on solid micro-foundations and includes relevant micro-level processes, chapters 4 and 5 provide analysis of case study, survey, and citizen participation data, providing a rare opportunity for observation of how several Mexican nonprofits tried to adapt to and survive in a risky environment. Chapter 5 also examines the impact of economic risk on other countries, namely Argentina, Chile, Thailand, and several rich countries including the United States.

Appendix to Chapter 3: Data and Methods

Operationalization of the Outcomes to be Explained

This analysis focuses on nonprofit sector strength, which, as defined here, includes two related dependent variables: philanthropy and nonprofit sector size. Philanthropy is measured using giving and estimated value of volunteering as a proportion of GDP from the Johns Hopkins Comparative Nonprofit Sector Project (CNP) conducted by Salamon, Anheier, and an international team of collaborators (e.g., Salamon et al. 2004). Nonprofit sector size is measured by total employment in the nonprofit sector as a percentage of the labor force from Salamon et al. (2004) and several country reports found at the Johns Hopkins Comparative Nonprofit Sector website. The calculation of employment in the nonprofit sector includes both paid and full-time equivalent volunteer labor input. To examine the robustness of my analysis, I also examine nonprofit sector spending as an alternative measure of nonprofit sector size.

Both indicators are included in the CNP dataset, which has been extensively used in cross-national nonprofit sector research (e.g., Gidron, Bar, and Katz 2003; Brinkerhoff 2002; Franco 2005). While other cross-national sets of nonprofit data are available, such as those developed by CIVICUS and the Union of International Associations (UIA), I chose the CNP because of this study's focus on philanthropy and nonprofit sector size. CIVIVUS and UIA do not include data on philanthropy. On the other hand, while the World Values Survey includes data on volunteering, which is a form of philanthropy, it does not include data on philanthropic giving.

Operationalization of Possible Explanations

The explanatory variables of interest are level of economic development and risk. Level of economic development is measured by GDP per capita, adjusted for cost of living differences across countries. Though controversial to some, as Ray (1998, ch. 2) points out, this measure is generally well correlated with the things that do correspond more highly with human welfare, such as child mortality, literacy, education, and health. Most importantly, GDP per capita is strongly correlated with the Human Development Index, which represents a broader indicator composed of opportunities (education), health (life expectancy), and income (Perkins, Radelet, and Lindaun 2006). Thus, economic development is operationalized by the natural log of average income per capita (purchasing power parity adjusted) from the World Bank's World Development Indicators (WDI) dataset.[3] Figures 1 and 2 in chapter 1 depict the nonlinear relationships between economic development, philanthropy, and nonprofit sector size, that is, the PKC.

In this study, nonprofit sector exposure to economic risk emerges from both systematic and idiosyncratic risk. Risk is, therefore, a "latent variable," which, rather than being directly observable, must be inferred from other observable variables. Factor analysis is invaluable in helping to estimate a latent variable (Kennedy 2003), assuming the variable is continuous and normally distributed. Risk is indeed continuous, and we can plausibly assume that it is also normally distributed. Indeed, its components are normally distributed in the sample. I estimated, therefore, a risk index using factor analysis, and more specifically its most common variation, principal components analysis. Systematic risk is operationalized using the natural log of the standard deviation of national economic growth between 1960 and 2000.[4] Often, economic growth is subdivided into trend and cyclical components using a mathematical tool, such as the Hodrick-Prescott or band-pass filter, to separate a term that is more sensitive to long-term variation (i.e., the trend) from the remaining (cyclical) variation (Bergman et al. 1998; Aiolfi et al. 2011). Such filters, however, can produce a distorted view of economic cyclicality and, consequently, I chose to follow Easterly, Islam, and Stiglitz (1999) in using the simple standard deviation instead.

Idiosyncratic risk is operationalized by calculating the Herfindahl index of nonprofit sector resources (see chapter 2). A less diversified sector is more vulnerable to idiosyncratic shocks and, therefore, faces higher idiosyncratic risk. As seen in table 3.1, both components are directly correlated ($r = 0.480$) and the computed risk index is highly correlated with its component variables as seen by its factor (component) loadings: macroeconomic volatility ($r = 0.859$) and Herfindahl resource concentration index ($r = 0.859$).

This nonprofit-related risk index is also strongly and directly correlated with measures of risk-aversion in the population. Risk-aversion is important because it determines the responsiveness of supporters to changes in risk level. An increase in systematic risk due to a crisis, for example, will have a stronger impact on risk discounting by more risk-averse supporters than by less risk-averse supporters. As argued in chapter 2, higher risk discounting reduces the "shadow of the future," on which cooperation rests, and thus discourages philanthropy and other nonprofit sector funding, especially for non-emergency programs. Risk aversion at the national level is measured using Hofstede's indicator of "Uncertainty Avoidance versus Risk-Taking Propensity" in national culture. Independent survey research found this indicator to be a significant predictor of impatience, or present bias, and long-term discount rates at both individual and cross-national levels (Wang, Rieger, and Hens 2010:24, 33). Cultures, or individuals, with a high score will refrain from taking risk and trying new methods, preferring instead traditional approaches.[5] As expected, this measure of risk-aversion is positively correlated with the risk index (r = 0.614). Figure 3.1 shows the remarkable relationship between various indicators of risk in nonprofit sector's environment.

The examination of the relationship between economic development, risk, and nonprofit sector strength must control for other determinants of nonprofit sector suggested by previous nonprofit sector research. Unless otherwise specified, all control variables refer to 1995 values. This is to ensure that they precede nonprofit sector data from the CNP, which were mostly collected between 1995 and 2000. To control for "government failure," I include ethnic fractionalization as a measure of social heterogeneity. Government failure is more likely in contexts characterized by high social heterogeneity, as the government tends to emphasize provision of standardized services demanded by the majority. In such contexts, the nonprofit sector emerges as an important service provider to unsatisfied minorities (Corbin 1999; James 1987; Weisbrod 1988). Ethnic heterogeneity is measured using the ethnic fractionalization indicator from Alesina et al. (2003) as included in the Quality of Government dataset (Teorell et al. 2008), which measures the probability that two persons drawn at random from a country's population do not belong to the same ethnic group. To control for non-income supply-side factors, I include an indicator for religious competition (see James 1989), resulting from religious diversity. This indicator, also from Alesina et al. (2003), reflects the probability that two randomly selected people from a given country do not belong to the same religious group. The natural log of trade as a proportion of GDP, from the World Bank's WDI dataset, is included as a control for globalization. To control for modernization, I use the proportion of the population living in urban areas from the World Bank's WDI dataset. Modernization theory suggests that increasing urbanization leads to greater fluidity in social relationships and a breakdown of traditional rural societies. To control for market failure, I control for trust in business from WVS data on "confidence in big business." To control for the role of government, and "interdependence" effects (see Salamon 1987), I use government final consumption expenditure as a proportion of GDP from the World Bank's WDI dataset.[6]

As discussed in chapter 1, democratic political institutions protecting political rights and civil liberties are important in the development of the nonprofit sector (see Douglas 1987; Hammack 2001). To control for their influence, I employ the widely used combined polity score from the Polity IV project. According to the Polity's Data Users' Manual (Marshall, Jaggers, and Gurr 2011:14–15),

> democracy is conceived as three essential, interdependent elements. One is the presence of institutions and procedures through which citizens can express effective preferences about alternative policies and leaders. Second is the existence of institutionalized constraints on the exercise of power by the executive. Third is the guarantee of civil liberties to all citizens in their daily lives and in acts of political participation. Other aspects of plural democracy, such as the rule of law, systems of checks and balances, freedom of the press, and so on are means to, or specific manifestations of, these general principles. . . . There is no "necessary condition" for characterizing a political system as democratic, rather democracy is treated as a variable.

The Polity IV index is highly correlated with other measures of institutional regime. Its Pearson correlation with the Freedom House's "civil liberties index" for the year of study is 0.780 and the Spearman rank order correlation, which is more robust to nonlinear relationships, is even higher (rho = 0.861). The correlation between the Polity IV index and

Freedom House's "Political Rights index" is very high ($r = 0.909$), and the Spearman rank order correlation is remarkable ($rho = 0.933$).

To explain different historical paths of nonprofit sector development, Salamon and Anheier (1998:228) suggested four "nonprofit regimes" as heuristic devices to describe broad types of "constellations of social forces" influencing the nonprofit sector. The detailed historical analysis needed to extend such a model from Salamon and Anheier's (1998) sample of seven rich countries to all forty countries from the CNP, which make up my smallest sample, is beyond the scope of this study. Nevertheless, to examine the influence of "social origins," and in particular of the legal framework, I employ a variable commonly used in cross-national comparative research—a dummy variable for Anglo-Saxon legal system—based on La Porta et al.'s (1999) indicator of legal system origins. An Anglo-Saxon legal system is associated with common law, which is generally seen as the most flexible legal system. Such flexibility is key to facilitating private enterprise and, consequently, the nonprofit sector (see Anheier and Salamon 1998; Salamon et al. 1999, La Porta et al. 1999; Archambault 2001).

Lastly, research on social capital suggests that social inequality undermines the social contract and weakens social trust (Uslaner 2002; Rothstein 2005). Since nonprofit sector strength, and especially philanthropy, is likely to be partly determined by the degree to which people trust each other, social inequality is also likely to influence the nonprofit sector. To control for social inequality I use the Gini coefficient estimated by the World Bank and included in the WDI dataset. Summary statistics are not included in this book, but are available from the author upon request.

Methods of Analysis

This study addresses two methodological weaknesses, which have thus far limited the contributions of statistical research on the nonprofit sector, especially at the cross-national level: failure to account for nonlinearity and reverse causation. The PKC is an inherently nonlinear (curvilinear) relationship and, as such, cannot be adequately examined using simple linear methods. Several curve-fitting techniques were employed to examine the actual nonlinear relationship between nonprofit sector strength and economic development. Surprisingly, the best possible, statistically significant, fit was not the obvious quadratic or cubic function but, instead, a power function with the form $Y = exp^{(a + bX)}$, which produced a very high score for goodness of fit ($R^2 = 0.73$ for philanthropy and 0.81 for nonprofit sector size!). The power function is equivalent to $\ln(Y) = a_0 + b_1 X$, so both philanthropy and nonprofit sector size variables were transformed by taking their natural logs. A new curve-fitting process was implemented on the transformed independent variables. After transformation, the best possible, statistically significant, fit was the quadratic form ($Y = a_0 + b_1 X + b_2 X^2$). Consequently, the analysis presented above focuses on the quadratic form after transformation of the dependent variable. This process permitted the use of traditional, linear methods to capture most of the nonlinear relationship between economic development and nonprofit sector strength. To check the robustness of this process, as explained below, I employed several non-parametric techniques in the analysis, namely Spearman's rank-ordered correlation, Lowess curves, and bootstrapping.

Another common weakness of statistical research on the nonprofit sector is the failure to disentangle cause-effect relationships. In this study, the analysis employs two-stage least squares (2SLS) and three-stage least squares (3SLS) regression to deal with the problem of potential endogeneity between economic development and nonprofit sector strength. As an instrumental variables method, 2SLS is commonly used when an experimental design is not feasible, as is generally the case in cross-national studies. In 2SLS, an instrumental variable (or set of instrumental variables), which affects economic development but does not directly impact nonprofit sector strength, is used to parse out the exogenous from the endogenous effect within the endogenous variables. Such an instrumental variable, therefore, controls for the potential reverse causality between economic development and nonprofit sector strength (Greene 2002; see also Duncan Chaplin's excellent explanation of Instrumental Variables Methods at the Urban Institute's website).[7]

The instruments used to estimate the exogenous effect of economic development (simple and quadratic terms) on nonprofit sector strength are the natural log of a country's population in 1980 and its age dependency ratio, measured by the proportion of dependents to the working-age population (16–64), in 1980. Both variables are from the World Bank's WDI dataset. Instrumental variables methods rely on two assumptions: the instrumental variables are distributed independently of the error in the structural equation, and they are sufficiently correlated with the included endogenous regressors (Baum 2006). A larger population permits economies of scale in production and consumption and, consequently, should stimulate economic development. A vast literature has examined the importance of the ratio between working-age and dependent-age population, generally arguing that a large dependent population hinders economic development (e.g., Perkins et al. 2006). Indeed, both age dependency and the natural log of population size are significantly correlated with linear and quadratic terms of income per capita (at $p < 0.01$). Moreover, both instruments were significant predictors of the endogenous variables in first-stage regressions, and the Anderson canonical correlation test rejects the null hypothesis of underidentification using the chosen instrument set. The instruments thus pass the requirement that they be correlated with the endogenous regressor. The other key requirement is that both instruments be exogenous in the mode—that is, independent of the error term in the structural equation. This assertion is, of course, essentially untestable. Nevertheless, both instruments are plausibly exogenous in the model as it is unlikely that the level of economic prosperity in 1995 determines population size or the age-dependency ratio in 1980. A larger population could be associated with greater social heterogeneity, which is a key influence on the dependent variable, nonprofit sector strength. However, because ethnic and religious diversity are also included as instruments in the regression, it is unlikely that larger population is associated with the error term in the structural equation. It is not clear how the dependency ratio might determine nonprofit sector strength once economic development is included as an independent variable in the equation. Dependents commonly have a lower income than working-age individuals, but have more time to participate in the sector (see Putnam 2000). The impact, if any, is probably indeterminate. Indeed, neither philanthropy nor nonprofit sector size is significantly correlated with the natural log of population size or age dependency ratio.[8]

Among the remaining independent variables, level of democracy is likely to be endogenous, potentially causing but also being caused by nonprofit sector strength. The instrument used to parse out the exogenous effect from level of democracy is "Muslims as a percentage of the population" in 1980 from La Porta et al. (2009). This instrument is plausibly exogenous in the model and not associated with the error term once the other variables are included in the model. Inspection of the partial correlations between level of democracy, the instrument, and nonprofit sector strength lend support to this claim as the instrument is strongly associated with and plausibly causes level of democracy, but it is not significantly correlated with either philanthropy or nonprofit sector size once we control for level of democracy.

Three-stage least squares (3SLS) regression offers another opportunity to disentangle cause-effect relationships and test the robustness of the 2SLS estimation. While 2SLS is a limited information method, 3SLS is a full information method (Greene 2002) that permits estimation of both cause-effect relationships simultaneously: how economic development influences nonprofit sector strength and vice versa. That is, 3SLS extends 2SLS to include all equations simultaneously. Generally, however, 3SLS is less robust than 2SLS because, since it computes both equations simultaneously, it depends on both being properly specified. The accuracy of 3SLS models, therefore, can be partly determined by a comparison between its results and the results of a properly specified 2SLS equation. Indeed, the high degree of consistency between the 2SLS and 3SLS coefficients for both income per capita terms lends great credibility to the results presented on table 3.3.

A different method, mediation analysis, permits the systematic examination of the means through which an explanatory variable exerts its effect on an outcome variable (MacKinnon, Warsi, and Dwyer 1995; Preacher, Rucker, and Hayes 2007). The hypothesis that risk exerts a mediating influence on the relationship between economic development and nonprofit sector strength can be tested by examining whether the explanatory variable (economic development) has an indirect effect on the outcome variable (nonprofit sector strength), that is, whether the explanatory variable helps to determine the mediating variable (risk) and, in turn, the mediating variable helps to determine the outcome variable when the explanatory variable's direct influence is included as a control. Mediation analysis helps identify the distinct, and potentially contradictory, direct and indirect impacts of the independent variable on the dependent variable.

The robustness of these mediating effects obtained using simple OLS regression was assessed using bootstrapped Sobel standard errors and confidence intervals. A growing literature now advocates the use of bootstrapping for assessing indirect or mediating effects (e.g., MacKinnon et al. 2002; Shrout and Bolger 2002). Bootstrapping is a way to overcome the limitations of statistical methods that make assumptions about the shape of sampling distributions, such as normality. Consequently, bootstrapping is recommended for small sample sizes (MacKinnon et al. 2002). According to Preacher, Rucker, and Hayes (2007:190), "In bootstrapping, the sample is conceptualized as a pseudo-population that represents the broader population from which the sample was derived, and the sampling distribution of any statistic can be generated by calculating the statistic of interest in multiple resamples of the dataset. Using bootstrapping, no assumptions about the shape of the sampling distribution of the statistic are necessary when conducting inferential tests." In other words, bootstrapping involves repeatedly sampling random observations with replacement from the dataset and computing the statistic of interest in each resample. After a large number of bootstrap resamples (2,000 in this study), an empirical approximation of the sampling distribution of the statistic can be generated and used for hypothesis testing (Shrout and Bolger 2002).

Lastly, analysis in chapters 4 and 5 also includes a comparison of qualitative case study data as well as longitudinal and hierarchical or multilevel statistical methods to examine survey data. The use of several different empirical methods of analysis was essential in helping to establish the robustness of the study's empirical conclusions, especially since cross-national statistical research on the nonprofit sector has thus far received limited empirical attention.

4 When Crisis Hits

CHAPTER 3 SHOWS the remarkable association between level of economic development, economic risk, and nonprofit sector strength across nations. Does this relationship hold over time as well? At present, the absence of longitudinal data prevents a cross-national time-series reply to this question. To more closely examine the hypothesis that economic risk mediates the relationship between economic development and the nonprofit sector, and to better understand how it occurs and what nonprofits may do about it, this chapter and the next examine the evolution of the Mexican nonprofit sector in the 1990s and early 2000s—before, during, and after the Tequila Crisis. The crisis is described as having "caused one of the worst recessions to hit an individual country since the 1930s" (Krugman 2008:39). With Mexico's population of nearly 100 million people at the time, the crisis brought suffering to millions of Mexicans and presented significant challenges to the nonprofit sector.

Developing countries face considerable economic and other types of risk, such as political instability, frequent natural emergencies, and large migration flows. Economic risk typically materializes in high macroeconomic volatility, inflation, interest rate, and commodity price shocks. Their adverse effects commonly overlap in macroeconomic crises with devastating consequences for poor countries' development prospects. During macroeconomic crises, national and household income fall and unemployment increases (Horton and Mazumdar 2001), leading to strong rises in poverty levels (de Janvry and Sadoulet 2000). In most developing countries, the impact on poverty is compounded by the absence of state benefits and a social safety net (Agénor 2002; World Bank 2005). In fact, Lustig (1999) has argued that economic crises typically have an asymmetric impact upon poverty; that is, the increase in poverty brought about by a 1% contraction in output is higher than the decrease in poverty brought about by a 1% increase in output. Crises can have, therefore, lasting negative impacts upon poverty reduction efforts, reversing many years of hard-won social and economic progress. Their severity and frequency make crises a key obstacle to development (e.g., De Janvry and Sadoulet 2000; Perkins et al. 2006) and global justice. Development, therefore, involves dealing with economic crises as well as chronic injustice problems (Sen 1999).

This chapter examines the context and nature of the crisis, introduces the situation of six nonprofit case studies prior to the crisis, and analyzes the immediate financial and organizational impacts of the crisis and nonprofit responses, up to the end of 1995. The following chapter focuses on the period following the crisis, from 1996 onward, revealing fundamental tensions and ironies of the long-term impact of the crisis upon the case studies, spearheading a reflection on nonprofit sector sustainability and social impact. By examining the precarious context in which these intrepid social actors operated, why leaders made the decisions they made, and what ultimately happened to them, we can increase our understanding of how risk impacts the nonprofit sector over time and at the organizational level.

The "Tequila Crisis"

Mexico has experienced more than its fair share of economic instability. Between 1870 and 1913 Mexico had the fastest-growing economy in the world (Rodrik 2009, table 1). The Mexican Revolution (1910–1920) put an abrupt end to this pattern. General political instability and the Great Depression contributed to a long period of economic stagnation. By 1950, however, Mexico still had a higher level of GDP per worker than Greece, Portugal, or Spain (Haber et al. 2008:57, fig. 2.6). During the Mexican "Miracle," from 1950 to 1981, Mexican productivity continued to grow faster than the rest of Latin America and the OECD average (though not as fast as Spain and Greece). By 1981, Mexico's GDP per worker was equal to almost 76% of the OECD average, up from around 60% in 1950 (Penn World Table data from Heston, Summers, and Aten 2002). Since then, and despite its relative wealth and political stability, Mexico has faced several macroeconomic crises—debt crises in the 1980s (1983 and 1986), the financial crisis in the 1990s (1994–1995), and the global crisis in the 2000s (2009), as well as some smaller economic downturns (1982 and 2001)—with devastating impacts on its political and economic development. Unfortunately, with an ever-widening gap between the level of economic development of Mexico and that of rich countries, Mexicans' "First World Dreams" (Dawson 2006) have been postponed sine die.

Salinas's "Miracle" and Zedillo's "December Error"

It is surprising how unprepared Mexicans were for the Tequila Crisis. The crisis had clear origins in political and economic policies adopted during the 1980s and especially during Carlos Salinas's presidency (1988–1994). Since the early 1980s Mexico has undergone momentous social, political, and economic changes that amount to a "Second Mexican Revolution" (Haber et al. 2008). In the 1980s and 1990s, Mexico was transformed from a country with an "official party" with a virtual monopoly on political power to a competitive democracy and from a largely closed economy based on an import-substitution model of economic growth to one of the most open economies in the Latin America (Williams 2001; Lustig 1999; Otero 2004; Haber et al. 2008). After 1982, when President de la Madrid was forced to declare a moratorium on debt interest payments, Mexico implemented a series of liberalizing reforms to the economy, eliminating subsidies and price controls, reducing barriers to imports, and closing or privatizing government-owned companies. The opening of the economy had its formal origin in 1986, when Mexico joined the General Agreement on Tariffs and Trade, the predecessor to the

World Trade Organization. In the early 1990s, Mexico was used as a poster child for the success of neoliberal, "Washington Consensus" reforms (Lustig 1999). In 1994, Mexico joined NAFTA, and by the mid-2000s, Mexico had signed free-trade agreements with the European Union and with all countries in Central America, as well as with many in South America (Paras and Coleman 2006).

The early 1990s—the period when most of the nonprofits examined in this chapter were created—were times of prosperity. During this relatively calm period, however, a storm was brewing. In 1987, the decision of the outgoing de la Madrid administration to abandon a floating exchange rate and adopt a "crawling peg"—the peso was tied to the dollar and fluctuated by a tiny amount on a daily basis—had the expected downward impact on inflation. The real exchange rate appreciated substantially over the Salinas presidency as the 1987–1994 stabilization agreements negotiated between the government, business, and labor left the peso closely pegged to the U.S. dollar, with a pace of depreciation insufficient to compensate for the difference between inflation rates in Mexico and the United States. With relatively cheap imports swelling well beyond exports, Mexican policy makers talked a brave game, pointing to the balanced fiscal accounts and insisting, first, that the real appreciation of the peso was due to confidence in the Mexican economy, and second, that private financing via portfolio investment was sufficient to cover the rising trade imbalance (Paras and Coleman 2006). "Crudely put, in the era of market reforms, Mexico's fixed exchange rate helped support domestic purchasing power—a function that a once-benevolent state had found it increasingly difficult to play" (Pastor and Wise 2004:8).

In sharp contrast to the early 1990s, 1994 was one of the most eventful years in Mexico's history. It began with the country's entry into the North American Free Trade Agreement, which was one of the greatest achievements of Mexican diplomacy and testament to the high level of external confidence in the Mexican economy. On the same day, the Zapatista army, under the leadership of "Subcomandante" Marcos, declared war against the Mexican government and invaded San Cristobal de las Casas, the capital of the southern state of Chiapas. The Mexican army fought back, and ninety-eight soldiers died in the battle. To add to the chaos, several bombs exploded throughout Mexico in the following days. In March of that year the main presidential candidate, Luis Donaldo Colosio, was assassinated. After this assassination Ernesto Zedillo became the main candidate, and eventually the next president of Mexico. In April, Mexico entered the Organization for Economic Cooperation and Development, commonly associated with the rich nations club—another powerful vote of confidence in the Mexican government and economy. In the meantime, several of Mexico's economic variables became increasingly worrying. To sustain an artificially high peso against the U.S. dollar, the country embarked in a desperate effort to attract foreign capital. Short-term borrowing from international sources rose strongly in the first few months of the year. By the time the presidential elections took place in August, short-term international borrowing had grown twelvefold since the start of the year (Pastor and Wise 2004). The interest rate had to rise sharply to attract such high volumes of international capital. Fortunately, the presidential elections took place without disturbances, and this led to greater confidence in Mexico's economy. In a fresh sign of political instability, however, the incoming speaker of the House, Ruiz Massieu, was assassinated in September. Despite the peaceful election of Zedillo, US$4.7 billion left the country in November. Overall, US$16.6 billion had left the country in the previous nine months. Foreign exchange reserves fell from US$29 billion in February 1994 to around US$6 billion in November 1994. This placed Zedillo in a very precarious position when he became Mexico's president in December (Paras and Coleman 2006).

The Crisis

Recognizing the challenge he was about to inherit, incoming President Ernesto Zedillo pressed for an orderly devaluation in late 1994. While investors clearly saw Mexico as an increasingly risky market—indicated by the extraordinary rate of capital withdrawals during the previous year—there was widespread hope that the country's entry into NAFTA would lift exports and help address the trade imbalance without a need for a drastic devaluation of the peso. The initial attempt at a step-devaluation, however, led to the peso's free fall and a subsequent collapse in national output. Between December 1994 and March 1995, the Mexican peso lost 43% of its value in relation to the American dollar. Another way to look at it: within a few months Mexico's share of global wealth fell by almost half! The devaluation continued. The exchange rate between nuevos pesos (N$) and U.S. dollars (US$) fell by more than 50%, from N$3.375 in 1994 to N$6.419 in 1995 and N$7.599 in 1996 (based on data from the World Bank's WDI dataset, average for the year). The sudden devaluation of the peso, which led to an abrupt rise in interest rates, often reaching a 90% annual rate, led to hundreds of thousands of debtors being unable to service their debt, which, subsequently, increased bad loans in banks. Business and consumers had become indebted due to the credit expansion of previous years and the expectation of stable interest rates. The deposit interest rate rose from 15.0% to 39.8% in 1995 and was still 26.4% in 1996 (WDI dataset). According to the *New York Times* (March 12, 1995), "With interest rates of 90 percent and higher on mortgages, credit cards and car loans will push many families into insolvency. Millions of Mexicans awoke on Friday morning to find that gasoline prices had jumped a third overnight and electricity costs were up 20 percent." Credit market woes paralyzed the economy. Output contracted so that its annualized growth rate in 1995 was −6.2% (Lederman et al. 2000). In constant dollars, Mexico's income per capita fell from US$4,600 in 1994 to US$3,660 in 1996. The output contraction led to a reduction in government tax revenues, which in turn led to rising taxes and scaling back of government social programs (World Bank 2005). Value added tax, which is similar to a federal sales tax, rose from 10 to 15%.

Unemployment, while low by global standards, almost doubled, from 3.9% to 7.4%, which translated into a loss of more than one million jobs in the formal sector. Employment also declined in the informal economy (World Bank 2005:439). Inflation rose from

6.9% in 1994 to over 34% in 1995 and 1996 (WDI dataset). Rampant inflation meant that real wages in the manufacturing sector fell by 39% (Székely and Lustig 1997). The fateful juxtaposition of rapidly shrinking income opportunities and rising costs had a devastating effect on the lives of ordinary Mexicans. As a result of these trends, the number of families under the poverty line doubled, and the middle-class was impoverished by a crushing debt burden. Using survey data, McKenzie (2003) found that households postponed having children. Overall, household incomes declined by roughly 30%, and the Gini index grew from 50.31 in 1992 to 54.93 in 2000 (WDI dataset). Extreme poverty more than doubled between 1994 and 1996 (rising from 10.1 to 26.5%), while moderate poverty increased from 43 to 62% (World Bank 2005:439). In terms of poverty reduction, the positive growth effects of the entire past decade were erased by the devastating effect of the 1994–1995 Tequila Crisis (Maloney, Cunningham, and Bosch 2004).

Economic distress led to signs of increasing social breakdown. "Crime in the capital, for example, rose by 6.85 percent from December through September when compared with the previous year, according to the Mexico City attorney general's office. The crime wave appears to be crisis-related: Although the number of rapes has fallen slightly, the number of cars stolen nonviolently has risen by more than 104 percent" (*Boston Globe,* December 12, 1995:4). "As unemployment rises and fear of crime increases, most Mexico City newspapers are dotted with advertisements for bulletproof cars, armed guards and executive lessons in hand-to-hand combat" (*New York Times,* March 12, 1995).

Clearly, the futures of the American and Mexican economies and polities are inherently bound (Roett 1996). In an age of rapid globalization, the impact of Mexico's economic crises is also felt across its northern border. The 1980s and 1990s witnessed a strong growth of illegal immigrants coming to the United States, probably trying to escape worsening economic conditions at home. Indeed, 1995 represented one of the strongest years of migration from Mexico to the United States (Homeland Security 2006).[1] According to a World Bank study, "The most common private risk management strategies during the Tequila crisis were out-migration to the United States and increased income diversification" (World Bank 2005:441). The decline in social spending also led to worsening health indicators and presented a potential security risk for receiving countries. Households responded to the sharp drop in income associated with the crisis by changing the composition of expenditure, reducing spending on durables and nonessential items (including primary health care) in order to maintain spending on basic food items (McKenzie 2003). The evolution of the tuberculosis infection rate in Mexico between 1990 and 1999 illustrates this point aptly. From an infection rate of under 15 per 100,000 in the early 1990s, the crisis years brought about a clear "jump" in the infection rate, which extended into 1997–1998, to reach 21 per 100,000 (Baez-Saldana et al. 2003). Migration complicates tuberculosis control efforts along the United States–Mexico border. To illustrate, Texas border counties have infection rates of 16.8 per 100,000 members of the population, against a infection rate in the United States of 6.8 per 100,000 members of the population. In those counties, Mexican-born immigrants account for 49% of all infection cases.[2] Mexico's troubles were literally contagious to its neighbors.

How then did international donors respond? International donors did come to the rescue of Mexico's *financial system*. The seriousness of the crisis and the possibility of the Mexican economy's collapse led the Clinton administration to initiate the largest financial commitment since the Marshall Plan, indeed until the Great Recession it represented the largest socialization of market risk in the history of international finance (see Glasgall 1995:38). A multilateral bailout package of nearly US$40 billion in loans to the Mexican government was assembled by February 1995. The American government committed US$20 billion and the IMF committed US$18.9 billion. According to the *Economist* magazine (January 21, 1995:18), at the time US$40 billion amounted to 10% of Mexican GDP, and twice what the United States spent on foreign aid every year at the time. Miguel Mancera, then head of Mexico's Central Bank, justified the rescue plan, saying, "Mexico and the United States would have suffered very large calamities. Countries are very much like banks. If everyone tries to collect their deposits from the bank at the same time, the bank fails" (*Boston Globe*, December 12, 1995:2). Meanwhile, it became increasingly evident that recently privatized banks had made a huge number of bad loans, and the government was forced to step in and shore up the banking system with loan purchases that would eventually cost over 20% of GDP (Pastor and Wise 2006).

Astonishingly, official development aid, excluding the extraordinary financial rescue package, actually fell during the crisis and immediately following years. Development aid from all international donor agencies declined from US$420 million in 1993 and 1994 to US$385 million in 1995, US$287 million in 1996, and just US$105 million in 1997 (WDI dataset, current dollars). Development aid per Mexican fell from US$4.7 in 1993 and 1994 to US$4.22 in 1995, US$3.09 in 1996, and US$1.11 in 1997 (WDI, current dollars). This reduction in foreign aid took place even as poverty doubled. Unfortunately, this international donor behavior during macroeconomic crises is not uncommon. For example, development aid also declined in Thailand during the East Asian crisis (1997–1998) (Raddatz 2005). According to Collier and Dehn (2001:9–10),

> Donors have lacked a modality for responding to (economic) shocks. Project aid, which is the majority of aid, cannot be increased rapidly since the flow of funds is determined by the timetables of project design and implementation. . . . Programs are set for a three-year period and increases in aid beyond those planned into the program are supposed to be accumulated in foreign exchange reserves rather than spent. This is an obvious disincentive for donors to provide shock-responsive aid. Hence, donors do not appear to have taken shocks into account in determining their allocations of aid.

Against this background, international remittances provided a major lifeline, rising very slightly in line with historical growth trends from US$3.47 billion to US$3.67 billion in 1995 and US $4.22 billion in 1996 (WDI, current dollars).

A Risky Environment for Nonprofits: The Crisis in Broader Context

The resource environment facing the Mexican nonprofit sector should be expected to be difficult—for the past three decades, Mexican nonprofits have faced a very volatile, and therefore risky, economic environment. After an economic crisis in the early 1980s and another in the late 1980s, the early 1990s displayed strong economic growth and a strong increase in the federal government's interest in partnering with nonprofits as part of an intensive social welfare privatization program under the rubric "co-responsibility" ("*Corresponsabilidad*") (e.g., Vázquez Mota 2005; Villalobos 2005). The Tequila Crisis brought an abrupt end to this expansionary period. While the post-crisis recovery period of the late 1990s was marked by a return to strong GDP growth rates, the government's fiscal constraints and preoccupation with the lack of resolution on consumer debt generally meant that financial support for the nonprofit sector stagnated. Consequently, the Mexican nonprofit sector has the lowest proportion of revenue from government in the world (Salamon et al. 2004). To make matters worse, government spending was procyclical between 1971 and 1997 (Alesina and Tabellini 2005), which means that it contracted when nonprofits were most likely to need it.

Despite a peaceful political transition from a de facto one-party system to a competitive democratic system in 2000, another recession hit Mexico in 2001. Mexico's economy grew at a modest pace in the early and mid 2000s. Economic dependence on the United States led to another major crisis in 2009. Consistent with Mexico's incessant economic risk and volatility, its population is among the most risk-averse in the world (Hofstede 2001). The general population's high level of risk-aversion, therefore, highlights the admirable effort by nonprofit staff, volunteers, and, especially, founders to build the nonprofit sector against such odds.

Another key obstacle to philanthropy is Mexicans have low levels of trust in one another, that is, generalized social trust. The level of interpersonal trust in Mexico is below that in Colombia, El Salvador, and Jamaica, among others. Mexicans exhibit strong trust toward family members, moderate toward neighbors, and low toward unknowns (Paras and Coleman 2006). Arguably, the combination of low levels of trust and high risk-aversion stymies philanthropy and volunteering among the general population. Indeed, Mexico's volunteering is the lowest in the world, while its philanthropic giving is the second lowest in the world (Salamon et al. 2004). Nonprofits, then, are forced to focus on commercial income as the key financing strategy. As a proportion of revenue, Mexico is more dependent on commercial income than any other country (see chapter 3 for a cross-national comparison of these variables).

The Tequila Crisis also presented Mexican nonprofits with an uncommon opportunity. Having grown significantly during the early 1990s in size and strength, nonprofits were given a chance to exert a defining impact upon the rapidly rising level of social needs neglected by the ailing market and state. Concurrently, however, an economic shock with the intensity of the 1995 crisis is always accompanied by a deleterious effect upon general resource availability. The crisis constituted therefore both a major opportunity and a test of the nonprofit sector's own economic limits and resilience. In their quest for growth before the crisis, however, few had the opportunity to lay a strong financial foundation, and by the time the crisis hit, many of them were vulnerable and faced a high level of financial risk. The stakes were high in 1995, as were the risks.

Nonprofit Case Studies

How did the nonprofit sector respond to the Tequila Crisis and Mexico's risky economic environment more broadly? The evolution of the Mexican economy since the 1980s offers a natural "laboratory" for the study of how economic volatility and concomitant risk impact the nonprofit sector. In particular, as a powerful macroeconomic shock, the Tequila Crisis provides a unique opportunity for an examination of how economic risk impacts the nonprofit sector while keeping confounding influences largely constant. The crisis comes as close as is possible in observational studies to isolating the risk mechanism, through which economic development impacts the nonprofit sector.

Since case study data were complemented by a survey of a larger, randomly selected sample of Mexican nonprofits, the nonprofit case studies were chosen purposefully to reflect variation in the dominant type of resource: entrepreneurial (Biocenosis), philanthropic giving (Fovaso), government funding (Centro), commercial fees (FIVA), international funding (Pronatura), and volunteering (El Barzón). As proposed in chapter 2, risk should affect different resources differently. Case study data permitted a preliminary exploration of this hypothesis and generation of new hypotheses about how nonprofit resources vary with the macroeconomic cycle and the broader impacts of risk. The case studies were also selected to ensure variation in terms of age, size, type of leader, and field. This variation led to further hypotheses about the impact of risk on nonprofits, which were subsequently examined using survey and sector-level data.

The crisis had different and at times contradictory impacts on these organizations, eliciting a wide range of financial and organizational responses, often in theoretically unexpected ways. This section introduces the nonprofits—their mission and resourcing—and presents the financial and organizational impact of the crisis, in increasing order of financial and organizational resilience. I then turn to the immediate effects of the crisis upon their programmatic work and social impacts.

Financial Distress, Adaptation, and Nonprofit Capacity

Biocenosis

The first case study, Biocenosis, depended primarily on entrepreneurial financial and labor investment. It was created in 1990. Its work focused on environmental conservation in rural central Mexico. During the observation period, its work included the drawing up of the land use plan for a local municipality, ensuring the demarcation of conservation areas and contributing to the environmental sustainability of an important environmental hotspot, the physical cleaning and recuperation of local streams, organic agriculture training for local farmers, and the diffusion of environmental technologies such as composting toilets. Biocenosis's external revenue was essentially derived from small contracts with local and state level government. It also depended heavily on volunteer work by the local community.

Biocenosis was clearly the hardest hit by the crisis. Just before the crisis, the organization was exposed to a high level of financial risk, that is, risk of funding, asset, and programmatic distress as well as risk of insolvency.[3] Its annual income had grown steadily since its inception in 1990, reaching almost N$50,000 by 1994.[4] In 1995, however, it did not attract any income at all. Its principal source of funding, state government spending, was abruptly cut during the crisis. According to Biocenosis's leaders, and as confirmed in interviews with government officials, during the crisis state government gave lowest priority to existing contracts with nonprofits and instead focused on financing its own fixed costs, such as its heavy salary bill. Consequently, most payments to nonprofits were suspended sine die, possibly to be resumed when the economy improved, though at the time no one knew for sure. Lacking other sources of external financial support, Biocenosis's income collapsed to zero in 1995, throwing it into a deep organizational crisis and programmatic paralysis. Its other key resource, volunteering, also fell abruptly during the crisis, undermining one of Biocenosis's signature projects, "Days for Nature" (*Jornadas por la Naturaleza*), which was based entirely on community volunteer labor. Several times a year volunteers would spend one day cleaning small streams (*arroyos*) that play a key role in the ecology of the local water basin and natural reserve system. This annual cleaning project provided essential preservation of the local ecological system, since over time such streams routinely become clogged with rubbish from human settlements. What had been a very successful project in the past, attracting dozens of volunteers, managed to attract only a handful of volunteers in 1995, most of whom were actually beneficiaries of a partner organization who were "conscripted" for the project.

In hindsight, the crisis came at a critical transition period in Biocenosis's life. In 1994, following a period of consistent growth, its leaders had decided to abandon other professional pursuits in order to devote themselves exclusively to expanding the organization. But in 1995, without external income or financial reserves, Biocenosis was forced to cut all costs. This meant closing its newly rented office, dismissing its secretary, and surviving on its leaders' volunteer labor, which that year was predominantly consumed by futile fundraising efforts. Without alternative sources of personal income, its leaders were forced to rely on their personal savings for most of 1995. By the end of the year, they felt compelled to pursue an alternative personal income generation strategy: growing and selling organic produce.

Although the organization was undoubtedly under heavy duress, its indefatigable leaders maintained a remarkably positive long-term attitude. One explained: "We will survive this crisis because we have cocooned ourselves [*nos encapullamos*]. We can dedicate ourselves to other activities for a while. . . . We can return to the organization [full time] and hire new staff when the [economic] situation improves."

Biocenosis's leaders saw the crisis as a serious but temporary setback, after which the organization would resume its pre-crisis growth trend. They believed in the organization's future because they saw an acute need for its services in the region, marked by strong human settlement pressure on a rich and diverse ecological system. When asked about the long-term sustainability of an organization completely dependent on state government funding, they affirmed that such dependence was temporary. As the organization became better known in the region, they would surely be able to attract local, and maybe even international, support. Indeed, with the onset of the crisis they began a diversification effort by forming links with bio-regionalist networks in the United States, hoping they might attract new funding in the near future. But, lacking the resources needed to effectively pursue such financial diversification projects, they eventually had to put them on hold, as with almost every other project. The crisis had brought Biocenosis to a state of organizational paralysis while waiting for a reversal in the economy and, they hoped, its finances. As expected, Biocenosis's concentrated funding portfolio aggravated financial and organizational distress during the crisis.

Fovaso

The second case study, Fovaso, depended primarily on philanthropic giving. Fovaso was created in 1990 with the support of a wide variety of local social actors. Its work focused on social welfare and poverty alleviation in rural Central Mexico, reaching over one thousand families annually during the study period. Initially it ran social welfare programs such as educating indigenous children, providing an education and daycare center for people with disabilities, a leisure center for the elderly, and a medicine dispensary, and building schools in indigenous communities. Later, especially after the crisis, it shifted its attention to community capacity building and micro-enterprise development in poor rural communities. Initially, Fovaso's income derived mainly from the donations of a few wealthy individuals and companies. Later, in 1991 it negotiated a matching funding agreement with the state and federal governments in which every peso fundraised from private sources was to be matched by another two pesos: one peso from the federal government and one peso from the state government, thus tripling the benefits from private fundraising efforts. According to a state government official the main justification for the widespread use of matching funding in government support to the nonprofit sector was that "we have more trust in organizations which civil society itself is willing to support. . . . We are partners, not creators of civil society." Because Fovaso had very good links with rich businessmen and the government, the nonprofit managed to create a relatively large reserve fund of nearly N$3 million[5] in its second year of existence. Fovaso depended solely on local (Mexican) funding, and because the government's promise to match private funding was only partly fulfilled, its dominant and most reliable source of income during this study was private philanthropy.

The crisis had a severe impact on Fovaso's revenue, despite its being exposed to a very low level of financial risk in theory. During the economically prosperous early

1990s, its annual income had averaged N$1,422,000 (almost half a million U.S. dollars)—an impressive revenue for a local nonprofit in Mexico.[6] As the country was entering the crisis at the end of 1994, Fovaso revised its 1995 budget from N$1.5 million to N$870,000. But worse was still to come. It managed to attract only N$370,000 in 1995,[7] less than one-quarter of its average pre-crisis budget forecast. Despite benefiting from tax-deductible status, which few nonprofits in Mexico enjoyed at the time, its philanthropic income plummeted as individuals and companies guarded against loss of income and profits.[8] Also, Fovaso was unable to raise its exiguous fees for services provided to beneficiaries because at the time most of its work focused on the poorest members in the community, such as indigenous groups, children with special needs, and the elderly, all of whom were facing acute financial distress.

Faced with a collapse in philanthropy and inability to raise user fees, Fovaso turned its attention to state and federal government for some financial relief. Since it was supposed to match philanthropic giving, the organization's matching agreement with the government would have been little help during the crisis, were it not for the government's own failure to keep up with agreed payments *prior* to the crisis. The matching system triples fundraising when philanthropic funds can be raised, but provides zero support when they disappear, exacerbating volatility in philanthropic income. In order to provide services to the poorest in the community, Fovaso required substantial philanthropic and government funding, and the sharp reduction in both sources of income at once spelled financial disaster. The terms of government funding were not altered during the crisis; rather, Fovaso pressured the government to catch up with outstanding payments that ultimately became the lifeline of the organization. Since the start of the matching funding agreement, federal and state government payments had been so irregular that by 1994 the state government was in arrears to the tune of over half a million pesos, while the federal government owed Fovaso a whopping N$1.82 million.[9] In 1995, despite the fact that only about 10% of this outstanding amount was paid, it provided a much needed lifeline ultimately comprising close to two-thirds of Fovaso's total income that year.[10] In this context, the otherwise detrimental tardiness of government payments actually reduced Fovaso's income volatility by reducing the correlation between philanthropy and government funding flows; that is, it provided revenue diversification.

A second critical source of funds during the crisis was the 19% of Fovaso's income derived from a video lending store created in 1993. Surprisingly, despite the negative impact of the crisis on most businesses in Mexico at the time, the video store was able to make a profit, providing precious income for the organization as well as creating four new jobs in the local economy at a time of fast-rising unemployment.[11]

These lifelines were not enough, however, to sustain Fovaso's pre-crisis activity level. Impending bankruptcy prompted a profound cost-cutting and reorganization program. When in 1995 Fovaso's budget dropped by nearly half, from N$1.5 million[12] to N$870,000,[13] difficult choices had to be made. Vigorous cuts were made to Fovaso's main fixed cost: paid staff. The number of staff was more than halved, from forty in September

1994 to fifteen in December 1995! This had profound implications for Fovaso's capacity and organization. It also shut down or made independent three of its seven program units. And despite these radical cutbacks, Fovaso still faced a large loss of close to half a million pesos in 1995,[14] corresponding to a deficit of 57% of its budget. Fovaso financed this deficit by dipping into its financial reserves, which it had painstakingly accumulated since 1990. Fovaso's nonfinancial assets, including three buildings, provided little shelter against falling income in a context of collapsing asset prices. The organization held off selling any properties since according to its financial officer they would probably fetch only a fraction of their pre-crisis value. Besides, Fovaso needed the buildings to carry out its increasingly valuable work. Borrowing was also not a realistic option as interest rates on loans had reached sky-high levels.[15]

Notably, Fovaso's cost-cutting effort was accompanied by increasing centralization and bureaucratization. To ensure financial restraint Fovaso's leadership introduced very strict financial and organizational control systems. Instead of the traditional monthly activity and financial reports, program directors were required to submit such reports weekly. Before the crisis, program directors had been able to make most of their own budgetary decisions, which reduced the need for supervisory approval and internal negotiation. Now, a hierarchical and formalized management structure replaced the old one, eliminating most staff participation in organizational decision making.

As financial resources evaporated, the department of services and administration, which the financial officer directed, became essential to the survival of the organization, and its power grew accordingly. Indeed, its newfound power is demonstrated by the facts that it did not have to make any staff cuts during the crisis and that the financial officer had weekly meetings with the managing director when program directors often had to wait over a month. The incentive structure in the organization was inexorably changed to give new precedence to cost-cutting over quality in service provision; program directors who emphasized cost control gained power within the organization, while the few who resisted making significant cuts were denied budget approval and funding. For example, the Center of Community Development initially resisted cost-cutting on the grounds that needs had not decreased. Despite unfailing logic in the justification for each of its program costs, its budget requests were denied for over two months, to the point that it almost had to suspend its operations. To avoid the program's insolvency, the director finally implemented a painful cost-cutting program that reduced its budget in half. At that point, program funding was resumed.

Perversely, the increased bureaucratization, which was designed to control costs and reduce wastage, absorbed precious labor at a time of sweeping labor cuts. With no administrative staff cuts and with increased reporting requirements for program directors, administration costs rose as a proportion of total costs at a time when resources were scarce, thus further reducing resources available for programmatic work. Its self-reported administration expenditure almost doubled, from 9% before the crisis to 16% in 1995![16]

Unfortunately, the list of Fovaso's organizational woes continued. The financial distress and ensuing reorganization led to a breakdown of internal communication, a shift from an organizational culture based on cooperation to one characterized by conflict, and widespread staff "burnout," all of which conspired to erode organizational capacity further. The quality of internal communication deteriorated considerably during the crisis. Initially, the managing director remained secretive about the organization's financial situation. Most members of staff, including program directors, found out about the funding predicament through internal gossip. Rumors of major cutbacks spread quickly and widely, and staff members in every department took the leader's silence as confirmation that they would be the prime targets of any cutbacks. As dismissals began early in 1995, this fear intensified. Moreover, stricter bureaucratic procedures were construed as a sign of the leader's low trust in program directors, and what was seen as a new haughty attitude in the financial officer was described as "rubbing salt on a fresh wound." Program directors were never involved in discussions about possible organizational responses to the crisis, which were instead confined to leaders, board of directors, and the financial officer. An initial organizational culture of high trust and optimism around the organization's work and public service to the community was overtaken by a culture characterized by fear, mistrust, and poor communication. Inter-unit and interpersonal conflict became rife. Undoubtedly, internal conflict hampered essential dialogue that could have facilitated learning and adaptation to the new challenges faced during the crisis. For example, during interviews a few staff members revealed that they would be willing to temporarily work for lower wages to prevent staff dismissals, but tragically Fovaso's managing director did not mobilize this dedication to the organization and its cause to minimize dismissals and capacity erosion.

As staff members coped with downsizing, increasing bureaucratic controls, and deterioration in the quality of communication within the organization, they simultaneously faced growing social demands. Most believed that expanding activities and serving larger constituencies would help to increase the indispensability of their program in the eyes of the managing director, reducing the probability of future cutbacks. Consequently, as resources were being drastically cut, the program units actually expanded Fovaso's beneficiary base. Remaining resources became stretched to the limit. Initially this expansion aggravated the financial situation as the budget was being spent more quickly than planned. As the administration realized the severity of the financial situation and imposed the cost-cutting agenda, program directors had to increasingly rely on unpaid staff overtime, and often in-kind contributions, in order to maintain expanded service provision. By mid-1995, most of the remaining fifteen employees were working thirteen hours a day. It was clear that a main motivating factor for staff was the fear of becoming unemployed amid a severe economic crisis, as even such demonstrated commitment did not guarantee a future in the organization. Anxiety was very high and morale very low. At least two employees who could afford to leave the organization did so, including the main assistant to the managing director, who invoked the rapidly deteriorating organizational morale and capacity to undertake its public service mission as the causes of her premature departure.

In sum, Fovaso experienced complex financial and organizational impacts as a result of the Tequila Crisis. Cost-cutting and increased bureaucracy reduced resource availability for program implementation and contributed to the emergence of organizational conflict and staff burnout, all of which conspired to rapidly erode organizational capacity. But the full effects of the crisis were unclear for months. By mid-1995 there was a unanimous sense at all levels of the organization that despite all efforts, Fovaso's path to insolvency could not be altered. In this environment, a factional reform movement emerged within the organization to redefine its mandate, as discussed below.

FIVA

The third case study, FIVA, was financed through commercial fees. FIVA was founded in 1993 as a joint venture between two community development nonprofits, the federal government and the Mexico State government. It was created through a government matching program so that 35% of the initial capital was provided by the two nonprofit partners, while federal funding provided 50% and the state government provided 15%. Despite the fact that government had provided the majority of its capital, FIVA was independent from government. It was set up as a nonprofit organization (*patronato*), and most of the members of the board of directors were not associated with the public sector. Its revenue consisted of interest and fees on micro-lending. The organization was designed and managed to operate with a small profit and not rely on any income from its founding partners.

Like Fovaso, FIVA also had a theoretically low level of financial risk before the crisis, but nevertheless the organization also experienced significant financial distress during the crisis. Its income halved, from a peak of N$2.8 million in 1994[17] to N$1.4 million in 1995.[18] Unexpectedly, the organization's significant financial equity as a micro-lender did not offer much relief. Most of its lending fund was not liquid because it had already been loaned out to borrowers and, therefore, could not be easily recalled and converted to cash to meet financial needs. Also, FIVA faced strong restrictions regarding how it could use its financial assets, determined by banking law and its own bylaws. The organization was therefore unable to use any of its founding capital to pay for organizational expenses such as wages or rent. Such expenses had to be paid out of current or accumulated profits from operations. At the beginning of 1995, FIVA's contingency fund, made up of liquid and unrestricted resources, was only 11% of its overall financial assets.

Despite these challenges, however, the organization never faced the risk of insolvency. It had very low fixed costs as it employed only two people, and, in the context of a national credit crunch, FIVA was able to enjoy high positive operating margins through its micro-lending program.[19] Even though the crisis weakened the financial position of its borrowers, FIVA managed to keep its bad or "nonperforming" micro-loans at an acceptable 7.2%, compared to a national average of 16.9% for commercial banks at the time (Graf 1999). Therefore, despite a halving of income, the organization actually had a surplus in 1995, increasing net assets by N$460,000![20] This financial feat did not escape the attention of Fovaso's leadership, a fact that played a pivotal role in Fovaso's strategic reorientation and future after the crisis.

Centro

The fourth case study, Centro de Educación Especial, was almost entirely funded by government. Centro was originally a program created by Fovaso in 1991 aimed at providing special needs education for disabled children from poor households, with a focus on mental disability. It became independent and responsible for its own resource mobilization in 1995, the apex of the Tequila Crisis. At the time, the program director who became managing director in the brand-new organization confessed that she thought Centro would not survive the crisis. The organization was "saddled" with high fixed costs from staff salaries, and, since its clients were generally poor, it was almost entirely dependent on state government funding for special education programs.

Unfortunately, one of the first letters Centro's managing director received as she became head of the newly independent organization stated that the state government was temporarily suspending payment on its contracts with Centro. Its payments would resume as soon as possible, "pending budgetary approval." With financial reserves of only two months of organizational expenditures, Centro's survival at that point depended entirely on new private support. As the managing director confessed, however, this was the worst possible moment for her to learn fundraising skills.

Because, at the time, it seemed that Centro could not count on philanthropy, fees from parents emerged as a potential way out of the budgetary emergency. Before the crisis, Centro had charged a modest fee of N$30 (US$6 at the time) per child per month. To put this fee into perspective, at the time a young teacher earned between N$1,500 and N$2,500 per month. Keeping fees low was essential in trying to reach the poorest populations. Nevertheless, as the only special education school in the region at the time, Centro also attracted a few children from middle-class families. Centro's managing director tried to mobilize additional resources by both doubling the minimum fee and asking for additional support from better-off families. Several meetings were held with clients' parents during the crisis to explain to them that unless the organization was able to attract more financial support, it was going to have to close its doors for all children. Centro's leader adeptly conveyed the urgency of its resource mobilization task. About one-third of revenue from parents (20% of total revenue) was given voluntarily by better-off families to try to keep the school open; even the poorest families contributed by paying the doubled fee at a time of great economic distress. The remaining revenue was mobilized from philanthropy. Against the odds, Centro was able to mobilize around 40% of its revenue through philanthropic donations from its board of directors. Some of Centro's board members were deeply committed to the special education cause because they had disabled children in their own families. According to the managing director, they also did not want the newly created organization to fail under their watch. While the organization did not dismiss anyone, two teachers left voluntarily and their spots were left open, permitting significant cost cuts at a critical juncture. It also had to postpone all nonurgent and nonessential spending. By the end of 1995, only a few months after the organization began its independent life, Centro was breaking even with a budget of N$260,000. Centro's leader, however, was concerned about the organization's future and the ability of poorer families to continue to pay the higher fees.

Pronatura

The fifth case study, Pronatura, received a little over half of its funding from international sources: international nonprofits (nongovernmental organizations, or NGOs) and official donor agencies. The organization presents an interesting contrast to the other case studies, which were funded entirely by local sources. Pronatura was founded in 1981. Its mission is to promote sustainable development, that is, community development and environmental conservation throughout Mexico. With an annual budget of N$40 million,[21] Pronatura is both older and financially larger than the other case studies. It received only 1% of its revenue from government. Other sources of support included individuals, sales, and interest on capital.

Pronatura faced low financial risk prior to the crisis and, not surprisingly, demonstrated strong financial and organizational resilience during the crisis. Extraordinarily, its income actually grew slightly, from N$7.81 million[22] in 1994 to N$8.039 million in 1995 (a 2.9% increase),[23] so the organization had a surplus, increasing its net assets by N$3.614 million.[24] But this apparent imperviousness to the crisis hides other important financial impacts. Pronatura's income from local (Mexican) sources fell sharply during the crisis. As in the case of Fovaso, philanthropy from individuals and companies declined abruptly, shrinking from N$847,000[25] in 1994 to N$425,000[26] in 1995. Despite the halving in philanthropic income, its total income rose slightly because of counterbalancing growth in international funding and investment income from its endowment fund. As Mexican real interest rates skyrocketed during the crisis, conservatively invested financial reserves produced high yields. Pronatura was thus able to almost double its investment income in 1995 as compared with the previous year (from N$1.543 million to N$2.5 million).[27] Also, the sharp decline in the value of the Mexican peso against international donor currencies between 1994 and 1995 meant that international funding transfers appreciated considerably in the amount of local currency they represented. Since a large share of Pronatura's income derived from international sources before the crisis, and most donors paid in foreign currency, Pronatura's international income grew proportionately to the peso's devaluation. Income from international sources grew from N$1.412 million in 1994 to N$2.126 million in 1995, a 50.5% increase.

Nevertheless, the crisis had two important negative financial impacts on Pronatura. First, it put a full stop to its prodigious income growth rate of the early 1990s (62.15%, compounded annually). Second, in 1990 close to two-thirds of income was derived from national income sources, and by 1994 44% of income was derived nationally. But in 1995 income from national sources fell to 22% of total income! So, while Pronatura's income remained stable during the crisis (in contrast to strong declines in most nonprofits observed) there were important changes in the composition of its funding portfolio and a significant departure from the previous financial growth trajectory.

El Barzón

The last case study, El Barzón, depended primarily on volunteers. A *barzón* is a leather strap used to hitch ploughs to yokes shouldered by oxen. The organization takes its name from a popular song about a poor farmer who despite all his work continued to sink under a debt burden. El Barzón's experience during the crisis provides an emphatic departure from the patterns described above. Theoretically, despite its low level of fixed costs, El Barzón was exposed to moderate level of financial risk due to low equity and a highly concentrated funding portfolio before the crisis. The organization was almost entirely dependent on fees from members who were in, or on the verge of, bankruptcy. Indeed the organization almost disappeared in 1994.

El Barzón emerged in Jalisco in 1993 as a social movement integrating medium and large farmers experiencing a sharp fall in revenues due to the opening up of the agricultural sector to international competition and the phasing out of food subsidies. The expansion of credit markets enabled these farmers to borrow extensively to modernize their production and be able to survive in this more competitive environment. As their revenues continued to decline, however, many farmers were facing bankruptcy in the early 1990s (Grammont 2001:45). Before the crisis, El Barzón was a loose confederation of farmers' organizations. The national office, coordinating ten state chapters, was located in a "rented second floor office in the capital city [of the state of Zacatecas] with one spare desk and filing cabinet" (Williams 2001:179). El Barzón grew after a few of its campaigning initiatives, such as occupying the mayor's building in a few smaller towns, attracted considerable media attention. Nevertheless, by 1994, the incipient movement was rapidly losing support as government and banks increased the effort to solve debt problems without stripping debtors of their assets (Williams 2001). However, despite a hesitating start in 1993 and weak prospects in 1994, the Tequila Crisis provided a bountiful environment for El Barzón's development, indeed constituting the defining period in the organization's history. As a debtors' organization, El Barzón campaigned publicly for debtors' rights and provided legal assistance to protect its members' property from repossession. As the crisis hit Mexico, however, small business and household debt exploded. Dollar-denominated debt and skyrocketing interest rates meant that debt service payments often more than doubled, which, combined with rising unemployment and lower business earnings, led to a nationwide debt problem. As banks sought to improve their balance sheets by intensifying their debt collection efforts, social discontent and the demand for the organization's services exploded. In this setting, El Barzón had the expertise and growing political clout to face banks' repossession efforts. Now as a formal organization, El Barzón filed thousands of legal action suits against banks to protect its members' property (Williams 2001). Under Mexican law, an *amparo* may be filed by an individual who believes his or her constitutional rights are being violated. El Barzón argued that compound interest, which underlies bank lending activity all over the world, violated the Mexican constitution. As several judges conceded the legitimacy of the *amparo* request and ordered a stay of bank attempts to recover their loans by seizing debtors' property, El Barzón was able to protect its members' interests. Thousands joined the organization social movement in a crusade against unfair lending practices. Consequently, in 1995 membership expanded from a few thousand to about one million by the end of the year, while the organization widened in scope from regional to national (Marchini 2004).[28] El Barzón was one of the most visible social actors during the crisis. It has, consequently, been the object of several studies (e.g., Cadena-Roa 2008; Grammont 2001; Williams 2001).

How did the crisis and such a spectacular growth affect El Barzón's finances and organization? Certainly, El Barzón was not the only nonprofit whose target beneficiaries were rapidly expanding in number during the crisis. What made El Barzón different was its resourcefulness, which fuelled its extraordinary growth in a resource-starved environment. The explosion in distressed debtors meant that the "market" for the organization's services was rapidly expanding. But at the same time most of its potential members were facing imminent bankruptcy and, as a result, had very little cash. El Barzón managed to turn this potential threat into an opportunity. Individuals facing repossession were encouraged to become members for a nominal membership fee of N\$10, a little less than US\$2 in 1994. After a successful action to save their property (e.g., a demonstration, a letter sent by one of El Barzón's "practically volunteer" lawyers to the bank or collecting agency), they were compelled to participate in actions for other members. The looming threat of repossession acted also as a selective incentive for individuals to remain active members in exchange for continued protection. Members were encouraged to make in-kind (*en especie*) contributions such as office supplies, food, or transportation to demonstration sites. The organization's limited financial resources were thus derived from meager individual membership fees paid by a fast expanding membership and by payments from a few wealthier members who preferred not to volunteer or make in-kind contributions (Williams 2001).

El Barzón's organizational structure also played a key role in its success during the crisis. Most of the organization's member mobilization, revenue collection, and activities were undertaken by small autonomous local chapters, with very little supervision by state or national levels. National and state coordinators were responsible for larger demonstrations and lobbying of the respective legislatures. They were financed from locally collected revenue according to an agreed formula. Local chapters kept 60% of the funds raised. State and national coordinators divided equally the remaining 40% (Williams 2001). This "bottom-up" financial and organizational structure, based on the organizational principle of subsidiarity (see Anheier and Themudo 2002), helped keep fixed costs to a minimum and enabled the organization to build a national presence on a resource base made up almost entirely of volunteering and in-kind contributions.[29] The largest cost in undertaking the organization's work was the cost of protesting, which was absorbed by participating members themselves. This cost included the opportunity cost of the time spent demonstrating, transportation to the demonstration site, food, sometimes for a few days, and when protests involved tractors, a significant fuel cost (Williams 2001). The organization's bottom-up structure eventually became a liability in the post-crisis period, but during the crisis it enabled the organization's rapid growth, as well as an equally rapid growth in its social impact, as discussed in the next section.

Even though most case studies faced acute financial distress, all of them succeeded in remaining solvent during the crisis, largely because of the significant unpaid labor of leaders, staff, and beneficiaries. Without their amazing commitment, the nonprofits' social impact would have been much more limited, and some of these organizations would have collapsed precisely when they were most needed.

Strategic Adjustments during the Crisis

The diverse financial and organizational impacts of the Tequila Crisis on the observed nonprofits would seem to intuit an equally varied effect upon their programs. Yet, with the exception of El Barzón, there was remarkable consistency in how the crisis affected their programs. The following analyzes the nature and extent of changes to their programmatic work and, correspondingly, their social impact, proceeding from the least to the most adversely affected case.

El Barzón

El Barzón is the only nonprofit studied that did not experience a reduction in its activities and beneficiaries. Before the crisis, the organization focused on campaigns against farmers' growing debt and declining income. But the crisis hit urban businesses, credit card, and mortgage holders especially hard as before the crisis banks had aggressively promoted credit expansion in urban areas. In 1995, the urban population began to experience financial problems similar to those experienced by farmers before the crisis. El Barzón's social mobilization and creative direct action tactics, such as blocking roads with tractors and occupying central squares and government buildings, commanded intense media attention. Its slogan, repeated countless times across the nation, denoted its members' responsibility and fairness: "I owe, I don't deny it, but I will only pay what is fair" (*Debo, no niego, pero pago el justo*). This message resonated with hundreds of thousands of urban Mexicans, who through no fault of their own found themselves having to service stratospheric interest rates on their loans. The organization's leadership therefore made a strategic decision to expand its activities into urban areas. In order to do this, and subsequently to attract urban supporters, the organization had to increase its emphasis on debt while playing down farmers' concerns; it had to show that it was concerned with the welfare of not only indebted farmers but all debtors. By focusing on debt issues, the organization managed to stay true to its original mission and even to deepen it by applying the same principles of fairness and equity to a broader population of now equally needy and vulnerable people. These strategic adjustments were central to the organization's exponential growth, and ultimately urban members greatly outnumbered rural members, irreversibly changing the organization's constituency and future.

The growth of its programmatic work through expanding membership and organizational infrastructure led to an emphatic increase in its social impact. Indeed, the organization is widely recognized as one of the most influential civil society actors in recent Mexican and Latin America history (e.g., Grammont 2001; Williams 2001).[30] Among its many achievements, it raised awareness about the plight of debtors and debunked automatic accusations of personal mismanagement and financial irresponsibility. The organization therefore had a cathartic impact on debtors, who were cleansed of the intense guilt of being unable to meet their financial obligations. El Barzón also lent important support to a growing movement, strongly boosted by the Zapatista rebellion, against the unrelenting advance of neoliberal ideology in Mexican society. The movement plainly blamed neoliberalism for the debt crisis, as it had promoted a blind faith in the quick liberalization of financial markets, which in the end had disastrous consequences. El Barzón worked to expose the hypocrisy of a government that after promoting credit market liberalization, then acted quickly to restore commercial banks' liquidity by absorbing a large share of their bad loans (Grammont 2001). In the meantime banks continued to try to collect those loans, often using intimidation tactics against borrowers. So while the banking system was rescued by the government and international donors, individual debtors were left to fend for themselves. By denouncing this inequitable treatment, El Barzón drew public attention to the corrupt nature of the political system, which focused on protecting the interests of the wealthy and powerful, commonly at the expense of the Mexican people. In so doing, El Barzón probably also contributed to the defeat of the long-established ruling party in the midterm elections of 1997, opening the way for the first truly democratic presidential elections in Mexico in the year 2000. Perhaps its greatest social impact, however, was in helping to balance the traditionally lopsided relationship between banks and individual borrowers by campaigning for increased legal protection of family property, using legal action against bank repossessions, and educating borrowers about their rights. Although difficult to quantify precisely, it is probably fair to say that as a result of its actions hundreds of thousands of Mexican families did not lose their homes during the crisis. The courageous work of El Barzón during the crisis had, therefore, incalculable benefits for Mexican society.

Pronatura

In contrast, the crisis hindered the social impact of the other nonprofits studied, as all of them sharply cut their program spending in 1995. Perversely, the cases that experienced the least financial and organizational distress proportionately cut their programmatic work the most, generating significant financial surplus during a period of widespread social need. Being at the crossroads of rapidly rising social needs and evaporating resource availability, even the less financially distressed nonprofits were vulnerable to pessimism about the future. Seeking resources and conserving organizational resources therefore became a priority to ensure future organizational sustainability. But in their effort to boost financial reserves to reduce financial risk, they compromised their social mission at a time of expanding opportunities for social impact.

Pronatura is an excellent example of this trend as, despite its increase in income during the crisis, the organization significantly constrained its activity level during the period. The organization attracted an enviable N$8.039 million in revenue, but it curtailed its expenditure to N$4.425 million, which at only 55% of income was well below its typical average of 90%![31] Such drastic cuts were achieved by essentially cutting variable costs, such as supplies for program activities,[32] and eliminating "less critical" activities, such as most advocacy projects. This enabled the organization to save almost all of the income from its endowment fund, N$3.8 million or 47.3% of annual income in 1995. Pronatura was able to conserve most of its staff, preserving its organizational capacity. But unless we accept that there was vast inefficiency before the crisis, maintaining the same staff level while significantly reducing programmatic spending undoubtedly led to a decrease in organizational effectiveness. For example, according to one of its officers, poaching threats to protected wildlife increased sharply during the crisis, as alternative income opportunities fast disappeared. At the same time, however, Pronatura's cuts in programmatic costs led to the postponement, due to the lack of needed construction materials, of a vital fencing project designed to stop poaching in an important conservation area. The damage to the environment caused by this delay is hard to quantify, but it was probably considerable. Because of its status as one of the largest and most prestigious environmental nonprofits, Pronatura's reduction of advocacy activity also weakened the environmental movement at a time when Mexico's Congress was considering critical legislation aimed at weakening environmental conservation.

Both its managing director and its financial officer explained that the main motivation behind the spending cuts was to boost the endowment fund and buttress defenses against the prospect of a long crisis and future financial difficulties in a volatile economic environment, that is, to reduce organizational risk exposure. This financially conservative attitude during the crisis generated some discontent among at least a few staff members, who thought that this strategy excessively reduced the organization's impact at a time of great social need. According to one of its management officers,

> Of course, we have to preserve the real value of our endowment, [but] we shouldn't be trying to increase it at a time when communities are cutting their trees to survive. . . . There is so much to do right now and even a little more spending can go a long way! . . . For example, our sustainable forestry projects have been very successful but the crisis has lowered demand for their products. . . . If we continue to phase out our support at this time [the long-term success of] the projects and the local environment will be in jeopardy.

Another common concern revealed in interviews with staff pertained to the organization's growing financial dependence on international donors. Between 1994 and 1995, dependence on international donors rose from just over 40% to just under 80%. Although Pronatura's endowment fund provided significant financial independence and the ability to reject funding with attached unpalatable conditions, there was a concern that Pronatura's international donors' priorities were not necessarily Mexican priorities, a problem that was particularly patent during the crisis. One example was a project to introduce into Mexican law a legal instrument commonly used in the United States: private conservation land. This program was sponsored by international donors, and Pronatura made it a top priority. However, one staff member confessed that at a time of chronic underfunding of existing government-owned conservation areas, a focus on an advocacy program with a distant future impact seemed misguided. Indeed, Pronatura's own leadership lent some credibility to this claim when they decided to cancel other advocacy programs as a main strategy to cut spending. While ultimately it is impossible to evaluate such a claim, the evidence is consistent with the theoretical argument that greater dependence on one type of donor may lead to mission drift and potentially even external control, reducing the organization's ability to achieve its original mission.

FIVA

Similarly, despite earning a profit in 1995 and facing no capacity erosion, FIVA scaled down its programmatic activity during the crisis. To keep its bad loans to a minimum and reduce its financial risk, the organization adopted much more stringent borrower selection criteria, such as introducing a requirement for business plans to be submitted with loan applications and giving preferential treatment to borrowers with collateral.[33] This led to a 45% decline in the number of clients served, from thirty-seven in 1994 to only twenty-two in 1995. This strategy in effect also restricted access to FIVA's microfinance work to individuals who already owned a business. This is evidenced, for example, by the shift toward loans for the restructuring of existing enterprises rather than the provision of credit for new enterprises. In 1994 restructuring loans corresponded to only 7% of the fund's capital as compared with a staggering 84% in 1995! In the effort to screen out riskier loans and reduce its own financial risk, FIVA denied capital to the poorest and less educated applicants at a critical economic juncture. And while the organization also offered capacity-building courses in business planning to potential and existing borrowers, poor applicants were not generally admitted into those courses, because in the words of its managing director, "they can't even read properly." In sharp contrast with the pre-crisis period, during the crisis it was difficult to discern any difference between FIVA's work and that of commercial banks down the road, apart from the fact that FIVA's loans were generally smaller. Famously, one of its largest loans during the crisis was given to a well-off owner of a local restaurant, who was thus able to obtain cheap finance for his business. FIVA's managing director approved this large loan on the grounds that it helped to protect jobs at the restaurant, an emphatic departure from its initial focus on helping indigenous women buy sewing machines to produce textiles. One of Fovaso's community development officers, who had earlier helped set up most of FIVA's loans to beneficiaries in rural communities, estimated that by mid-1995 FIVA's lending portfolio included only a couple of poor borrowers.

Based on the "product portfolio map" (James and Young 2007:113), FIVA's strategic shift amounts to a move from "saint" to "cash cow" *clients* with a considerable reduction in ability to pursue its social mission and impact. The main reasons for the new emphasis on profitability at the expense of social impact were the pressure to demonstrate positive financial performance and a perceived urgency in boosting its contingency fund in a context of high financial volatility. It is surprising that this profound change in the organization's main constituency was never questioned by its board of directors. But the organization's vaguely defined purpose of providing credit to the "the poor" was easily set aside by considerations of rising financial risk, which ultimately affected much more tangible financial results.

Since FIVA was the only institutional micro-lender in the region, its strategic shift could not have come at a worse moment for the people whom the organization had been created to serve—the poor in rural communities—most of whom were immiserated by debt, unemployment, and inflation and could now obtain credit only at exorbitant interest rates from local informal lenders or "loan sharks" (*coyotes*). While FIVA's interest rate averaged 33% in 1995, informal reports by some of FIVA's clients put the interest rate charged by informal lenders at over 10% per month (equivalent to an annual rate of 214%!) and sometimes much more, depending on the relationship between the borrower and lender.

Biocenosis

Perhaps less surprisingly, financially and organizationally distressed cases, Biocenosis and Fovaso, also cut programmatic spending. By eroding organizational resources and capacity, the crisis had insidious effects upon Biocenosis's social impact. Since the organization did not manage to attract any funding during the crisis, the organization had only one project in 1995, "Days for Nature," which due to resource scarcity was scaled down considerably. Biocenosis's leaders manifested deep frustration with this situation, particularly since they felt a strong sense of urgency in promoting the organization's mission of environmental protection and poverty reduction. According to one of its leaders,

> Even as we speak opportunistic squatters are invading conservation areas [in Valle de Bravo]. The government has other concerns and is not going to evict them if there is any ambiguity about ownership and rightful land use. . . . That is why we urgently need a Land Use Plan for [this region], which defines conservation areas unequivocally. . . . This way, a clear definition of conservation areas will also help to implement a program of "payment for nature services" [*pago por servicios ambientales*] which pays poor communities for conservation and reduces their incentives for logging.

The crisis had not of course reduced the need for Biocenosis's work. On the contrary, the weakness of state and local governments and the national obsession with the economy had diverted attention from pressing social issues like those targeted by the nonprofit. But, for the time being, those issues would have to wait.

Fovaso

Of all the nonprofits studied, the most profound programmatic and social mission impact occurred in Fovaso. Before the crisis, Fovaso's enviable financial and programmatic success emanated from its inspiring vision of charity and attention to basic needs: "Fovaso is a place where there is water for every thirst and love for every heart" (*Fovaso es un lugar adonde hay agua para toda sed y amor para todo corazón*). This vision inspired the organization's programmatic focus on ensuring that "those who need the most" (*los que mas necesitan*) had access to "basic needs" such as food, education, health care, and a clean environment. Its outreach strategy focused consequently on helping the poorest and most vulnerable in the community: indigenous groups, children with special needs, the sick, the elderly, women, and the environment. Since its founding, the organization's core values of love, charity, and public service had inspired a number of individual donors and attracted extensive government support, fast making Fovaso one of the principal service providers in the region. By 1994, only four years after its founding, Fovaso annually helped to meet the basic needs of over 1,100 families, providing food, special education, grants for primary education, grants for community development, medicines, doctor consultations, and a meeting place for the elderly and indigenous people when they came to the village to sell their products.

The crisis irreversibly put this model in check. Initially, the financial crisis led Fovaso to reduce its spending across all programs. But the unrelenting financial downslide led to a deeper questioning of its charitable vision of basic needs provision, which depended on a continuous transfer of resources from the rich and the government to the poor. As philanthropy plummeted in 1995 and organizational finances deteriorated, the financial crisis eroded the organization's ability to sustain this resource transfer and endangered organizational survival. Eventually, two members of the board of directors and the financial officer began to question the organization's vision and service-provision model, coalescing as a reform movement led by the board treasurer. This internal "elite movement" was very powerful, as it integrated the key people responsible for the management of financial resources, who had power to approve or deny funding to different parts of the organization. They also had easy access to the managing director and board of directors. The reform movement advocated that the traditional model needed to be supplanted by a new model that focused instead on creating income opportunities for beneficiaries. The traditional organizational vision should give way to a new vision: "Fovaso, a capitalizing institution that improves, grows and harvests . . ." (*Fovaso, una instituición capitalizadora que mejora, cultiva y cosecha . . .*).

The proponents of the new model made a pragmatic case for the strategic shift. They dismissed the traditional model as "inspiring, but unrealistic in a country like Mexico." Fovaso's traditional programs operated with negative margins, requiring a continuous subsidy. Since the organization was not able to generate sufficient income internally to meet this requirement, it had to rely on continuous external financing. Reformers argued that "loss-making service provision programs" were essentially unsustainable as Fovaso could not guarantee the continuation of external funding. Instead, they proposed that a focus on helping communities through income-generating programs such as micro-enterprise would be much more sustainable. A very appealing characteristic of such a model rested on the premise that helping communities raise their income level would at the same time address Fovaso's own lack of financial sustainability: the communities' inability to pay for services they needed. Moreover, they saw the traditional service-provision model as generating long-term community dependence on Fovaso, contributing to a perpetuation of their poverty.

Initially, the managing director rejected the reformers' onslaught. However, the reform movement gained momentum with the relatively successful experience during the crisis of FIVA's micro-lending as well as Fovaso's commercial enterprise (the video store). FIVA was heralded by the reform movement as an example of "best practice." With large positive operating margins, FIVA was able to generate all of the income needed to pay for its lending program and management costs, making it much more financially sustainable than Fovaso's traditional programs. But after months of fruitless fundraising, the managing director's commitment to the original vision began to waiver. Even a few program directors confessed that it was difficult to justify their service-provision programs if they could not attract sufficient external resources. By mid-1995, the managing director had embraced the new organizational vision and service-provision model, partly hoping that, as suggested by the treasurer, it would lead to new philanthropic opportunities among wealthy business leaders who might prefer to support an innovative market-oriented model of poverty alleviation. The managing director rejected the claim that the new vision was a radical departure from the traditional vision. For example, in an interview in late 1995, she stated: "To love is to give [beneficiaries] what they need. Right now they need income opportunities and training on how to sell what they produce. . . . Then they can send their children to school and buy their own medicines. We can't keep on subsidizing medicines forever."

But in practice the strategic shift to a market-oriented model was consolidated by wide-reaching constituency and programmatic changes, with a profound effect on the organization's social impact. In order to quickly make its programs sustainable, Fovaso had to focus on target groups who could be reached cheaply and be expected to implement income-generation projects within a short period of time. Generally this was not possible with Fovaso's poorest beneficiaries, such as the elderly or children with special needs. Therefore, the organization made a critical shift from its initial focus on "those who need the most" (*los que mas necesitan*) to those "with limited opportunities" (*con oportunidades limitadas*) or "with less opportunities" (*de menores posibilidades*) after the crisis, as indicated by organizational documents such as annual reports and interviews with staff members.

This change in Fovaso's primary constituency was matched by analogous changes in its programs. Fovaso divested all service-provision programs that were incompatible with the new market orientation, that is, where the potential for generating a financial surplus was very limited. The Center for the Elderly and Medical Dispensary were promptly shut down. The Center for Special Education was made independent and responsible for its own fundraising, despite the fact that without Fovaso's support its financial future looked very bleak. Most of the remaining programs were largely redirected to support a new signature program for young community leaders, "Youth for Change" (*Jovenes por el Cambio*). This new program was proposed by the reform movement as the "new face" of Fovaso. It aimed at training a small number of young indigenous boys and girls in "financial self-sufficiency strategies," mostly micro-enterprise, so that in turn they could educate their own communities about micro-enterprise, serving as new "catalysts" for community development. The youths were trained in the basics of accounting and running small income-generation projects such as producing handicrafts, rearing rabbits, and cultivating mushrooms and cash crops. A fundamental aspect of the new program, and a radical departure from previous programs, was that it was conceived to be autonomously sustainable. Fovaso was to be reimbursed for all incurred program costs from the income generated. It was also to keep 20% of all profits, which should enable the organization to cover administration and extraordinary costs. Indeed, initially almost all of the income generated by the program was used to pay for its startup costs. So, aside from a limited training impact, the program did not produce any significant social impacts in 1995. Moreover, the difficult economic context meant that this new program still represented a significant gamble, as it depended on the participants' ability to sell their products. Nevertheless, this strategy helped pay for the program and reduced the need for external financing, which made it much more financially sustainable than traditional programs. Combined with the extensive cost-cutting effort, the new model enabled the organization to courageously keep on working for the local community.

While justified by very pragmatic financial considerations, these extraordinary changes in organizational vision, programs, and outreach strategies are tantamount to a profound ideological transformation that redefined the organization's framing of the nature of poverty and therefore its role in society. Initially following a basic-needs model, the organization defined poverty primarily as a lack of access to basic needs. Its main strategy to address this problem was therefore providing access to basic services such as education, medicines, and day care. After the crisis, Fovaso shifted toward a model of service provision in which poverty was primarily defined as a lack of opportunities to generate income. Consequently, fighting poverty should rest with strengthening the poor's access to capital, technological capacity to transform capital and labor into products, and access to markets. Toward these goals, Fovaso provided training on income-generating technologies to increase the poor's productive capacity and help with the marketing of the products. As a partner organization, FIVA would be responsible for providing access to capital through micro-loans. So despite the continuing focus on poverty alleviation, the neoliberal model offered a substantially different ideological "theory of change," or service-provision model, with significant implications for the nature of the organization's social impact.

Given the initial high level of resistance to the new vision, which the majority of Fovaso's staff initially manifested in interviews, it was surprising to observe how little opposition this radical organizational change ultimately faced from the rank and file. Several reasons explain this acquiescence. A few staff members who disagreed with the new direction voluntarily left the organization. Also, the crisis brought about the dismissal of many staff members, many of whom were among the most disgruntled. One of the fired employees, who used to work for the Center for Special Education, described the movement to change the organization's mission as a "private sector coup" (*un golpe de la IP*) to refer to the fact that the movement was led by a businessman who wanted to bring private sector obsession with the "bottom line" to a social mission organization. The forceful reduction in personnel made most staff members feel very vulnerable, which together with a general increase in unemployment due to the economic crisis led to a high level of anxiety about job security. The increasing bureaucratization, centralization, and collapse of communication and staff participation channels further contributed to the top-down change. Staff members were reluctant to oppose this movement of powerful organizational members with easy access to the managing director. Finally, those who still believed in a basic-needs approach to poverty reduction could not explain how it would be sustainable when philanthropy and government funding proved to be undependable funding sources. The financial crisis provided, therefore, much of the legitimacy for a thorough change in Fovaso's personnel, organizational structure, and mission. The conflict of visions about the rightful role of the organization was reflected in most interviews in mid-1995, but by the end of a year that was characterized by a dearth of revenue opportunities, most staff had accepted the pragmatic case for the new organizational ideology. As always, a few never fully accepted the change, remaining skeptic of its purported advantages over the old system. For example, the community development director stated: "Our main objective is still to fight poverty. Now we promote income generation, rather than special education or providing [grants] for the development of community infrastructure. If the [beneficiaries] sell textiles or mushrooms they will be able to pay for their roads and schools themselves . . . but if the crisis lasts much longer they may not be able to sell [enough to make a profit]."

As it turned out, the persuasiveness of these strategic changes was reinforced through pervasive denial. As programs were being cut and in a desperate need to attract resources, Fovaso consciously and unconsciously inflated its performance rhetoric. For example, Fovaso claimed in its public communications that it had increased the number of beneficiary families from 1,130 in 1994 to 1,305 in 1995, a year in which Fovaso lost close to two-thirds of its programmatic staff! Proponents of the new vision nonetheless used this rhetoric to legitimize the new orientation. However, a community development officer referred to this alleged increase as "meaningless" as these figures included families who benefited both "directly" and "indirectly," so whole communities were included when the actual beneficiaries were a small number of participating families. The deception was also internal. Different program directors tried to paint a favorable and unrealistic picture of their work so as not to lose as many resources, creating a destructive internal competition based on fictitious metrics. The result was that, even within the organization, mistakes were rarely acknowledged, and consequently organizational learning was limited. Measuring social impact is, of course, very difficult in the best of circumstances, but this evidence indicates that it may be even more challenging during periods of financial crisis and organizational decline, which are often characterized by denial and internal strife.

Short-Term Impacts and Responses to Risk

Analysis of the Tequila Crisis's short-term impacts is consistent with the risk framework proposed in chapter 2. The sharp rise in economic risk resulting from the Tequila Crisis led to profound consequences for nonprofits and their social impact in the short term. In line with the procyclicality prediction, case study evidence showed a general decline in nonprofit revenues as the economy deteriorated. At the same time, as interest rates soared and consumer debt became an urgent problem, El Barzón was able to reverse its decline and mobilize thousands of people in well-publicized protests around the country, thriving during the crisis. El Barzón was able to capitalize on increased social discontent and focus on a major short-term problem: protecting debtors' assets from banks. Even within the cases facing declining support, the crisis led to increasing pressures for organizations to move away from traditional, long-term programs in favor of new, short-term programs. Those pressures took different forms. In Fovaso, some of the board members and a few donors pushed for a move away from the traditional, long-term welfare support model in favor of the commercial, income-generating model of community development. In FIVA, the leader moved away from poorer and riskier clients who generally needed capacity building in favor of richer clients who already understood financial transactions.

A risk perspective is essential to explain why FIVA and Pronatura increased their reserves during the crisis, at a time of falling or stable revenue and growing social need. Concerned about the economy in the long term, their leaders decided it was wise to increase organizational reserves during the crisis. They were able to use surpluses from commercial revenue to boost reserves. By running a surplus rather than the expected deficit, nonprofit leaders show that they continue to greatly value the future even in face of high risk. In most case studies, stakeholder differences in attitudes toward risk and discounting of long-term impacts led to considerable philanthropic friction, manifested in reduced donor support, voluntary staff departures, and lower volunteer participation. Even within Pronatura, which did not experience a revenue decline, some staff members expressed dissatisfaction with the leaders' decision to protect organizational reserves and, consequently, long-term impact at the expense of immediate impact during the crisis. I could also detect several instances when there seemed to be a sharp reduction of trust in nonprofit leaders among staff and in nonprofit organizations among supporters and even beneficiaries.

In line with predictions of increased discount rates and philanthropic friction, philanthropic giving and labor contributions by volunteers declined in most case studies during the crisis. Other types of income were less susceptible to the crisis, that is, had a lower beta risk. Indeed, international resource flows and some types of commercial income (e.g., interest on micro-loans and interest-bearing accounts) actually increased during the period. Such types of revenue provided an invaluable opportunity for hedging beta risk and attenuating procyclical tendencies. Most Mexican nonprofits, however, have limited access to such countercyclical revenue opportunities. Moreover, some of these opportunities entailed a move away from traditional beneficiaries toward richer and less risky ones. In this context, therefore, risk management may result in higher resource availability but lower social impact.

Other factors also contributed to organizational resilience. The most obvious are equity and low fixed-cost structure. Equity was most useful when it was highly liquid and unrestricted, such as in the form of a contingency fund. Fovaso, FIVA, and Pronatura relied on their contingency funds to compensate for temporary drops in income flows. On the other hand, without a contingency fund, Biocenosis was dependent on its cash inflow to remain operational, and since it did not attract any income, it did not operate in 1995. The nonprofits studied therefore suggest that, as advocated by Woods Bowman (2007) and Kevin Kearns (2007), nonprofits need to create contingency funds during times of plenty to survive and maintain their activity levels during recessions. A contingency fund is particularly important to meet fixed expenses such as most staff wages, avoiding significant losses of organizational capacity during the crisis. Secondly, Young (2007) argues that large fixed costs can turn into a major liability during economic downturns. This was indeed demonstrated by Fovaso. Conversely, El Barzón owed much of its financial success to its bottom-up structure and very low fixed costs, which enabled the organization to thrive in a cash-starved environment.

Previous research suggests that a higher ratio of administrative to total costs (AC ratio) can provide a financial margin to protect program spending during difficult times by offering the option of cutting (administrative) costs instead. An organization with low administrative costs does not have such a margin. Therefore a high AC ratio can be an important element of organizational resilience to financial shocks (e.g., Tuckman and Chang 1991). Based on the case studies, however, a higher ratio of administrative costs to total costs (AC ratio) was a poor predictor of lower financial distress. Against theoretical predictions, Fovaso's, FIVA's, and Pronatura's AC ratio actually rose during the crisis. To deal with shrinking income they cut variable, mostly programmatic, costs, leaving administrative costs unchanged, as administrative spending was essential to support the renewed cost control and fundraising efforts.[34] As a result, despite having the highest AC ratio during the crisis, Fovaso faced a high level of financial distress.

At the same time, the courage and importance of these nonprofits during the period must be underscored. Despite the hemorrhaging of resources, throughout the crisis most cases studied continued to courageously fight for a meaningful social impact and for their survival, animated by the hope that they would later be able to return to the pre-crisis level of programmatic activity and impact. Indeed, by the end of 1995, none of the observed nonprofits had become insolvent—a major triumph for these organizations and a sign of nonprofit resilience during the worst of times. In this process, nonprofits commonly relied on the extraordinary commitment and unpaid labor of leaders and staff. Their many vital contributions to social welfare during the crisis included providing food to poor families, education and business training to indigenous youth, adult literacy classes, micro-finance loans, protection for endangered species, community capacity building in sustainable forestry practices, and protection for Mexican families facing bankruptcy. Although the crisis wiped out close to N$6 million from the combined expenditures of the case studies, they were still able to spend or lend over N$5 million in 1995—close to US$1 million in 1995 dollars. Since only a small proportion of this funding originated from the government, it represents a nontrivial net increase in the amount of resources available for public policy in Mexico during a critical period. Certainly, for clients the crisis could have been much worse without the efforts of these brave actors.

Their noble contributions aside, we need to better understand what the nonprofit sector can do to increase its relevance at times of great social need. The theoretical and policy implications emerging out of the crisis period now beg a continuation of the analysis into the long-term. Were the studied nonprofits able to quickly recover, financially and programmatically, and return to or even surpass their former levels of social impact? Or were the depressing impacts of the crisis more long lasting? The following chapter investigates what happened to the case studies in the post-crisis recovery period, alongside a survey of a broader sample of nonprofits and several nonprofit sector indicators, to analyze the influence of an expanding economy on sector resources, organization, and impact. It extends the analysis of key factors illuminated in this chapter, considering in particular the roles of attitudes toward risk, philanthropic friction, and organizational vulnerability alongside the strategies pursued to manage risk and promote sustainability in the long-term.

5 The Long-Term Impact of Economic Risk on Nonprofit Sector Strength

How DID THE Mexican nonprofits studied and the nonprofit sector more generally fare in the post-crisis period? To the surprise of most, Mexico's 1995 adjustment program worked to quickly boost the economy. The dizzying drop in the peso led to an export boom, so that by 1996 the economy was growing again. Private investment rebounded, and by 1999 it registered the highest share of GDP since 1970 (Pastor and Wise 2006). While it may be the case for some that, as H. G. Wells once said, "the crisis of today is the joke of tomorrow," most Mexican nonprofits took several years to be able to fake a laugh, and many never got to laugh at all. This chapter looks closely at the evolution of Mexican nonprofits after December 1995 and examines the generalizability of its findings.

I begin by examining the dramatically different impacts the case studies experienced, despite their common exposure to the same macroeconomic recovery. I show how, in line with the risk framework developed here, the level of economic risk that nonprofits experience during macroeconomic recovery depends upon the sensitivity of particular resource flows to the macroeconomic cycle (i.e., their beta risk), resource diversification, financial reserves, relationship with the government, and attitudes toward risk among leaders and supporters. I then analyze the impact of economic volatility and risk on the broader nonprofit sector in Mexico, combining results from an original survey, with several independent macro-level indicators of nonprofit sector support and activity. I then consider the cross-national generalizability of these longitudinal findings by using comparative and historical evidence from Thailand, Argentina, Chile, and several rich nations, including the United States. The final section summarizes lessons from quantitative and qualitative evidence on nonprofit sector evolution. Two powerful impacts of economic risk on the nonprofit sector stand out: (pro)cyclicality in the short term and capacity erosion in the long term.

Cases of Recovery, Expansion, and Demise

As the economy recovered in 1996, most nonprofit case studies' resource availability improved. However, significant economic risk continued to influence them in the post-crisis period, revealing different mechanisms through which risk influences the nonprofit sector.

Biocenosis

Despite the resounding reversal in Mexico's economic fortunes and prospects in 1996, Biocenosis's leaders remained concerned about the organization's economic prospects.

After the crisis, they were concerned about their financial vulnerability, especially their revenue concentration and lack of a reserve fund. To keep fixed costs to a minimum, they initially decided not to rehire a secretary or any other worker. They also decided to pay themselves an honorarium that was proportional to their involvement in funded projects, rather than a fixed salary. To diversify the organization's resource base, they continued to offer one-day courses on organic agriculture. They also continued their efforts to establish links with American nonprofits, which could lead to future funding opportunities. In particular, they pursued a link to a small and tightly knit network of nonprofits with interest in permaculture. The network had several email and online discussion lists, which allowed them to seek potential clients for their courses for free. These efforts paid off, and together with the late payment of state government funding, in 1996 Biocenosis returned to its pre-crisis growth trend, which had been so forcefully disrupted in 1995.

The first year of the economic recovery was the organization's most successful year, financially and programmatically. In 1996, Biocenosis was able to generate an unprecedented level of income, about twice as much as in 1994 and a dramatic reversal of its zero income during the crisis. Similarly, Biocenosis found it much easier to attract volunteers for its Days for Nature program after the crisis. Following a year of programmatic inactivity, in 1996 Biocenosis was able to have significant programmatic impact. Its main output was the elaboration of the Land Use Plan, which was a key piece in the regulation of human activity in the region's rich ecological system. The plan clearly identified protected zones as well as zones that enabled human settlements. Because local and state governments approved the plan, it became an essential tool to fight squatter incursions into the natural protected areas. The Days for Nature program attracted the largest number of volunteers yet, leading to the cleaning of most of the water basin's hundreds of capillary streams, injecting much needed new life into the previously deteriorating local environment.

Unfortunately, however, this prosperity was short lived. In 1997, Biocenosis's revenue collapsed again. Its leaders' efforts to attract international funding and further diversify the organization's funding portfolio were unsuccessful. Moreover, the state government did not renew their contract, and demand for their courses began to waiver. "Burned out" by their experience during the crisis, the organization's leaders saw little hope in being able to attract enough stable income through state government and organic agriculture classes, which could have provided the kind of financial growth needed for them to dedicate themselves fully to the organization. They continued to provide some classes in 1997 and 1998. They provided them at cost because they believed they were providing an important service to the community and their clients could not afford higher prices. They also began to look for alternative, and more stable, employment opportunities. In 1999, Biocenosis's leaders migrated out of Mexico to pursue their personal careers, and the organization became largely inactive. Their only activity has been the accompaniment of the Days for Nature program, which was still undertaken in some years with

Biocenosis's expertise and the collaboration of other local nonprofits. Biocenosis leaders' distressing experience during the crisis combined with their inability to diversify organizational revenue into international funding eventually led to the organization's collapse. Mexico and especially Valle de Bravo lost two exceptionally committed activists who were internationally renowned for their environmental expertise.

Fovaso

As described in the previous chapter, the crisis took an especially heavy toll on Fovaso, more than halving its pre-crisis budget and number of staff members. In 1996, organizational income improved, though not to the levels enjoyed before the crisis. Fovaso's cost-cutting effort initiated during the crisis also appeared to be paying off, and the organization was able to stabilize its finances, avoiding any further dismissals. Nevertheless, its leaders remained cautious. As a result, the organization had to cut its 1996 budget further, to N$318,000.[1] Fovaso's leaders were confident that in the long term, the organization's new focus on micro-enterprise would increase both the organization's effectiveness and its funding prospects. By cutting many of the programs with a negative operating margin, Fovaso created a new focus that was more economical than the previous one. For example, in the Youth for Change program, participating youths successfully designed and implemented income-generating projects such as growing mushrooms and vegetables, raising rabbits, and collecting and selling old clothes. This income was a main source of finance for the program, making it almost financially self-sustainable. By recouping its program setup costs, Fovaso was able to expand the program and free other income for the other programs. The bureaucratic demands of the programmatic changes, however, contributed to a further rise in self-reported administration expenditure in 1996 to 19%, from 16% in 1995 and 9% before the crisis!

Initially, Fovaso's new emblematic program, Youth for Change, attracted a lot of attention from the press and even a few academics. The promise of creating young community leaders who could catalyze their communities into greater economic and social development was appealing. Unlike its older welfare-oriented programs, Youth for Change was a pioneering model in Mexico and probably even Latin America. Due to the continuing scarcity of philanthropic giving in 1996, the program was initially financed by the managing director's son, who was a prominent local politician, and his wife.[2] The video shop also continued to generate more income for the organization, with profits growing consistently every year.

In 1997 and 1998, Fovaso continued to regain financial strength. The organization's financial performance became increasingly tied to its ability to generate commercial revenue. This was largely due to its difficulty attracting philanthropic giving, which, in turn, under the matching agreement also meant low government revenue. The organization's new emphasis on micro-enterprise made it a hard sell among many previous donors who had supported special education, the medical dispensary, and the elderly center. On the other hand, the treasurer's plan of creating a club of sponsoring companies for the community development projects never came to fruition. In fact, over time it became clearer that it was harder to fundraise for the new model of development based on micro-enterprise than it had been for more traditional charitable services.

Initially, the new Youth for Change program was a success. Several classes of indigenous youths were trained, and their income-generation projects implemented in local communities. By the late 1990s, however, the new model was evidencing grave deficiencies. Fovaso had faced major difficulties in transposing to the communities the learning and pilot projects undertaken in its training center. When they tried to replicate these projects in the communities, they often would not produce the desired outcomes, and most did not even generate enough income to pay for the initial investment (made by both Fovaso and community members themselves). Several factors contributed to this. Timing was not ideal. Communities were chronically starved of resources after the crisis. They also found it difficult to penetrate other markets. There are significant marketing costs, which were generally ignored at the project design stage, with the implicit assumption that the products would find their way to the markets using existing marketing mechanisms. Indeed, indigenous communities have a long history of selling textiles in urban centers. They have a lot less experience of selling food, especially perishable types such as mushrooms and rabbit meat. Vegetables, mushrooms, and rabbits require little investment, and the sale price is well above the production cost, often several times higher. However, one reason for such a large margin is the very cost of marketing of these products. Underestimation of such costs led to very compelling business plans, but the inadequacy of their traditional marketing strategies and the margins expected by local retailers rendered the ventures ineffective in generating income for the communities. They did benefit from consuming much of the production, but that was a marginal benefit. The pilot projects had worked because Fovaso sold their products in its urban headquarters. That did not seem to be a viable strategy, however, as the projects were replicated and production expanded. But perhaps the most serious problem was that the projects were too ambitious for young high school students to pull off. The technical and business training they received in the program was very basic. It would have been difficult to pull off such commercial ventures in the best of times, but it proved nearly impossible after a major crisis, in the resource-starved community economy.

By the end of the 1990s, Fovaso's finances were fast deteriorating again. The promise of a return to its pre-crisis glory, by focusing on a model that supposedly had great appeal for rich businesspeople, never materialized. Few expected that the organization could possibly collapse, but the macroeconomic recession in 2001 sealed Fovaso's fate. Fovaso ceased all operations in 2002.

Centro

Perhaps ironically, Centro de Educación Especial, which Fovaso made independent ("abandoned" was the term used by Centro's director) during the crisis, managed to

stabilize its revenues and was still operational in 2007. Its survival immediately following its legal constitution as an autonomous organization had depended on fees from
parents and philanthropic support from both better-off parents and board members. In
the long term, survival was also possible because Centro reduced its financial vulnerability by pursuing government funding sources. From the perspective of the risk framework, Centro was able to transform its long-term educational mission into a short-term
emergency. The process was partly planned and partly serendipitous. The organization's
managing director made a considerable effort to communicate its dire prospects to all
relevant stakeholders. The possibility of failure in its very first year (of autonomous
operation) was a constant preoccupation. In fact, according to its managing director,
the board was determined to not let such an important organization die in its first year.
In this sense, newness was not a "liability"; instead it was a challenge. As in the case of
Fovaso, "staff volunteering" was an important resource as a smaller number of teachers
cared for a growing number of children. By 2007, Centro employed ten teachers, up
from six in 1995, and reached close to 160 children. Its long-term survival and operation
as a charitable nonprofit was possible when Centro forged new, longer-term contract
agreements with the state government that did not depend on a philanthropic matching
formula. It still relied on philanthropy, but most of its revenue came from public funding and small fees from the parents.

FIVA

FIVA's "temporary" adaptation to the crisis by shifting from micro-loans to the poor to
larger loans to local businesses continued after the crisis, despite the improving local
economy. Initially, this strategy was justified on the grounds that the local economy was
recovering very slowly. The local economy was largely dependent on domestic tour-
ism, which had been decimated by the crisis. FIVA's managing director continued to
see lending to the poor as too risky. On the other hand, lending to local businesses
helped to protect existing jobs and prepared them for the imminent economic recovery.
By 1997, the local economy did appear to improve: restaurants were busy again, local
shops were open longer hours, and conversations turned less frequently to the previously favorite topic: La Crisis. However, FIVA continued to ignore its original mandate
to provide micro-credit to the poor in 1997 and 1998. Part of the problem is attributable
to a few bad experiences of loans to communities under the Youth for Change micro-
enterprise program. FIVA used these examples as proof that it still was providing credit
to poor communities and as justification for not providing a significant portion of its
capital, as too risky. Despite its having been set up to provide credit to the poor, and not
to compete with commercial banks for small business loans, by the year 2000 FIVA's
leader continued to blatantly disregard its social mission. It was able to do so because
its board of directors was simply rubber-stamping the executive's decisions. Following
the collapse of the two founding nonprofits, and the inability of the managing director
to implement a change in the organization's governance structure, in 2004 the federal

government began the process of dissolution and absorption of FIVA's assets. The reason was the extinction of its two nonprofit founders, which left the state government as the only remaining member of the board of governance. Because FIVA was a nonprofit, a government-led governance composition was not seen as legitimate; consequently, the government dissolved the organization and confiscated its assets.

FIVA's mission drift was product of what is often called the "underinvestment problem" in corporate finance (Doherty 2000). This problem refers to the tendency for managers to avoid risky, but potentially very profitable, projects to protect their organization's finances and their jobs, despite the fact that it is in shareholders' interests that companies undertake such projects. Managers, therefore, tend to underinvest in the most profitable projects. The only solution to this problem would have been closer supervision by the organization's board of directors. However, the joint-governance between two (at the time) nonprofits in financial and organizational trouble and the state government proved ineffective in providing sufficient supervision of management. Ironically, despite strong financial stability secured by its manager's unrelenting pursuit of high operating margins, a large investment fund, and a contingency fund, the organization was dissolved.

Pronatura

Pronatura's reserve fund and international funding provided a high degree of insulation from the crisis. As in the other case studies, Pronatura's leaders remained cautious after the crisis. Indeed, as interest rates fell and international donors adjusted their grants to take the peso devaluation into account, in 1996 Pronatura's income fell 1.6% or N$129,194.[3] Following the crisis, then, the organization began an effort to hedge its macroeconomic risk exposure by increasing revenue from domestic sources. Pronatura also invested in a funding diversification strategy through more attention to commercial income, gifts in-kind, and an individual membership-sponsorship program. Despite the slight revenue decline, Pronatura was able to significantly increase its spending by N$1.22 million, increasing its spending as a proportion of income from 55% in 1995 to 71% in 1996. The increase in spending was primarily due to its investment in new commercial enterprises and higher spending on fundraising and advocacy. Non–advocacy program spending also rose 21%. The rise in spending during a year in which income fell slightly was possible because the organization's leaders were more confident about the financial future of the organization (having boosted its financial reserves during the crisis) and the country. Its commercialization effort, which included conducting an ecotourism program and selling a conservation magazine and memorabilia, was a resounding success. The improvement in the economy and the increase in tourist flows to a much cheaper Mexico meant that commercial ventures such as ecotourism attracted a large market and produced an income of N$857,840 in 1996 from zero in 1995. Combined, commercial income and philanthropy rose N$1.262 million, or 16% of total 1996 income (philanthropy rose from N$29,000 in 1995 to N$389,000 in 1996)! Overall, however, this impressive rise in income from new sources did not compensate for the fall in interest income and international funding.

From 1997 to 2000, the organization continued to grow its programs and resource base. Most notably, gifts in-kind grew every year, so that by 1999 they constituted 5.37% of its income (from zero in 1995). Despite strong rise in advertising income, the magazine struggled to make a profit. The organization saw the magazine as an opportunity to spread the organization's message and demonstrate the quality of its work (it is a very glossy magazine with beautiful photos). Income from the ecotourism venture remained stable throughout the period, adding a valuable element of risk diversification to the portfolio. Pronatura's diversification strategy paid off, leading to a very sustainable doubling of its programmatic spending in five years (almost 15% annual growth rate!). According to several donors I interviewed, the Pronatura "brand" became highly valued among national and international donors.

In stark contrast to most of the other case studies, Pronatura was able to capitalize on the crisis in the post-crisis period. By the organization remaining financially sound when most of its competitors were weakened, the crisis presented significant growth opportunities, which the organization ably seized. For example, the organization was one of the few Mexican nonprofits receiving a grant from the Fondo Mexicano para la Conservación de la Naturaleza in 1996. The FMCN is one of the largest environmental donors in Mexico. Yet, in its first funding round in 1996, FMCN was not able to disburse all its grant money because it did not receive sufficient quality proposals to fund! As a result, Pronatura's income rose sharply after the crisis, and by the year 2000 its annual income was N$14 million,[4] representing an increase of almost 80% over its pre-crisis income. Pronatura's financial success in the post-crisis period turned the organization into a dominant player in Mexico's environmental nonprofit field.

El Barzón

Due to its emergency focus and the countercyclical nature of its key resource, volunteering, El Barzón was uniquely positioned to take advantage of the crisis, experiencing very rapid expansion in 1995. Those same characteristics, however, constituted a major handicap as the economy recovered and risk fell. Thus, the post-crisis economic recovery ultimately led to El Barzón's decline and eventual demise. As interest rates declined, and the economy recovered, the problem of personal and small business debt was deflated. Moreover, El Barzón's continuing pressure greatly contributed to further concessions by the Mexican government and commercial banks. While banks were the main beneficiaries of the international rescue package, in 1996 the Mexican government decided to extend financial relief to debtors as well. The government offered debtors the opportunity to join various debt conversion programs such as *Unidades de Inversión* (UDIs, Investment Units) and the *Acuerdo para el Apoyo a Deudores* (Debtor Support Agreement). These plans included a temporary reduction or moratorium on interest payments, suspension of judicial proceedings, restructuring of credit, and limitations on what banks can demand from debtors (Grammont 2001). El Barzón urged its members not to restructure their debt, which the organization claimed was illegal. The fact that a very large number of debtors restructured their debt constituted a major blow to the organization. As the economy continued to improve El Barzón began losing large numbers of supporters.

Another contributing factor was the increasing tendency for the movement's leadership to demonstrate left-leaning political sympathies, eventually leading to the involvement of some leaders in party politics. El Barzón rose in power partly because it maintained a focus on the issue of debt and it did not get involved in traditional party politics. Eventually it became a household name, and its reasonable demands inspired great trust and power. *Barzonear* became a verb (Williams 2001). Before the 1997 midterm elections, this essentially meant not getting involved with the ruling party, the PRI. However, the founders had clearly leftist inclinations, demonstrated, for example, by the open manifestation of mutual support between the Zapatistas and El Barzón when both parties signed the *Tratado de Intocabilidad* (Untouchability Treaty) in 1996. Consequently, the leftist Party of the Democratic Revolution (Partido de la Revolución Democrática), which was sympathetic to the organization's demands and believed that the crisis had been caused by the ruling party, made efforts to forge a closer relationship with El Barzón's leadership. This led to a split in El Barzón. One faction, El Barzón–Unión favored its leaders running for elected office. Twenty organizational leaders decided to run for office in the 1997 midterm elections, and three were elected to Congress. Such a relationship with a left-leaning party did not sit well with a large conservative section of its middle-class membership. The other faction, El Barzón–Confederación, favored independence from political parties (Cadena Roa 2008). This split was another serious blow to El Barzón. Mexico's Supreme Court delivered a third blow when it ruled that, contrary to El Barzón's arguments, compound interest was constitutional and banks were legally allowed to charge it. These political factors added to the economic resolution of the debt problem to render El Barzón largely redundant by the end of the 1990s. Its website claims that "El Barzón's decline was brought about by its success." This is only partly true. The timing of Mexican government concessions suggests that the improving economy might have played a role as important as El Barzón's campaigns. Moreover, as in Fovaso's case, the organization's decline was also partly due to the abandonment of its original mission in adaptation to the Tequila Crisis. Despite Mexican farmers' worsening living conditions under NAFTA, El Barzón did not return to its original focus on the Mexican countryside after the crisis. In trying to expand and diversify its resource base by including urban debtors, El Barzón partly alienated many of its original, rural supporters. When the economy recovered, El Barzón lost both short-term support from urban debtors and long-term support from farmers. Their lack of a clear long-term focus undermined support in the lower-risk period of the late 1990s. Indeed, the Monterrey section of El Barzón was able to formulate long-term goals and has remained active, while other sections have largely disbanded. By the early 2000s, El Barzón had lost most of its members and mobilization power, but the Monterrey section still had a membership of around five hundred families. It had no paid staff and received no outside funding (Brumley 2004). A sad, but telling, anecdote to illustrate El Barzón's decline is that when I "Googled" "El Barzón" in June 2006, the first hit was a Mexican restaurant in Detroit, Michigan!

Wider Impacts: Survey, Startup, and Participation Data

The nonprofit case study evidence provides invaluable details about how risk impacts nonprofits largely consistent with the risk theory of the nonprofit sector, and also reveals key lessons, to which we will return. But first, are such impacts generalizable to other nonprofits in Mexico, and possibly in other countries as well? This section considers broader data on the nonprofit sector in Mexico as well as in a few other Latin American and rich countries, providing a quantitative assessment of their generalizability.

The nonprofit sector is inherently difficult to measure. It takes many forms and cannot be subsumed under one single measure without significant loss of accuracy and relevance. Nevertheless, previous research has employed several informative indicators, which can help capture different dimensions of the sector. Unfortunately, Mexico does not have a reliable and comprehensive longitudinal dataset on nonprofit organizations such as the "990 form" databases in the United States.[5] It is therefore necessary to look more broadly and creatively for reliable empirical sector evidence. The following independently collected datasets provide a diverse, yet surprisingly coherent, representation of complementary dimensions of the Mexican nonprofit sector before, during, and after the Tequila Crisis. To provide insights into the impact of other macroeconomic cycles, whenever possible a larger time period is included in the analysis.

Survey on Risk Attitudes and Nonprofit Resource Mobilization

Due to clear limitations in available data on the Mexican nonprofit sector over time, and especially on its finances, in 1999 I undertook an independent survey of the leaders of forty-seven nonprofits included in CEMEFI's dataset (described below).[6] The survey paints a general picture of the evolution of philanthropy and different dimensions of nonprofit sector size with a special focus on the evolution of key nonprofit resources between 1994 and 1998. Data collection was based on telephone interviews with nonprofit leaders, typically the managing director or, in a small number of cases, a high-ranking manager.[7] When the leader did not have immediate access to the financial information requested I followed up in a second, and sometimes even third, call. A few leaders sent detailed financial spreadsheets by email, but most simply answered the questions by phone. I was impressed by the degree of cooperation and transparency among the participating leaders, given the fact that most Mexican nonprofits are not required to divulge their financial results publicly.

The sample was selected randomly to minimize potential researcher bias and maximize sample representativeness. To get to the target sample size, I tried to contact eighty-three nonprofits. Of those, I was unable to locate sixteen nonprofits. A further fourteen nonprofits were excluded because their leaders refused to participate in the survey. I could not identify any systematic reason for why some nonprofit leaders refused to participate so I assume nonresponse was randomly determined and does not bias the results reported here. Leaders in six organizations told me that their organizations had ceased to operate between 1995 and 1998. The final sample, therefore, consisted of forty-seven nonprofits. Given the survey's focus on the impacts of the Tequila Crisis, the survey focused on nonprofits created before 1995. Its findings, therefore, may not represent the experience of nonprofits created since then. As a retrospective study, moreover, the survey was based on nonprofit leaders I could locate in 1999, and, consequently, it provides limited information on the bankruptcy rate during and after the crisis. It is very possible that some of the sixteen organizations I was unable to locate in 1999 had disbanded for reasons that were related to the crisis. It is also possible, however, that some of these organizations may have simply relocated or ceased to exist for reasons that were unrelated to the crisis. Follow-up calls and, more recently, Internet research were unfruitful in generating further insights about those organizations.

This survey is one of the first empirical efforts to assess the impact of economic volatility and risk on the nonprofit sector in developing countries. To ensure comparability over time, all estimates reported below are adjusted for inflation.[8] Aside from generating detailed financial data from participating nonprofits before, during, and after the crisis, the survey also included a "choice experiment," which was adapted from Michigan University's Panel Study of Income Dynamics, and was designed to assess nonprofit leaders' degree of risk-aversion. This experiment helped me understand their risk calculations, generating new insights into how and why different nonprofits respond to economic risk.

The basic statistics relating to survey data can be found in table 5.1. Philanthropic giving displayed a remarkable rate of annual variation. Between 1994 and 1995, average revenue from philanthropic giving fell 75.2% (see figure 5.1 and table 5.1). In 1996, despite significant macroeconomic growth, average revenue from giving rose only 11.1%. A paired t-test, moreover, shows that that the increase is not statistically significant at the 95% confidence level. Despite continuous growth in the next two years, by 1998 the level of philanthropic giving was still 40.3% lower than it had been before the crisis. This long-term reduction in philanthropy is consistent with the theoretical analysis developed in chapter 2, which predicts that high-risk periods generate considerable philanthropic friction that might remain intense long after the economy has fully recovered.

Another hypothesis developed in chapter 2 was that commercial income will be less susceptible to economic volatility and risk than other types of income because it is generally associated with an immediate benefit for the client, and consequently its benefits do not attract a heavy risk discount. Moreover, to the extent that clients can evaluate the quality of the service they are purchasing from the nonprofit, there is less risk involved in commercial transactions than transactions in support of more diffuse social benefits: evaluation of public goods provision is subject to significant risk (i.e., uncertainty) due

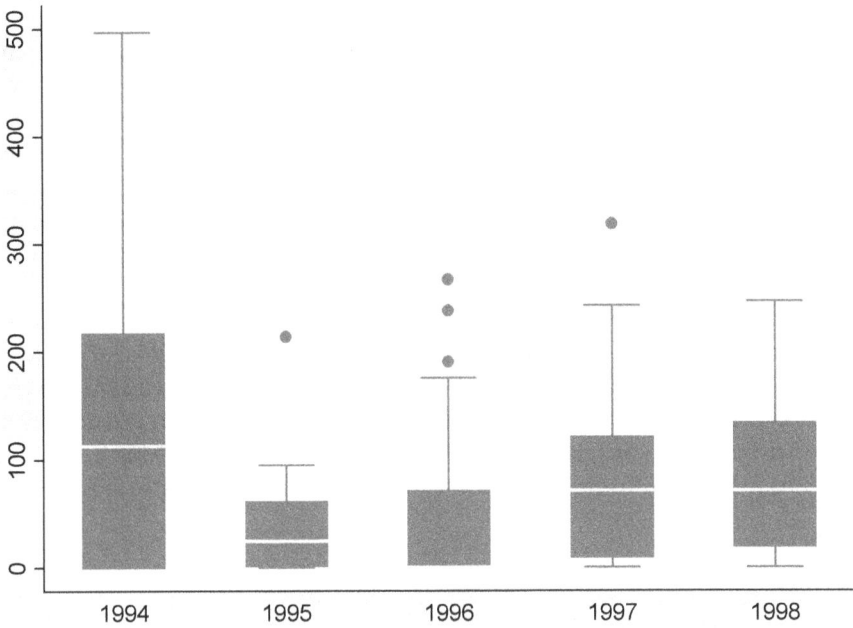

Figure 5.1. Philanthropic giving, 1994–1998. Notes: Based on author's survey of forty-seven non-profits. Figures in thousands of nuevos pesos.

to the general absence of consensus on appropriate evaluation methods. Consistent with these arguments, average commercial revenue was the financial bedrock for most surveyed nonprofits. It fell only 4.8% during the crisis and the decline is not statistically significant. In 1996, commercial revenue surpassed its pre-crisis level, and consistent rises in the following two years meant that by 1998 it was 9.3% higher than before the crisis.

Both government and international funding to nonprofits were more stable than philanthropic giving, but more volatile than commercial revenue (see figure 5.2). Government funding declined abruptly during the crisis, falling 54.8% between 1994 and 1995. The following year it grew sharply by 58.8%. Government funding grew again in 1997, but declined in 1998. By 1998, revenue from government sources was still 26.7% lower than it had been in 1994. Similarly, international funding declined 54.4% during the crisis and grew only slightly in 1996. By 1997, international funding grew sharply, helping to close the gap in relation to pre-crisis levels. That year, international funding was just 10.8% lower than in 1994. Surprisingly, international funding fell almost 15% the following year. By 1998, therefore, revenue from international sources was still 24%

lower than it had been in 1994. The evolution of international funding seems inconsistent with the experience of Pronatura, which saw a sharp rise in international funding during the crisis due primarily to the fact that the peso had lost almost half of its value in relation to the U.S. dollar that year. It indicates that, rather than passing the favorable exchange rate difference to their Mexican partners, international donors generally adjusted the value of their giving to pesos. The devaluation, therefore, hurt Mexican nonprofits as the rising cost of imports contributed to inflation in the post-crisis period. Unfortunately, consistent with previous research on international aid, international donors failed to respond to the economic emergency in a timely manner, actually cutting aid to local nonprofits during one of the worst crises in Mexican history.

Increased reliance on commercial revenue in high-risk environments can also be seen in the evolution of resource dependence among surveyed nonprofits (see table 5.1). Dependence on commercial revenue rose from 41.4% of total revenue before the crisis to 64.1% during the crisis. By 1998, dependence on commercial revenue (52.4%) was still higher than before the crisis. Resource dependence on philanthropic giving fell from just under 20% to just over 10% in 1995 and 8.7% in 1996. By 1998, it had returned to slightly

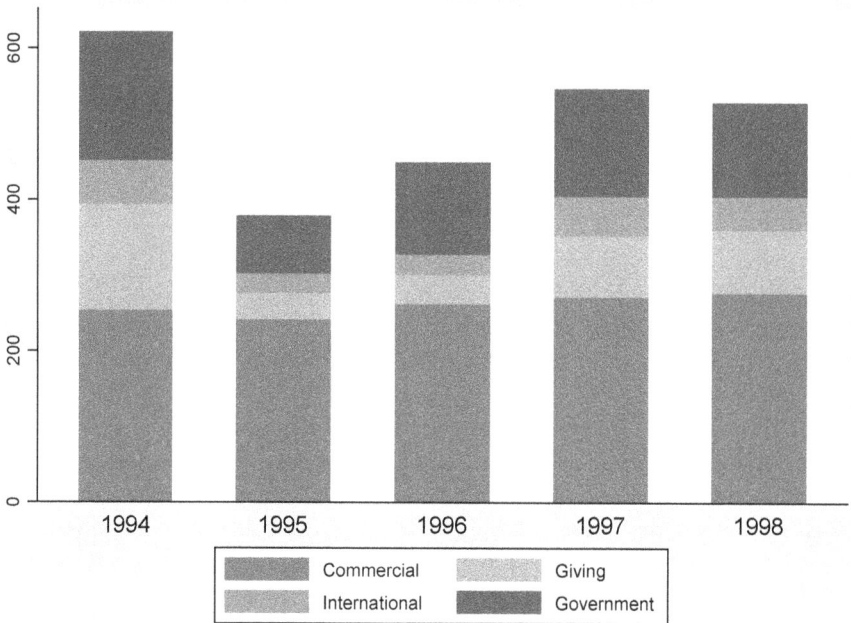

Figure 5.2. Nonprofit revenue composition, 1994–1998. Notes: Based on author's survey of forty-seven nonprofits. Figures in thousands of nuevos pesos.

under 20% (table 5.1). Lastly, dependence on government funding fell from 32.7% in 1994 to 20.5% in 1995, and it was only slightly above that level in 1998 (i.e., 21.2%).

Case-by-case inspection reveals that only two nonprofits had higher revenues in 1995 than they did in 1994. Moreover, the two nonprofits experienced a decline in revenue and volunteering as the economy improved from 1996 to 1998. That is, like El Barzón, the two nonprofits had countercyclical support. Unlike El Barzón, however, both organizations had a high level of resource dependence on commercial revenue (60.8 and 80%). At the same time, three nonprofits experienced growth in philanthropic giving during the crisis, and those three nonprofits continued to experience growth in philanthropic giving as the economy recovered. Like Centro, these nonprofits were able to increase philanthropic giving at a time when such support was generally falling quite rapidly and to sustain it when the economy recovered. Unfortunately, a follow-up on these extraordinary organizations was impossible within this study.

Turning to labor resources, while most nonprofits reported a decline in volunteering during the crisis, volunteering was relatively more stable than paid staff and most types of revenue throughout the period. Not surprisingly, changes in paid employment were closely associated with variation in nonprofit spending (table 5.1). Volunteering, therefore, offered vital support during the crisis and is an essential component of resource diversification in high-risk environments. This finding lends support to the hypothesis that within philanthropy, volunteering should be more resilient to risk discounting than philanthropic giving. Of note, broader evidence on political participation during this period (analyzed below) suggests that the willingness to volunteer evolved in a countercyclical fashion, but actual volunteering evolved in procyclical fashion. This puzzling fact is consistent with the hypothesis that philanthropic friction may increase during high-risk periods and the mismatch between nonprofit goals and volunteer preferences may lead to a substantial gap between potential (i.e., willingness to volunteer) and actual volunteering. As El Barzón illustrates, the capacity to rapidly change organizational goals to match rapidly changing donor preferences (i.e., from farmers' debt and subsidies to urban consumers' debt) provides a major competitive advantage in volatile environments. In so doing, El Barzón was able to generate considerable countercyclical support—a major resource advantage when we consider the fact that none of the nonprofit resources examined here were generally countercyclical (see table 5.2).

As explained in chapter 2, the *beta risk* is an indicator of systematic risk that measures elasticity, or susceptibility, with respect to the economic cycle. Table 5.2 displays beta risk values for different nonprofit resources. Since the sample is relatively small, beta risks were calculated through bootstrapping—a resampling technique described in chapter 3. Bootstrapping eliminates the need for the normal distribution assumption, which characterizes traditional statistical methods but which might be unrealistic in this setting. On the other hand, bootstrapping requires the assumption that the sample distribution be the same as the population distribution. Since the sample was randomly selected, I can reasonably assume that this requirement was met.

Table 5.1. Basic statistics of survey

Year	1994		1995		1996		1997		1998		Total	
	Mean	(S.D.)	Mean	(S.D.)	Mean	(S.D.)	Mean	(S.D.)	Mean	(S.D.)	Mean	(S.D.)
Revenue, N$000	621.797	(401.431)	379.408	(299.705)	449.913	(375.636)	547.585	(364.713)	529.698	(374.314)	505.68	(371.173)
Giving, N$000	140.35	(147.425)	34.76	(39.587)	39.083	(70.53)	81.532	(78.044)	83.846	(69.761)	75.914	(95.802)
Commercial, N$000	253.782	(220.107)	241.697	(209.626)	262.327	(231.654)	271.713	(220.291)	277.323	(215.954)	261.369	(218.131)
Government, N$000	170.125	(181.152)	76.901	(120.167)	122.146	(114.498)	142.976	(183.921)	124.735	(170.399)	127.377	(158.616)
International, N$000	57.541	(115.837)	26.05	(50.766)	26.356	(66.108)	51.363	(86.012)	43.794	(76.367)	41.021	(82.282)
Dependence giving	.196	(.163)	.106	(.102)	.087	(.157)	.163	(.101)	.199	(.198)	.15	(.155)
Dependence commercial	.414	(.226)	.641	(.202)	.566	(.141)	.524	(.186)	.524	(.231)	.533	(.211)
Dependence government	.327	(.262)	.205	(.223)	.309	(.167)	.234	(.213)	.212	(.208)	.258	(.221)
Dependence international	.063	(.113)	.049	(.09)	.039	(.089)	.079	(.114)	.064	(.093)	.059	(.1)
Expenditure, N$000	577.333	(378.242)	341.69	(364.959)	348.314	(282.793)	466.528	(354.734)	495.426	(388.374)	445.858	(364.087)
Surplus	44.465	(180.741)	37.719	(247.441)	101.599	(185.939)	81.057	(169.784)	34.272	(118.84)	59.822	(185.513)
Expenditure/Revenue	.931	(.311)	.879	(.498)	.826	(.284)	.835	(.235)	.953	(.236)	.885	(.329)
Employment	29.155	(15.849)	20.196	(16.897)	16.319	(11.163)	23.621	(15.42)	25.974	(16.886)	23.053	(15.9)
Volunteers	6.415	(8.666)	4.723	(6.688)	4.085	(5.871)	5.366	(7.525)	5.57	(8.077)	5.232	(7.41)
Volunteer employment	.243	(.328)	.285	(.359)	.26	(.349)	.244	(.339)	.241	(.338)	.254	(.34)
Paid employment	22.74	(15.009)	15.472	(16.879)	12.234	(10.239)	18.255	(14.137)	20.404	(16.242)	17.821	(15.022)
Herfindahl	.476	(.169)	.572	(.146)	.503	(.091)	.463	(.118)	.505	(.184)	.504	(.149)

Notes: Based on author's survey of forty-seven nonprofits.

All resources were procyclical during the period of study. Giving is by far the resource that is most responsive to changes in economic growth. Its beta risk shows that for every 1% of economic growth/decline, giving grows/declines 16.8%. In contrast, commercial revenue is remarkably stable, growing/declining only 1.26% for every 1% the economy grows/declines. Moreover, its beta risk is significant only at the 90% confidence level, suggesting that commercial income may in fact be acyclical, that is, unrelated to the economic cycle. Government and international funding have intermediate beta risks. Though clearly procyclical, volunteering is the most stable labor resource. With a beta risk of 4.3, volunteering is more stable than paid staff, which has a beta risk of 6.3. Nonprofit capacity, measured as total employment including both paid and volunteer labor, is quite volatile but less procyclical than income or spending. Not surprisingly, survey evidence suggests that paid employment is almost as responsive as revenue to economic fluctuations.

What were the consequences of these volatile types of funding for nonprofits' total revenue and spending? As predicted in chapter 2 and consistent with general case study evidence, average revenue was highly volatile during this period. Between 1994 and 1995, revenue fell 39%! Overall, revenue has a beta risk of 6.5. This figure is consistent with the 39% contraction in nonprofit sector funding that took place when the economy contracted over 6% during the Tequila Crisis. Nevertheless, due to the relative stability of commercial revenue and its increasing share in nonprofit revenue, especially during the crisis, revenue was less procyclical than philanthropic giving, government funding, and international funding (see table 5.2). The surprising economic turnaround in 1996

Table 5.2. Beta risk values for different nonprofit resources

	Beta	Bias	Bootstrap S.E.	Bts. Confidence Interval 95%	N.
Giving	16.829***	.087	2.243	[12.616, 21.442]	112
Government	5.933***	−.028	1.977	[1.986, 9.798]	98
Commercial	1.258*	−.008	.695	[−.187, 2.545]	167
International	5.945**	−.058	2.693	[.604, 11.330]	39
Revenue	6.485***	−.023	.713	[5.118, 7.900]	169
Spending	7.597***	−.002	1.133	[5.401, 9.882]	164
Paid	6.285***	.021	1.257	[3.870, 8.761]	131
Volunteers	4.326***	−.003	.525	[3.345, 5.360]	98
Employment	5.296***	−.007	.863	[3.541, 6.867]	180

Notes: Unstandardized beta coefficients based on ordinary least squares regression based on log differences formula: $(\ln Y_t - \ln Y_{t-1}) = a + b(\ln X_t - \ln X_{t-1}) + e$. Number of observations reflects both number of nonprofits and number of available annual variation. Bootstrapping estimation based on 2,000 repetitions. ***$p < .01$; **$p < .05$; *$p < .10$ (two-tailed).

brought some relief to surveyed nonprofits. Despite strong macroeconomic growth, however, average revenue in 1996 was only modestly higher than in 1995. In 1997, revenue experienced a more significant growth, but in 1998 revenue lost some ground again, so that revenue was still 14.8% lower in 1998 than in 1994. As expected, average nonprofit spending was more volatile than revenue during this period. It fell 41% during the crisis, largely in line with the 39% decline in revenue. The next year, however, spending grew only 1.9% while revenue grew 18.6%. As a result, average surplus grew an astonishing 169% between 1995 and 1996! Indeed, as a proportion of total revenue, surplus grew from 6.9% in 1994 to 12.1% in 1995 and 17.4% in 1996. Surplus remained high in 1997 (16.5%) and fell significantly only in 1998, when it represented 4.7% of revenue.

How can we account for the surprising finding that nonprofits generally had countercyclical surpluses? The hypothesis of a direct relationship between income and spending would suggest that changes in organizational spending should be roughly in line with changes in revenue. A spending-smoothing hypothesis, on the other hand, would suggest that spending should remain fairly constant over time so that surplus should vary procyclically; that is, nonprofits save in good years and spend those savings in bad years. Countercyclical variation in nonprofit budget surplus, however, is entirely consistent with the risk explanation. The gap between organizational revenues and spending shows that organizational savings peaked in 1996, which suggests that nonprofit leaders remained concerned about future risk even after the economy began to recover. This concern about the future was evident in my interviews with case study leaders. They justified their organizations' budget surplus during the crisis and two subsequent years by alluding to the need create a contingency fund to insure against future economic risk. Unfortunately, this strategy is also likely to lead to an increase in philanthropic friction, as the case of Fovaso illustrates. Indeed, the dramatic decline in philanthropic giving in 1995 and 1996 is consistent with higher friction during high-risk periods.

Chapter 3 shows that risk-aversion attitudes among the population tend to peak in middle-income countries. The influence of risk is also apparent in the different attitudes toward risk among different types of nonprofit leaders. At the same time, Dennis Young (2006) hypothesizes that entrepreneurs tend to be less risk-averse than professional managers. This hypothesis is consistent with previous research on the business sector (Djankoff et al. 2007). To test Young's hypothesis, I examine the relationship between the level of risk-aversion among nonprofit leaders (i.e., entrepreneurs and managers) and their respective organizations' behavior, employing several statistical methods. I assessed risk-aversion among nonprofit leaders by including in this study's survey an adaptation of the risk-aversion instrument used in the Michigan University's Panel Study of Income Dynamics. Answers to several hypothetical questions entailing different risk-reward combinations produce an ordinal-scale assessment of nonprofit leaders' level of risk-tolerance (that is, the inverse of risk-aversion). Figure 5.3 displays the results of the "choice experiment" by type of nonprofit leader (a rank of 1 corresponds to the lowest level of risk-tolerance and 6 to the highest).

A Mann-Whitney test confirms the impression from visual examination of figure 5.3 that entrepreneurs have higher risk-tolerance than managers on average (at $p < .05$). A key weakness of this comparison between managers and entrepreneurs, however, is that it is based on choices among abstract scenarios. To help address this issue, the examination of how leadership type relates to organizational surpluses provides a more "consequential" assessment. The more risk-averse leaders are, the more likely their organizations will try to reduce risk exposure by generating surpluses and creating a reserve fund.

Figure 5.4 contrasts spending and surplus between entrepreneur-led and manager-led nonprofits. During the crisis, entrepreneur-led nonprofits operated with a mean *deficit* of N$40,700. That same year, manager-led nonprofits had a mean *surplus* of N$134,900. Since countercyclical surpluses are an indication of risk-aversion (which encourages self-insurance through savings at times of high risk expectations), figure 5.4 lends further evidence in support of Young's (2006) hypothesis. Of course, higher surpluses in manager-led nonprofits could also be due to manager-led nonprofits being

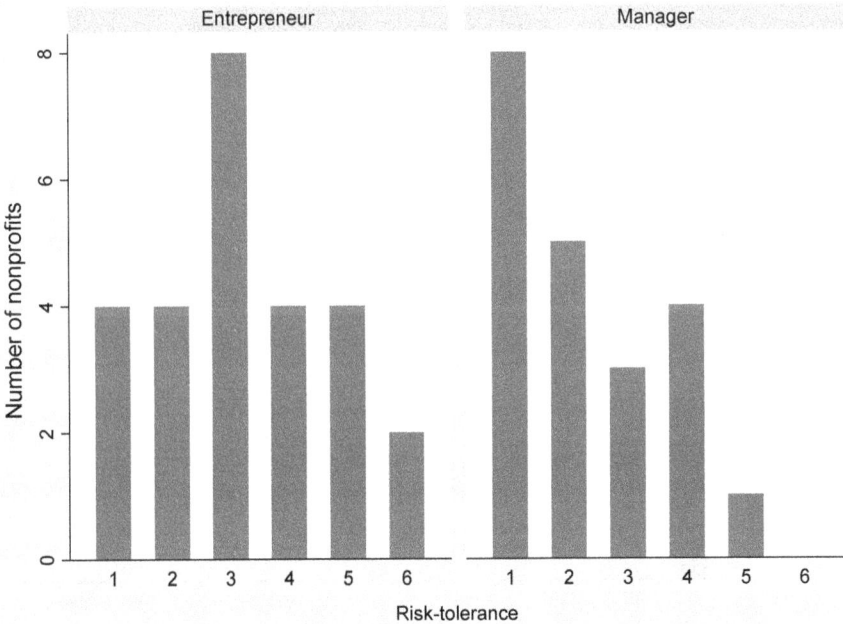

Figure 5.3. Risk tolerance by type of leader. Notes: Based on author's survey of forty-seven nonprof-its. Risk-tolerance measure adapted from the Michigan University's Panel Study of Income Dynamics. While the study refers to this measure as "risk-aversion," higher levels correspond to lower risk-aversion and, to make it more readily understandable, it is referred to here as a risk-tolerance measure.

generally larger and older than entrepreneur-led nonprofits. The significantly higher spending associated with manager-led nonprofits is consistent with such a qualification. We need, therefore, further analysis to control for the potential impact of confounding influences.

Table 5.3 presents results of a statistical analysis of survey data. Due to the complexity of the data—involving both hierarchical and longitudinal effects—the analysis employs three different methods: (1) ordinary least squares regression; (2) Prais-Winsten regression with panel-corrected standard errors to maximize learning from the longitudinal nature of the data, while controlling for serial autocorrelation; and (3) hierarchical, "mixed-effects" models to examine the influence of clustered data and to account for the influence of variables that vary at the organization level, such as age, and those that vary at the national level, such as GDP per capita (see, e.g., Musick and Wilson 2008 on the justification for the use of hierarchical methods to analyze multi-level datasets).

The outcome variable in all models in table 5.3 is organizational surplus as a proportion of total spending (i.e., surplus/expenditure). Defining surplus as a proportion of spending generates a measure of surplus that is independent from organizational size.

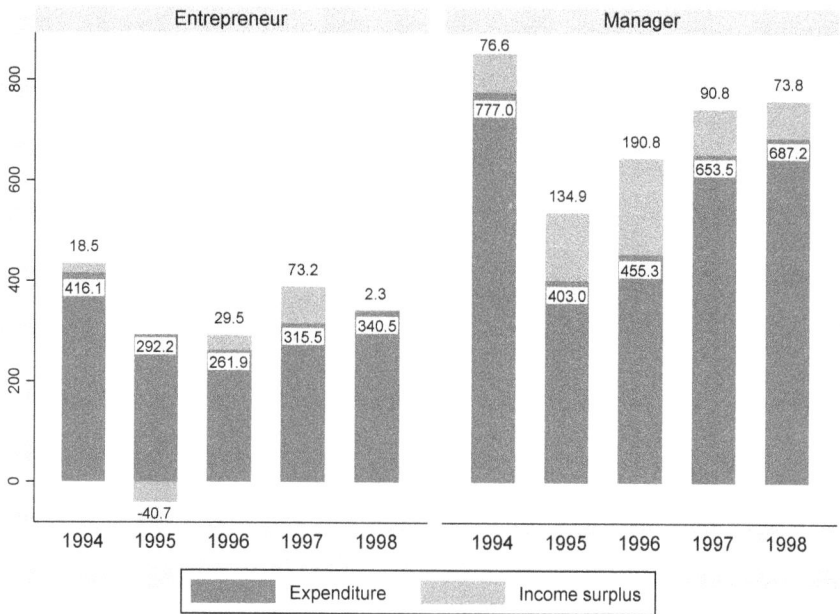

Figure 5.4. Spending and surplus by type of nonprofit leader, 1994–1998. Notes: Based on author's survey of forty-seven nonprofits. Figures in thousands of nuevos pesos.

In all models, manager-led nonprofits tend to generate higher surpluses than entrepreneur-led nonprofits. This is the case even when other potential causes of higher surpluses, such as age and revenue, are included in the analysis. In fact, the inclusion of several controls does not significantly change the estimated effects, although the coefficient does not reach statistical significance in one of the models. Longitudinal and hierarchical methods produce similar findings. Level of economic development has an inverse, strong, and statistically significant association with the size of organizational surplus. This means that nonprofits tend to increase their surplus when the economy declines. This is counterintuitive but consistent with both theoretical predictions based on the influence of risk (see chapter 2). Of course, we must interpret this finding within the context from which the sample was taken and not extrapolate it to mean that the poorer a country is, the higher the surplus its nonprofits will generate.

At the same time, once leadership type is included, organizational age does not seem to have a significant effect on organizational surplus. All models indicate very small effects, which reach statistical significance in only one of the models. Organizational size measured in terms of total revenue has a positive effect on organizational surplus, and the effect reaches statistical significance in one longitudinal and both hierarchical models. Dependence on commercial fees has a strong, direct relationship with organizational surplus. This affirms the argument made in previous research that commercial revenue is associated with lower financial vulnerability within nonprofits (Tuckman and Chang 1991; Keating et al. 2005). Resource dependence on philanthropic giving, on the other hand, does not seem to have a systematic relationship with organizational surplus. This finding is somewhat surprising and inconsistent with theoretical predictions that, in risky environments, donors pressure nonprofits to spend their contributions within a short time period. This result could be due to entrepreneurs and board members often making significant philanthropic contributions to build their organizations' capital base. Unfortunately, I was unable to test this new hypothesis, which I must leave for future research. Organizational size based on the total number of employees has an inverse association with organizational surplus, while the number of volunteers relates directly to organizational surplus. Both relationships reach statistical significance in all models. Because paid staff are typically nonprofits' more significant fixed cost, it is not surprising that organizations with more employees (i.e., with a higher proportion of labor costs) tend to have lower surpluses. In contrast, volunteers help nonprofits generate surpluses. This is not surprising since volunteers are also typically cash and in-kind donors (e.g., Center on Philanthropy at Indiana University 2002) and help keep labor costs low.

Evidence from survey data, therefore, highlights the importance of nonprofit leaders' attitudes toward risk in determining how their organizations responded to changes in the riskiness of their environment. Differences in risk-aversion between entrepreneurs and managers, which are consistent with Young's (2006) hypothesis, can explain the apparent puzzle of widespread countercyclical budget surpluses. Risk-aversion in leaders, and arguably supporters as well, has a profound influence over how nonprofits

Table 5.3. Regression analysis of survey results

	1	2	3	4	5	6	7
Method	OLS	OLS	Hierarchical Mixed	Hierarchical Mixed	Mixed	Prais-Winsten	Prais-Winsten
Manager dummy	.198***	.178**	.178**	.165	.162#	.210***	.159***
	(.071)	(.087)	(.087)	(.137)	(.100)	(.056)	(.044)
Ln(GDP per capita)	-1.633**	-1.696**	-1.696**	-1.170*	-1.482**		-1.064***
	(.798)	(.822)	(.811)	(.683)	(.646)		(.619)
Organizational Age		.000	.000	-.006	-.003	.003	-.010**
		(.006)	(.006)	(.010)	(.007)	(.002)	(.003)
Ln(Revenue)		.021	.021	.279***	.367***	.012	.383***
		(.035)	(.035)	(.054)	(.049)	(.011)	(.029)
Dependence Fees				.668***	.581***		.466***
				(.211)	(.203)		(.059)
Dependence Philanthropy				.188	.145		-.017
				(.155)	(.148)		(.081)
Employees				-.027***	-.032***		-.032***
				(.003)	(.003)		(.002)
Volunteers					.044***		.047***
					(.007)		(.005)

	(1)	(2)	(3)	(4)	(5)	(6)	(7)
Year 1994						-.051** (.021)	-.121*** (.020)
Year 1995						.258*** (.022)	.242*** (.022)
Year 1996						.203*** (.018)	.027 (.024)
Year 1997						.166*** (.012)	.051** (.021)
Intercept/Fixed effects	15.525** (7.030)	15.962** (7.207)	15.962** (7.116)	10.314* (5.937)	12.464** (5.634)	.934*** (.075)	
Random Effs. intercept			-3.884 (15.175)	-1.131*** (.186)	-1.593*** (.205)		
Sigma epsilon			-.674*** (.055)	-.973*** (.059)	-.988*** (.056)		
Adjusted-R²	.046	.048					
N.	208	208	208	208	208	208	208

Notes: Dependent variable is organizational surplus as a proportion of total spending (i.e., Revenue/Expenditure). Standard errors reported between parentheses under unstandardized coefficients. ***p<.oı; **p<.o5; *p<.05; #p<.15 (two-tailed).

responded to the Tequila Crisis and ensuring recovery. Broader lessons from the survey of Mexican nonprofits are discussed at the end of this chapter. Before that, the next sections examine the representativeness of both case study and survey evidence by examining sector-level data in Mexico as well as findings from previous research in several other countries.

Nonprofit Registration

The Mexican Center for Philanthropy (CEMEFI) has gathered a fairly comprehensive quantitative dataset on the Mexican nonprofit sector. As of 2006, the dataset included 10,791 nonprofits. Its records refer essentially to organizations that have been legally registered and thus possess a minimum level of human and financial resources to comply with the registration process.[9] The dataset provides important insights into variation in startup activity within the nonprofit sector since it includes data on when nonprofits were registered.

Figure 5.5 shows the remarkable relationship between annual variation in GDP and annual variation in the number of nonprofits created between 1982 and 2003 ($r = 0.700$, $p < 0.001$).[10] These correlations are equally strong if only cyclical (detrended) data are used.[11] Aside from the vertiginous economic decline during the Tequila Crisis, the data also include the different troughs of the 1980s' debt crisis and the recession of the early 2000s, spanning therefore multiple economic cycles. Visual inspection shows that economic crises (1983, 1986, 1988, 1995, 2001) always led to decreases in nonprofit startup activity, and, conversely, periods of economic boom tended to lead to an increase in nonprofit startups. Typical determinants of nonprofit registration activity such as legal registration requirements, tax regime, or even political cycles cannot account for the wide variation shown here. It is therefore difficult to conceive of alternative hypotheses for this remarkable overlapping pattern between the economic and nonprofit sector startup cycles.

These data suggest that the number of nonprofits grows faster in times of economic growth and grows much more slowly during recessions. Current nonprofit sector theory is unable to account for this remarkable finding. Unfortunately, complementary data on organizational deaths were impossible to obtain. The lack of data on organizational deaths or inactivity is common in most nonprofit sector research, and its implications in light of this study's findings are discussed in the conclusion. Nevertheless, it seems reasonable to expect that nonprofit deaths and inactivity are more common during economic crises, when resource availability declines sharply and the probability of insolvency rises proportionally. In that case, we should expect the number of active nonprofits to be even more procyclical than the available data on the number of nonprofit startups suggest, with deeper nadirs in times of economic crises and higher peaks in times of economic prosperity.

The risk theory suggests that high-risk periods such as the Tequila Crisis should have a weakening impact on the sector's long-term development. To examine this

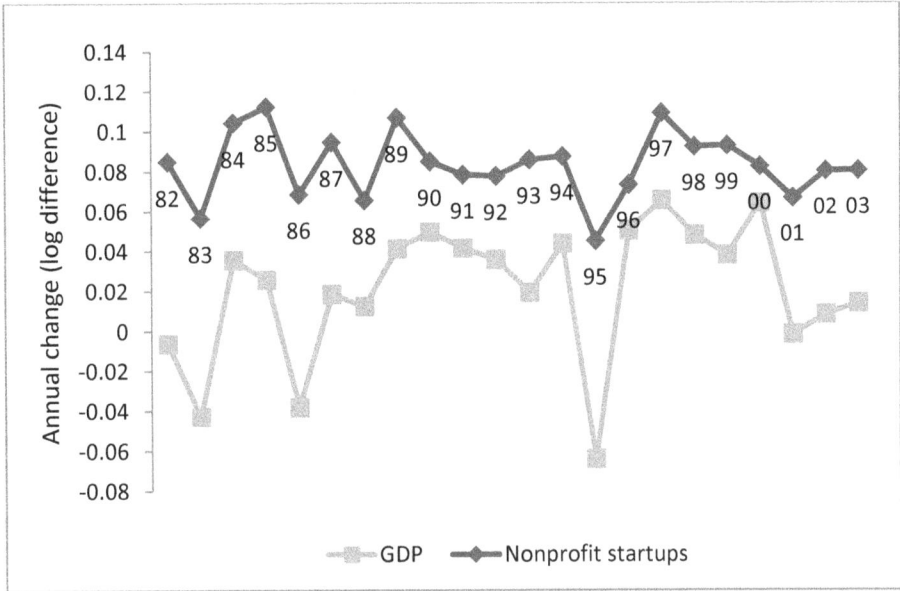

Figure 5.5. Annual change in GDP and nonprofit startups, 1982–2003. Note: Based on author's analysis of nonprofit registration data from CEMEFI and GDP data from World Bank's World Development Indicators dataset.

hypothesis empirically, I adapted a methodology developed by Cerra and Saxena (2008) for the examination of the response of output growth to economic crises.

Figure 5.6 displays the long-term trend and actual annual growth in the number of nonprofits between 1985 and 2003, based on CEMEFI's registration dataset. Taking the peak year as the starting point of our analysis (1994), the trend line extends the average annual growth rate of nine pre-peak years (1985–1993) into nine post-peak years to the end of the period (1995–2003).[12] This long-term trend represents a projection of the pre-crisis trend, suggesting the most probable trend over the whole period had the Tequila Crisis not taken place (our hypothetical "counterfactual"). This trend line can then be compared with actual growth rates after the peak year.

This analysis shows that the Tequila Crisis had a significant effect on the long-term evolution of the Mexican nonprofit sector. Before the crisis, the total number of non-profits was growing at 8.74% per year. After the crisis, growth rate trend fell to 7.13%. In 1995, around 59% fewer nonprofits were created than their long-term trend suggested. Despite a marked improvement, the continuing lower rate of growth between 1996 and 2003 contributed to a widening of the gap between actual and long-term (projected) growth rate. By 2003, this gap meant that there were around 5,600 (or 34%) fewer

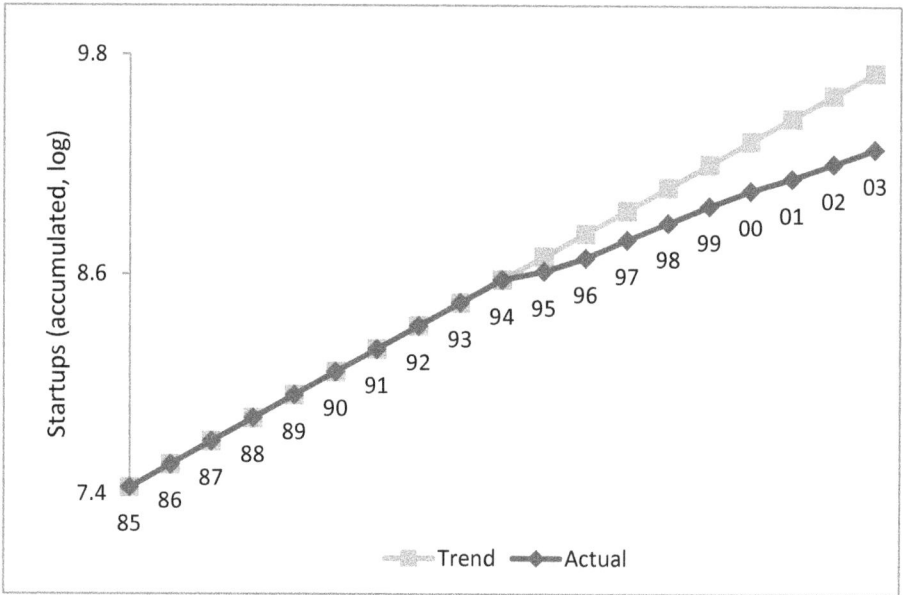

Figure 5.6. Trend and actual growth in the number of nonprofits, 1985–2003. Note: Based on author's analysis of nonprofit organizations' registration data from CEMEFI.

nonprofits than projected by the long-term trend. As noted earlier, available quantitative data do not include organizational deaths, and therefore it is reasonable to assume that, since economic crises probably increase organizational death rate, the real impact of the Tequila Crisis and economic instability more generally is likely to be even more pronounced than that shown on figure 5.6.

A nationwide survey of nonprofit leaders undertaken in 1998 is consistent with a pattern of long-term weakness. Three years after the crisis, the survey revealed that "almost 80 percent of those surveyed knew of some [nonprofit] organization that had ceased to operate within the last year for lack of financing" (Verduzco and Reveles 2001:10). Similarly, results of my own survey indicate a long-term weakening effect as discussed above.

While other factors may have contributed to the long-term deceleration in nonprofit startups, this fact is consistent with the risk approach, which suggests that high risk reduces the present value of future nonprofit impacts, discouraging social support for the sector. On the other hand, as risk falls after the crisis, social support for the sector should rise again. A return to a pre-shock level of nonprofit sector strength, however, is hindered by the persistence of risk expectations among supporters and, in this case, entrepreneurs. Risk may also depress the startup rate because not only does it increase the risk of failure, it also increases the level of investment in capital, fundraising capacity, and funding diversification that is necessary to avoid failure. In other words, it increases the costs of the entry into the sector, which should reduce the startup rate.

Analysis of main stated purpose across nonprofits founded in different periods is also consistent with the risk framework's predictions. Thirty-one (41.3%) of the seventy-five organizations created in 1995 had an explicit assistencialist focus (*asistencia social*), such as fighting hunger and poverty. Of the remaining nonprofits, three focused on sports and culture, nine on human rights, fifteen on social development, five on education and research, two on environmental protection, and eight on health. By contrast, only twenty-one nonprofits (22%) of the ninety-five nonprofits created in 1994 had a social welfare stated purpose. Of the remaining nonprofits, five focused on sports and culture, eighteen on human rights, nineteen on social development, ten on education and research, six on environmental protection, and seven on health. Moreover, only thirty nonprofits (20.4%) of the 147 nonprofits created in 1998 had a social welfare orientation. Of the remaining nonprofits, five focused on sports and culture, twenty-eight on human rights, twenty-six on social development, ten on education and research, five on environmental protection, and twenty-one on health.[13] Of note, the case studies suggest that the actual shift toward more emergency and short-term assistentialist programs within the sector is probably even more dramatic than nonprofit registration data indicate. Despite having long-term stated purposes such as social development, environmental conservation, and human rights, all of the case studies increased their focus on short-term programs during and immediately after the crisis.

Evidence on Civic Engagement

Complementing data on resources and startups, a final area for the examination of hypotheses about the impact of risk on the nonprofit sector is nonprofit activity. Such data is rarely collected in a systematic fashion, because of the great diversity of nonprofit sector activities (see Anheier 2004). Luckily, two datasets on civic engagement in Mexico during the 1990s provide key insights into how startups and resources were actually translated into activities, offering another angle on the influence of economic volatility and risk on the nonprofit sector.

The first dataset was compiled by the Mexican government's National Ecology Institute (Instituto Nacional de Ecologia) on the prevalence of water-related protests between 1990 and 2001. The data were collected through content analysis of national and local newspapers, which found five thousand references to such protests during the period. It includes a wide variety of actions, from peaceful demonstrations and sit-ins to the violent bombing of water wells and taking over of the mayor's building.

Analysis of water-related protest activity (figure 5.7) suggests a procyclical pattern. After a period of growth in the early 1990s, the decline in nonprofit advocacy activity during the Tequila Crisis is striking. The decline is proceeded by another period of strong activity (1997–1999) in line with the growth phase in the macroeconomic cycle.

The correlation with the economic cycle here is weaker than the previous correlation with the number of nonprofit startups. Nonetheless, water-related protests have a positive and statistically significant correlation with variation in GDP over time ($r = .427$, $p < .1$) in line with a procyclical argument. It is plausible that this unexpected pattern is partly caused by the weakening of nonprofit capacity and possible friction between potential participants' preferences for urgent problems during times of crisis and more long-term water-related goals. While many water protests may relate to urgent problems, others may target more long-term issues. The risk approach would suggest that the latter would be particularly vulnerable during periods of heighted economic risk. Clearly, an alternative explanation for this pattern might suggest that a reduction in water scarcity due to changes in rainfall caused the reduction in protests during the crisis. This is unlikely however, since data from the National Climatic Data Center of the United States Department of Commerce show that in 1995 Mexico had average rainfall but experienced one of the hottest years on record. That year, temperatures reached maximum levels greatly above average, with 61.3% of days when the daily maximum temperature was above the 90th percentile; much hotter than years with more protest activity as in 1993 with 35.5%, 1997 with 29.0%, and 1998 with 45.2%.[14]

It is worth noting that the dissonant slowdown of protests in 1999 and 2000 is probably due to changes in the political system. The year 2000 was marked by what is commonly described as the first truly free presidential election in Mexico's history. Not surprisingly therefore, intense political campaigns marked 1999 and 2000. It is possible that political activity was focused on the national presidential campaigns during this period, rather than much more localized water-related protests. The data also lend some support to the claim that severe crises, such as the Tequila Crisis in 1995, can lead to an immediate decrease as well as a slow recovery in nonprofit activity (1996 and 1997) despite a rapid macroeconomic recovery.

Data on individual-level participation in advocacy events offer an opportunity for triangulation of event-level protest data. Moreover, a better test of the philanthropic friction hypothesis needs data both on actual philanthropy and on donors' intention to give. Friction results from the inability of donors to find appropriate recipients and vice versa. Such data are difficult to gather. Fortunately, data collected through the World Values Survey provides an approximation. The survey regularly asks respondents about their civic participation as well as their intention to participate in civic events.[15] Comparing data from the Second and Third Waves of the survey for Mexico, the proportion of respondents saying that they attended demonstrations fell sharply from 22.0% in 1990, a year of strong economic growth, to 11.5% during the crisis in 1995. Similar reductions took place in most other forms of civic participation such as signing a petition and participating in a boycott. If the "market" for civic participation were frictionless, we should probably conclude that the reduction in participation in demonstrations was due to a fall in Mexicans' interest in politics. The same survey data, however, suggest that this is not the case. The fall in political activity took place despite the fact that

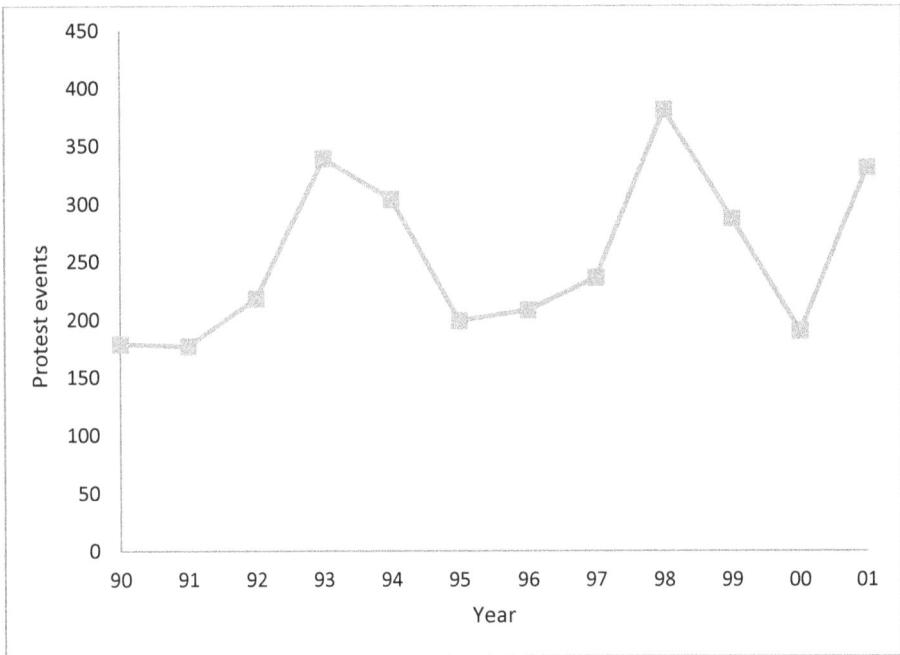

Figure 5.7. Evolution of water-related protest activity, 1990–2001. Note: Based on author's analysis of data from the Instituto Nacional de Ecología, a Mexican government agency.

interest in politics rose between 1990 and 1995. Those who said they were "very" or "somewhat" interested in politics rose from 38.9% in 1990 to 44.6% in 1996. Indeed, in 1996, 71.2% of respondents thought giving people more say in politics is an "important" or "very important" national goal. Even more intriguingly, while the number of respondents who participated in a demonstration fell sharply, the number of those saying that they *might* attend a demonstration—an indicator of willingness to participate—actually increased from 43.2% to 47.1% between 1990 and 1996. At the same time, there is a decline of individuals saying they signed a petition, from 34.7% in 1990 to 31.7% in 1996, despite a growth in the number of those saying that they might sign one, from 43.2% to 48.0%. The rise in the number of those willing to participate combined with the fall in the number of those who actually participated suggests a decreasing "action-intention ratio," that is, the proportion of actual participants ("action") divided by the proportion of those willing to participate ("intention"). In relation to participation in demonstrations the action-intention ratio was approximately 50%. In 1996, the ratio had fallen to 24%. As the economy recovered it rose again, reaching 36% by 2000 (data are available only for 1990, 1996, and 2000). The case studies suggest that this may be caused by friction between rapidly changing volunteer participant preferences and slower-adapting nonprofits, which prevented nonprofits from taking advantage of the growing social grievances during the crisis, as indicated by increased willingness to participate in demonstrations and other forms of protest. El Barzón's ability to build on this willingness to participate was key to its success during this period.

In sum, analysis of available data on different dimensions of nonprofit resources and activity reflects some of the great diversity within the nonprofit sector. The variation in resources and activity levels is, in absolute terms, quite remarkable: one year may witness more than twice as many nonprofits being created as the previous year. Advocacy events may fall by over 30% from one year to the next. Philanthropic giving fell by almost three-quarters in just one year! The data clearly suggest that variation in different indicators is positively correlated and generally consistent with fluctuations in economic activity. It also suggests that nonprofits, such as El Barzón, were able to draw strength from rising social discontent, which is countercyclical, as indicated by data on the intention to participate in civic events. This may help explain the apparent disagreement between the procyclical pattern identified here and other studies that suggest that social movement activity and citizen participation intensified during the Tequila Crisis, most of which focus at least partly on the case of El Barzón.[16]

The qualitative and quantitative evidence assembled in this study lends strong support to the argument that risk, which accompanied the profound changes in Mexico's economy during this period, has influenced the evolution of the Mexican nonprofit sector in both short and long terms. These independent datasets provide a multifaceted perspective on the Mexican nonprofit sector. Given their measurement imperfections and the multiple influences on any form of nonprofit activity, the possibility that such independent indicators might be correlated would be surprising. For example, many water-related protests may be undertaken by ephemeral citizen groups, which would not be counted in CEMEFI's nonprofit registry because they never establish a formal structure. Analysis reveals, however, a surprisingly high consistency over time among data from the different datasets. Years of strong advocacy activity such as 1994 tended to also display at the same time a sharp rise in the number of new nonprofits and nonprofit revenue. Of course, the correlations among these nonprofit sector measures are far from perfect. No single indicator can capture all nonprofit forms with perfect fidelity. Indeed, we probably would not want to, and that is why I analyze them separately above. Before drawing further conclusions, the next section examines comparative evidence on the relationship between economic risk, philanthropy, and the nonprofit sector.

Comparative Evidence

How generalizable is the analysis of nonprofit sector evolution in Mexico presented here? Cross-national statistical data examined in chapter 3 show that, rather than being a puzzling outlier, Mexico fits closely within the U-shaped PKC pattern. At this point, however, available statistical data on the nonprofit sector do not permit an evaluation of the representativeness of the Mexican nonprofit sector's evolution *over time*, and specifically of the influence of economic risk. This section seeks to answer the question of generalizability by examining data on how the nonprofit sector responded to macroeconomic risk and crises in other middle-income countries—namely Thailand, Argentina, and Chile—as well as in several rich countries, including the United States.

United States

Tornell, Westermann, and Martínez. (2003:90) argue that "economic fluctuations in Mexico since 1980 are closer in magnitude to those of the 1930s and 1940s in the United States than they are to what we in [the United States] now call the business cycle." The historical experience of the American nonprofit sector during the Great Depression, therefore, offers a valuable comparison to Mexico's recent experience. The Great Depression, which hit the American and later most of the global economy from 1929 to 1933, remains "the worst economic disaster of modern history" (Ferguson 2008:9). The combination of feverish growth during the "Roaring '20s" and ill-advised policy led to a dramatic economic contraction (Krugman 2008). The Dow Jones Industrial average fell from a high of 381 in the fall of 1929 to 90 in November of 1933; by January 1940 it remained at 151, less than half of its 1920s peak. The unemployment rate rose from under 5% in 1929 to almost 25% in 1933, and by 1940 it remained at just under 15% (Shlaes 2007). As a proportion of nonagricultural labor, unemployment increased from 5.3% to a staggering 37.6% in 1933 (Hammack 2003:265). Concerns about unemployment were so great that the government forced or encouraged migration of hundreds of thousands of Mexican Americans to Mexico, in an effort that is often referred to as the "Mexican Repatriation" (Hoffman 1974). Marked suffering across the country, in both urban and rural areas, created the political support needed for President Roosevelt's New Deal, which lay the groundwork for the American welfare state (e.g., Rauchway 2008). Its global impact also cannot be overestimated. "The Great Depression came close to destroying both capitalism and democracy, and led more or less directly to war" (Krugman 2008:15).

How did the nonprofit sector fare during this period? Unfortunately, systematic research on this question is still limited. A few accounts highlight the sector's resilience and critical contributions at a time of widespread government and market failure (e.g., Beito 2000; Skocpol 2002; Rauchway 2008). At the same time, as many nonprofits faced increasing financial difficulties (Smith and Lipsky 1993; Hammack 2001), the Great Depression highlighted the limitations of a purely philanthropic response to social protection (Salamon 1993; Grønbjerg 2001). For David Hammack (2003:268), the "Great Depression posed a challenge that proved far too great for American philanthropy."

Estimates by the Center on Philanthropy at Indiana University (2009:3) show that annual itemized giving by individuals fell 35% between 1929 and 1934 (from US$5.1 billion to US$3.5 billion, inflation adjusted). As in the Tequila Crisis, philanthropic giving continued to decline during the first year of the economic recovery, 1934. Giving returned to pre-crisis levels only by 1937, after four years of economic recovery. The 1938 recession brought another decline in giving, but this time by only 6%. This analysis is consistent with Colin Burke's (2001) analysis of total giving as a proportion of national income based on data from the *Historical Statistics of the United States*. His analysis shows that giving as a proportion of the economy fell by over 20% between 1929 and 1934 (Burke 2001:186, figure 10). Giving recovered as the economy recovered in the mid-1930s, but it declined again during the 1938 recession.

Robert Putnam (2000) offers a different perspective on the impact of the Great Depression on the nonprofit sector. He collected data on the average membership rate in thirty-two national voluntary associations between 1900 and 1997. For Putnam (2000:54, 192), the

> sharp dip [in the 1930s] in this generally rising line of civic involvement [during the first half of the twentieth century] is evidence of the traumatic impact of the Great Depression on American communities. The membership records of virtually every adult organization in this sample bear the scars of that period. In some cases the effect was a brief pause in ebullient growth, but in others the reversal was extraordinary. . . . [F]inancial worries and economic troubles have a profoundly depressing effect on social involvement, both formal and informal.

Putnam's data show that by 1933 membership levels had fallen to 1921 levels. As the economy recovered in the mid-1930s, membership began to rise again. This pattern is repeated in membership levels of Parents and Teachers Associations (p. 57) and eight national professional associations (p. 84). Similarly, Theda Skocpol (2003:69) finds that "the 1930s were stressful for many . . . voluntary associations, because economic times were so hard for the working and middleclass men and women who paid dues to them. Most voluntary federations experienced membership downturns during the Great Depression, sometimes very sharp declines. But most also revived along with the economy in the late 1930s." This evidence lends strong support to the hypothesis of procyclical support.

More recent data on American nonprofits' income also lend support to procyclicality in philanthropic giving. According to Center on Philanthropy at Indiana University (2002:57):

> In eight years of recession between 1971 and 2000, the growth rate for individual giving averaged 6.7 percent (−1.4 percent adjusted for inflation). In years of economic expansion, individual giving grew at an average annual rate of 8.5 percent (3.9 percent adjusted for inflation). . . . Individual giving is closely tied to the economy. More than any other factors tested by Giving USA using economic models, personal income and stock market are the best predictors of individual giving in recession, crisis, or a combination of the two.

Likewise, during the recession in 2001, inflation-adjusted giving by individuals dropped 1.7%, giving by bequest dropped 7.1%, and giving by companies dropped 14.5%.

These falls took place despite the major giving effort to the victims of the 9/11 attacks (Center on Philanthropy at Indiana University 2002).

The most recent downturn, often referred to as "the Great Recession," also had a powerful impact on philanthropic giving. According to Center on Philanthropy at Indiana University (2010) estimates, between 2007 and 2009, total philanthropic giving fell 5.5% in constant dollars. This was the second steepest decline in giving in over fifty years and at least since the organization's reports began in 1956. All types of giving declined during this period. Individual giving declined 5.7%, bequests declined 1%, foundation giving declined 7.2%, and corporate giving declined 4.3%.

Consistent with the risk framework's predictions, the recession had a different impact on nonprofits in different fields. The poor economic environment "particularly affected charitable recipients that otherwise receive contributions for new buildings, endowment campaigns, and long-term planning. These include education, arts, foundations, and freestanding donor-advised funds (which are part of public-society benefit). The types of charities that showed estimated growth typically provide immediate services, such as human services, health, international aid, and even environment" (Center on Philanthropy at Indiana University 2010:1). Indeed, against this dire general background, giving to human services rose an estimated 2.7% adjusted for inflation, which "seems to reflect efforts that donors made to continue emergency aid services as an increasing number of people suffered from the continuing recession" (2). This very recent evidence lends strong support for the risk perspective.

Some evidence suggests that government funding to nonprofits in the United States has been procyclical. Nonprofit Finance Fund (NFF) research suggests that government financial support to the nonprofit sector is procyclical, even in the context of the United States' acyclical fiscal policy (see Alesina and Tabellini 2005)! Based on 990 form data from a random sample of 6,585 mid-sized nonprofits (with financial expenses between $500,000 and $20 million), the study found that a greater proportion of "organizations that are entirely supported by government feel the pinch during challenging economic times than those with even 10% of funding from another source" (NFF 2008:1).

As a result of declining philanthropy and public funding, the NFF study also suggests that total nonprofit revenue is procyclical. Based on an evaluation of income from all sources, nonprofit revenue growth fell in 2001 and 2002, as the economy stagnated, and recovered in subsequent years as the economy improved. "Over 40 percent of the nonprofits reported a deficit in 2001, as well as in the two years immediately thereafter" (NFF 2008:2).

Turning to the long-term impacts of risk, the long-term weakening hypothesis suggests that countries beset by high economic volatility will have a weaker nonprofit sector, other things being equal, than countries benefiting from a stable economic environment. Historical evidence on the American nonprofit sector is generally consistent with this hypothesis. Putnam's (2000) research shows that, while the American economy was growing again from 1933 and GDP had recovered to its pre-crisis level by 1936, pre-crisis membership levels were not reached again until 1943. Moreover, a visual examination of Putnam's (2000:54, figure 8) evidence is consistent with the long-term weakening impact by showing that, despite exponential growth during the 1940s, membership rates never regained their 1920s pre-crisis growth trend. This is also true of the 1909 economic crisis. Despite formidable growth during the 1910s and 1920s, membership rates never regained their early 1900–1908 growth rate. More recently, NFF's data support a longer-term weakening effect, as the "number of nonprofits that suffered deficits grew by 20 percent in fiscal year 2001, and had not returned to 2000 levels by 2005" (NFF 2008, 2).

The unprecedented level of economic stability in the United States and other OECD countries since the 1950s (e.g., Krugman 2008) has probably been a main driver of growth in their nonprofit sectors. Indeed, as discussed below, analysis of a sample of rich countries shows that the level of economic instability between 1880 and 2000 is strongly associated with nonprofit sector and social capital weakness today. Overall, evidence from economic instability in the United States lends support to the debilitating impact of economic risk and volatility.

Thailand

Despite the fact that Mexico has a comparatively weak nonprofit sector, limited available evidence in this area indicates that the patterns described in this chapter should not be confined to Mexico. There are clear parallels between the impact of the Tequila Crisis on the Mexican nonprofit sector and the impact of the East Asian crisis on the nonprofit sector of Thailand, another middle-income country. The East Asian crisis began in Thailand in mid-1997 and spread to Indonesia, South Korea, Malaysia, and the Philippines, with devastating consequences to these countries. Like the Tequila Crisis before it, the East Asian crisis seems to have caught most people by surprise (Radelet and Sachs 1998; Krugman 2008), hitting many of the countries that had previously been known as "the Asian Tigers."

While the impact of the crisis on Thailand's government and businesses has been widely discussed, there has been almost no attention to the corresponding impact on the nonprofit sector. One exception, Preecha Dechalert (2003), provides a vivid depiction of Thailand's collapsing economy on its nonprofit sector. Dechalert's research indicates that nonprofit activity in Thailand was also procyclical in the 1990s, rising rapidly in the early 1990s due to a strong economic boom, contracting abruptly during the crisis, and eventually returning to a growth pattern as the economy recovered. To survive, however, most nonprofits had to transform their operations over the course of the macroeconomic cycle. During the crisis most nonprofits reduced their staff and activity level to match available resources; tried to diversify their funding base, often turning to "cash cow" and commercial enterprises to attract new funding; and changed their activities and sometimes even their mission to accommodate the interests of the only remaining international donor agencies. Nonprofits relying on international funding managed to steer through the crisis in much better shape than those relying solely on a domestic resource base. During the crisis, most government agencies terminated their contracts with local nonprofits just as local philanthropy dried up. One of the Thai nonprofits Dechalert examined was able to turn the crisis into an opportunity. It drew the public's attention to the rapidly deteriorating welfare of children during the crisis, which resulted in an increase in philanthropic donations (many from international companies working in Thailand) for the cause in 1998, as the economy began to recover.

In the long term, many nonprofits were ultimately unable to survive the economic shock, suggesting that, like its Mexican counterpart, the Thai nonprofit sector may have been weakened by the crisis. In a different study, Gary Suwannarat (2003:5) finds that the impact of the crisis on nonprofit finances led to widespread capacity erosion, so that by the early 2000s the nonprofit sector in Thailand was weaker than before the crisis in 1997. He suggests that a general lack of trust in the nonprofit sector has been hindering its recovery. "A recent survey by the King Prajadhipok Institute confirms the low opinion society holds of [nonprofits], ranking them at the low end of the spectrum just above the police and media" (Suwannarat 2003:11). The nonprofit sector in Thailand, thus, must strengthen public understanding of nonprofits and their roles in society and increase their accountability to supporters and the communities with whom they work (Pongsapich 1997; Suwannarat 2003).

Research on the nonprofit sector in Thailand displays startling similarities to the Mexican story described in this book. Unfortunately, the lack of sector-level evidence on Thailand, as well as developing countries more generally, limits the opportunities for further exploration of this intriguing comparison at this point.

Mexico, Argentina, and select OECD countries since 1880

Even in rich and relatively stable countries, nonprofit sector evidence is highly consistent with the risk perspective developed here and the evolution of the Mexican nonprofit sector. The Great Depression, East Asian crisis, and Tequila Crisis are, fortunately, rare events. Is there any comparative evidence that, as in the case of Mexico, broader economic instability can influence the long-term evolution of the nonprofit sector? To generate a comprehensive and fair comparison of economic volatility levels between rich and developing countries, I compiled economic recession data on several OECD countries from 1880 until 2000. The data are from previous studies (namely, Aiolfi et al. 2007; Bergman et al. 1999; IMF 2002, ch. 3). Because most countries for which we have accurate data are rich countries, Argentina was added as a Latin American control case that is in many ways similar to Mexico. By looking back 120 years, the analysis seeks to avoid a potential economic development bias. Today, rich countries are generally much more stable than Mexico, which weakens comparisons based solely on recent data. However, a few decades ago rich countries were much more unstable, facing a level of economic volatility more characteristic of poorer countries today. Comparative data on nonprofit sector strength are from the CNP dataset (e.g., Salamon et al. 1999, 2004) and social trust data from the fifth wave of the World Values Survey (2006).

Figure 5.8 displays the relationship between nonprofit sector strength, measured as total (paid and volunteer) employment as a proportion of the labor force, and economic instability, measured as an index of crisis frequency and maximum crisis depth, obtained though principal component analysis (see chapter 3). This method reflects the fact that the impact of economic instability is proportional to the intensity of major crises, such as the Tequila Crisis, and the frequency of economic downturns, both of which, following the arguments in this book, should lead to considerable long-term damage to the nonprofit sector. Each variable was also analyzed separately as reported below.[17]

Figure 5.8 clearly shows that countries that have historically faced greater economic instability, such as Mexico, Italy, Argentina, and Japan, have a weaker nonprofit sector than those with more stable economies, lending support for the hypothesis that economic instability leads to long-term underinvestment and nonprofit sector weakness. The correlation between economic instability and nonprofit sector size is strong and negative ($r = -.62$, $p < .01$). Nonprofit volunteering and income are also negatively associated with economic instability (respectively, $r = -.89$, $p < .001$, and $r = -.37$, insignificant at $p < .1$). The correlation between nonprofit sector size and maximum loss over the period, or crisis depth, is strong and negative ($r = -.66$, $p < .01$), while the correlation between nonprofit sector size and crisis frequency is less strong ($r = -.41$, $p < .1$). This suggests that instability characterized by few severe economic crises can mark long-term nonprofit sector development more profoundly than volatility from frequent shallow downturns. These observations also suggest that economic instability is closely associated with weaker nonprofit sector within the sample.

To test the sensitivity of these results to the operationalization of "nonprofit sector size," I examine the relationship between economic instability and social trust, a key element of civicness and social capital (e.g., Putman 2000; Norris 2003). These data produce a very strong and inverse correlation between economic instability and social trust ($r = -.90$, $p < .001$). Social trust is also strongly and inversely associated with crisis frequency ($r = -.80$, $p < .001$) and maximum depth ($r = -.58$, $p < .1$).

This evidence provides support for the hypothesis that, in the long term, economic instability leads to nonprofit sector weakening. More research on the relationship between economic stability and nonprofit sector development could examine the validity of this claim in different contexts to generate a more nuanced analysis. For example, are there any exceptions to the general pattern; that is, can economically unstable countries produce a strong nonprofit sector? Does economic stability have equal relevance for the development of different nonprofit sector dimensions, as the risk perspective suggests? Unfortunately, lack of historical data on economic instability forbade the inclusion of poor countries. Future research must systematically examine the impact of economic instability while controlling for other possible influences and using larger samples. Nevertheless, the comparative analysis presented here is surprisingly robust. By including mostly rich countries, the sample included natural controls for several key social and political development variables.[18] The inclusion of Mexico and Argentina

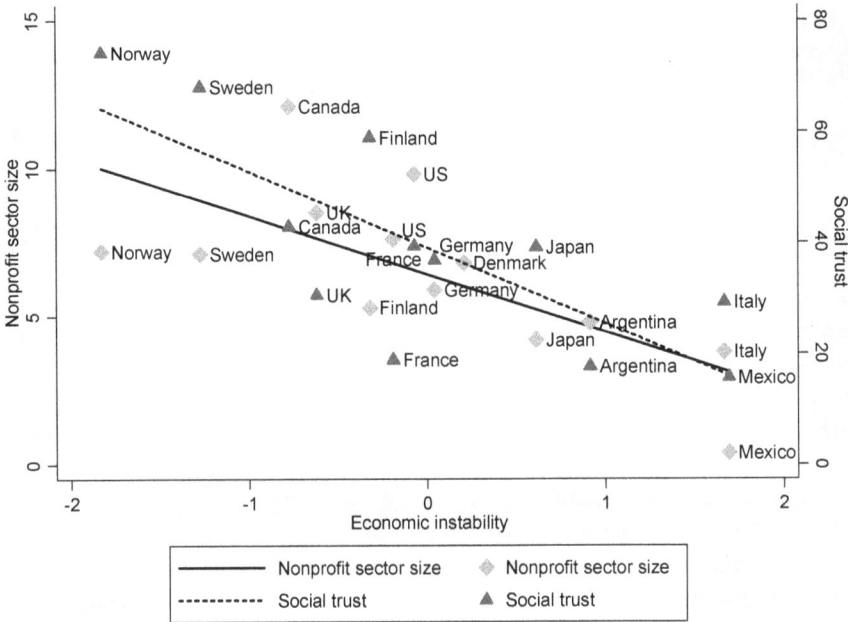

Figure 5.8. Nonprofit sector size, social trust, and economic instability, 1880–2000. Notes: Based on author's analysis of nonprofit data from the Johns Hopkins CNP dataset, social trust data from the Fifth Wave of the World Values Survey (2004–2006), and economic instability data from Aiolfi et al. (2007); Bergman et al. (1999); and IMF (2002). Nonprofit sector size measured as total nonprofit employment as a percentage of labor force (Salamon et al. 2004).

increases confidence in the comparison between rich and middle-income countries. Moreover, the consistency between results based on nonprofit sector size and social trust data from two independent datasets demonstrates that these results are not due to a single indicator's caprices. Taken together, these findings suggest a strong influence of economic instability on nonprofit sector strength in the long term.

To be sure, nonprofit sector development is subject to many other influences. As figure 5.8 depicts, economic instability alone cannot explain differences in nonprofit sector strength between Canada and the United Kingdom, for example, because both sectors have experienced roughly the same level of economic instability, yet the Canadian nonprofit sector is considerably larger. Likewise, economic instability cannot explain the different levels of nonprofit sector size and social trust between Mexico and Italy, because both countries have had a similar level of exposure to economic instability, yet Italy has considerably higher levels of social trust and nonprofit sector size. Indeed, the case of Chile suggests policy can alleviate the depressing influence of economic risk on the nonprofit sector, as discussed below.

Chile as an Example of "Bridging across the PKC"

Nonprofit sector theory would predict that Mexico and Chile should have a similar level of nonprofit sector strength. Like Mexico, Chile is a Latin American, middle-income country with a history of dictatorship and recent democratization. Both countries also have similar levels of social and religious diversity. Yet, based on CNP data, total nonprofit sector employment as a proportion of the labor force is thirteen times larger in Chile than in Mexico! And volunteering as a proportion of the labor force is twenty-five times larger in Chile than in Mexico! Can the risk explanation account for this difference? At first, it would seem that it can't. Like the Mexican nonprofit sector, the Chilean nonprofit sector has experienced considerable macroeconomic volatility since 1960, which suggests that it should be considerably weaker than it is today, ceteris paribus.[19]

Further examination, however, reveals that the nonprofit sector in Chile displays a much lower level of vulnerability than in Mexico. Thus, the contrast between the Chilean and Mexican nonprofit sectors offers important lessons about the influence of risk. Because risk includes both exposure to potential shocks and vulnerability to those shocks, the nonprofit sector in Chile faces significantly less risk than in Mexico. The risk approach suggests that Chilean nonprofit sector resilience is due to three key factors. The first is its low level of resource concentration. While the Herfindahl index is equal to 0.596 in Mexico (the highest in the world) its value is only 0.347 in Chile. Resource concentration at the sector level in Chile is even lower than in the United States, which has a Herfindahl index of 0.362. The Chilean nonprofit sector's low level of resource concentration—a proxy for diversification—suggests that its exposure to idiosyncratic risk is significantly lower than that of the Mexican nonprofit sector.

The second factor underlying the lower level of vulnerability in Chile is its much higher level of government support when compared to Mexico. As Irarrázaval et al. (2006:32) found in their research into the nonprofit sector in Chile, "public sector subsidies and reimbursements constitute the primary revenue source, accounting for 46% of total revenues. This is twice as high as in developing countries (23%) and is in closer resemblance to European-style welfare partnership type countries (55%)." While the relationship between government and the nonprofit sector in Mexico rests on retrenchment and rhetorical partnership, in Chile the relationship rests on privatization and genuine partnership. The Chilean government policy aims

> to foster citizen participation in the design and assessment of social programs; the development and strengthening of the third sector and a permanent connection between the State and Civil Society, aside from generating a new style of relationship between the government and citizens, strengthening regional and local links in the promotion of citizen rights. . . . The principles underlying and fostering this national policy are based primarily on the recognition of diverse civil society expressions,

the incorporation of the concepts of citizen association and participation in the formulation of public policies and programs; the creation of a legal framework for the development of civil society; and technical and financial support for its organizations. (Irarrázaval et al. 2006:50)

The Chilean government's countercyclical fiscal policy (see Alesina and Tabellini 2005) should further contribute to its extraordinary nonprofit sector resilience. In the absence of international donor support, and since most nonprofit resources evolve procyclically, countercyclical government support offers an opportunity for beta risk hedging by combining procyclical and countercyclical revenue streams and, thus, limiting the impact of macroeconomic volatility. Given the general procyclical tendency for virtually all types of nonprofit resources identified here, countercyclical government support should greatly contribute to nonprofit sector resilience in the face of macroeconomic volatility.

The third factor is Chile's high level of volunteering and civic participation. Volunteer support is essential in helping to diversify the resource base and limit dependence on the government. Indeed, Chile has resisted the temptation to rely too heavily on government support, balancing it with a solid philanthropic base of giving and volunteering and some commercial revenue. This has been in part the result of an effort to avoid state control and appear as mere government agents (Irarrázaval et al. 2006). Interestingly, the Chilean nonprofit sector's resource dependence on commercial fees is one of the lowest in the world, receiving only 35% of its revenue from commercial transactions as compared to 85% in Mexico and 57% in the United States.

Chile aptly illustrates the possibility of "bridging across" the PKC (see figure 1.4). Despite its having experienced high levels of macroeconomic volatility like Mexico, significantly lower resource concentration in Chile's nonprofit sector translates into lower levels of economic risk, facilitating the development of a much stronger sector. The nonprofit sector does not have to suffer continuous erosion as the economy moves from poor to middle-income, risking being caught in a "risk trap" such as the one in which the Mexican nonprofit sector appears to find itself. Government support to the nonprofit sector is a main determinant of the sector's financial vulnerability and, therefore, size and sustainability.

Unfortunately, however, nonprofit sector strength and institutional quality are often mutually constitutive (see Putnam 2000). It is very likely that the supportive role of government in Chile has helped nonprofit sector development, and at the same time, a stronger nonprofit sector has helped promote a stronger and accountable government. In contrast, weak nonprofit sectors tend to coexist with weak and unaccountable governments. The fact that nonprofit sector strength is correlated with government support for the nonprofit sector, both as a proportion of GDP and as a percentage of total nonprofit revenue, lends some support to this conjecture. In such instances, international donors must play a leading role. I return to this and other policy implications in the next chapter.

Risk and Nonprofit Sector Evolution

In line with theoretical predictions, evidence on nonprofit sector evolution in Mexico presented in this and the previous chapter highlights two key impacts: the powerful influence of systematic risk on nonprofit activity and capacity, which leads to (pro)cyclicality in the short term, and the impact of broader risk on capacity erosion in the long term. At high levels of economic risk, capacity erosion may lead to a long-term "risk trap," which severely limits opportunities for nonprofit sector growth while risk remains high. Comparative evidence from the United States, Thailand, Argentina, Chile, and various rich countries suggests that these findings may have much wider applicability. This section discusses each of these impacts in turn.

(Pro)cyclicality: The Powerful Influence of Systematic Risk

Systematic risk, which in this study manifested itself primarily in the cyclical variation of economic growth, exerted a profound influence on the Mexican nonprofit sector. As a systematic shock, the Tequila Crisis impacted all case studies and surveyed nonprofits. In line with the risk theory, most nonprofits suffered revenue declines and, consequently, cut spending and even staff, but some nonprofits dependent on international and commercial funding experienced less severe revenue declines, and a few, which were dedicated to urgent problems, actually expanded during the crisis. On the other hand, as the economy recovered and became more stable in the post-crisis period, revenue in most nonprofits improved considerably, even though the effects of the crisis continued to be felt into the late 1990s. By 1998, most surveyed nonprofits had not returned to their pre-crisis revenue level. By contrast, El Barzón and two surveyed organizations, which had grown during the crisis, experienced a sharp decline during the recovery period. As risk expectations declined and the urgent causes they focused on became less significant, their support declined accordingly. Only a small minority of nonprofits were able to grow consistently throughout the period (namely, Pronatura and two surveyed organizations).

These cases demonstrate the importance of moving beyond traditional financial vulnerability indicators to assessing beta risk as an essential step toward understanding nonprofit sector risk exposure. Beta risk, which is a common operationalization of systematic risk in finance, enables the assessment of whether the income source's uncertainties are correlated with the market or other macroeconomic risks. If so, then the resource has a high beta. If not, then the income source has a low beta. If the income source is negatively correlated to the economy, then it has a negative beta. Assuming the susceptibility of different resources remains largely constant over different economic cycles, beta risk can provide an invaluable indicator of nonprofit financial vulnerability. As an illustration, and based on the generic beta risks of different resources, which were estimated using survey evidence, in 1994 Biocenosis had a beta risk of 8.9, Fovaso had a beta of 7.8, and FIVA had a lower 2.9 beta risk. This organizational beta risk is obtained by multiplying the generic beta of each resource by the case study's resource dependence on that resource and adding the results, that is, their weighted average (see chapter 2). Based on their beta risk alone, all of these organizations should have revenues that were more volatile than the economy. During the crisis, Biocenosis should be the most affected, followed by Fovaso and FIVA, which indeed matches the actual experience. On the other hand, both Biocenosis and Fovaso should have benefited from their high beta risks during the recovery period. Indeed, in 1996 Biocenosis experienced a strong growth in revenue. The recovery did not last, however, as its financial dependence on government funding meant that the organization had no revenue when government unexpectedly did not renew the contract in 1997. This idiosyncratic shock illustrates the relevance of idiosyncratic risk, as discussed below. Fovaso also experienced a financial recovery, but as the economy recovered, philanthropic friction, due to its programmatic reorientation that alienated many previous donors and the inability to find a long-term sponsor for its new programs, led to a gradual deterioration in revenues. Compared to other cases, FIVA had much more stable finances during this period. Predictions based on beta risk would have been less accurate in relation to Pronatura's finances during the crisis, but the same beta risk is consistent with its rapid growth during the recovery period. The nonprofit had a beta of 6.8 in 1994, which is not consistent with its stable revenue during the crisis. This was primarily due to the organization being able to receive most international funding in dollars, which in 1995 had doubled in terms of the number of pesos they were worth. The exchange rate surplus and the jump in interest rates, which increased returns on its conservatively invested reserve fund, compensated for the abrupt decline in philanthropy and moderate decline in commercial funding the organization experienced in 1995 (both of which are consistent with generic beta risk assessments). Survey evidence on international funding suggests Pronatura's ability to benefit from currency exchange and interest gains was uncommon. In fact, among surveyed nonprofits average international funding declined in 1995. Centro and El Barzón similarly demonstrate that beta risk provides a useful initial indicator of financial vulnerability, but many factors will ultimately influence individual organizations' revenues. With a beta risk of 5.2 when the organization became independent, the initial shortfall in Centro's revenue in 1995 was consistent with a dependence on philanthropic giving and government funding. Its efforts to involve highly committed philanthropic sponsors and get the parents to pay fees, combined with significant volunteer labor by staff, enabled the organization to make up most of the shortfall and keep it operational until government funding became available again during the recovery in 1996. Its post-crisis growth is consistent with its beta risk. Its slight decline during the crisis is less so.

El Barzón offers an important cautionary tale. With a beta risk of 3.4 before the crisis, El Barzón should have experienced a decline in resource availability during the crisis. Its exponential growth during the crisis and decline during the recovery, however, suggests that the nonprofit actually had a countercyclical beta risk. The fact that none of the generic betas was negative suggests such countercyclical organizations might have been rare. Indeed, of the forty-seven nonprofits included in the sample only three were countercyclical. Since the beta calculation aims at finding mean values of resource responsiveness to the macroeconomic cycle, it will often fail to accurately describe resource vulnerability among outliers. Nevertheless, once El Barzón's organization-specific negative beta risk became clear, the subsequent forecast of a decline during the economic recovery would have accurately predicted the organization's resource mobilization risk after 1996. As a nonprofit focusing on an economic emergency, El Barzón's experience of rising support as risk increased is consistent with a shrinking "shadow of the future," which encourages attention to short-term issues and disregard for long-term ones. El Barzón was not the only case benefiting from risk-aversion and short-termist attitudes among existing and potential supporters. In fact, all case studies pursued commercialization and short-term programs that produced immediate or near-future benefits.

Beta risk generally provides invaluable insights into the level of financial vulnerability that different resource portfolios are likely to experience. Among the studied cases with a positive beta, the lower the beta risk the less financial distress nonprofits tended to experience during the crisis, suggesting that, as a major component of financial risk, beta risk is an essential element of a comprehensive financial risk assessment. Ideally, when an organization has a sufficiently long historical record, beta risk can also be calculated at the organizational level, probably generating more accurate predictions than beta risk calculated at the sector or field level. Without consideration of systematic or beta risk it is impossible to comprehend why spending procyclicality was pervasive despite the clear advantages of countercyclical spending for social impact and organizational capacity preservation (e.g., by not dismissing staff during downturn).

Indirectly, the influence of systematic risk on nonprofits is also evident in the fact that almost all Mexican nonprofits studied responded to raised risk by increasing commercial revenue after the crisis. To be sure, nonprofit commercialization is not a Mexican phenomenon. A vast literature has documented a similar tendency within in American nonprofits (e.g., Tuckman 1998; Weisbrod 1998; Young and Salamon 2002; Guo 2006). Nevertheless, close inspection of why the case studies turned to commercial revenue sources during and after the crisis, which this study permitted, shows a clear cause-effect relationship as predicted by the risk perspective. The case studies suggest that this was due primarily to how it contributed to reducing organizational vulnerability to systematic risk. Survey evidence on a random sample of Mexican nonprofits shows that commercial income has a lower sensitivity to systematic risk than either government or philanthropic giving. Commercial revenue is generally more resilient to economic risk, because the typical simultaneity between costs and benefits make it less vulnerable to risk discounting (see chapter 2). Commercial income may also contribute to diversification, thus reducing idiosyncratic risk. Past research, however, has not examined the relationship between commercial revenue and systematic risk. Increasing dependence on commercial income, therefore, will provide systematic risk hedging—another powerful driver for commercialization. Without this insight, it is hard to understand nonprofit efforts to adventure into new commercial enterprises at a time when markets were more depressed than they had been in decades!

These findings are consistent with empirical research in a much more stable environment (i.e., the United States) suggesting that dependence on commercial revenue increases financial resilience (Keating et al. 2005). But they also reveal *a new puzzle:* if commercial income increases nonprofit resilience, why does the highest level of nonprofit sector dependence on commercial income coincide with the smallest sector in the world? More generally, why do middle-income countries have the highest dependence on commercial income and weakest nonprofit sector? This puzzle can be answered by the fact that economic risk causes both nonprofit sector weakness and dependence on commercial fees among most surviving nonprofits. An explanation based on the impact of risk also highlights the limitations of commercial revenue in generating nonprofit sector development on its own. Mexican evidence suggests that, for example, commercial revenue may be more resilient to economic slumps, as indicated by its low beta risk, but this also means it will experience the lowest rate of growth during recoveries. Without access to philanthropy and government funding, therefore, nonprofits enjoy limited growth prospects.

Evidence on the impact of the Great Depression and more recent economic slumps, including the Great Recession, in the United States as well as on the impact of the East Asian crisis in the late 1990s generally affirms the conclusions from Mexican data that systematic risk has a powerful impact on the nonprofit sector, which, as a result, tends to be procyclical in terms of resource acquisition and level of activity.

The present effort to understand the impact of systematic risk will hopefully stimulate more research on beta risk in nonprofit finance in an effort to increase our understanding of how economic cycles impact different nonprofit resources. The relevance of systematic risk for nonprofit sector evolution has become even more obvious after the past decade, which displayed levels of macroeconomic volatility not seen since the Great Depression.

Adaptation Dilemmas and Long-Term Weakness

The previous analysis of Mexican nonprofit sector evolution since the 1990s raises larger questions about the impact of risk. Why were the case studies generally so vulnerable? Research on nonprofit finance has focused on proximate causes of vulnerability (e.g., resource concentration), commonly eschewing questions about its more fundamental causes (e.g., why resource concentration). Consistent with previous nonprofit finance research, other *proximate causes* of resource vulnerability, such as lack of a reserve fund, resource concentration, and low dependence on commercial revenue, were important in determining how different nonprofits fared during the study. The case studies demonstrate that, having made considerable personal commitments to their organizations, nonprofit leaders were tireless in their efforts to create a resilient and sustainable resource base. To adapt to their high-risk environment, nonprofits' leaders pursued several risk-management strategies, including variable and fixed cost-cutting, resource diversification, building of financial reserves, and programmatic and even mission change. Why then did some nonprofits apparently fail to reduce their vulnerability? Why didn't those same nonprofits build a reserve fund and diversify their resource base? To answer questions about *fundamental causes* of financial vulnerability, we need to focus on attitudes toward risk among leaders and supporters as well as the intimate relationship between risk and the ability of nonprofits to pursue risk-management strategies.

One of the paradoxes of risk is that *while higher levels of risk call for greater risk-management efforts, the options available for risk management are limited by higher levels of risk.* In particular, the analysis presented here suggests that economic shocks erode nonprofits' limited resource base, increase risk-aversion and discount rates among supporters and other economic agents, promote philanthropic friction, and encourage supporter distrust of nonprofits.

Economic shocks led to significant and persistent erosion of nonprofits' resource base: reserves were drawn down, human capital was eroded by staff dismissals and departures, and social capital was destroyed through philanthropic friction, intra-organizational conflict, and community dissatisfaction with nonprofits' responses. *These losses could not be easily reversed.* It takes only a moment to fire a good program officer, but it takes many years to hire and train another one. Loss of community trust and a bad reputation may never be fully repaired. Nonprofit sector capacity may take many years, and significant economic growth, to return to pre-crisis levels. Case study, survey, and startup data lent strong support to this long-term weakening effect of economic shocks, which helps to explain why a recession can have such a detrimental impact despite the fact that it is commonly surrounded by boom years.

The long-term erosion of organizational capacity depended greatly on the level of nonprofits' financial reserves. Larger reserves helped organizations avoid dismissals and preserve their physical and human capital investments. It also enabled nonprofits to limit programmatic changes, which can aggravate philanthropic friction in the long term. The risk perspective, however, sheds new light on the disadvantages of nonprofits holding financial reserves. In high-economic-risk environments, the present value of future nonprofit spending is heavily discounted, and therefore supporters may be generally unwilling to contribute to nonprofits' capital projects since most of such projects' impact is in the long term. Supporters' attitudes toward risk, which as the cross-national statistical evidence presented in chapter 3 shows is strongly associated with general macroeconomic conditions, play a critical role in nonprofits' ability to build their capital base and, consequently, reduce their vulnerability.

The fundraising literature often claims that donors typically prefer to contribute to operations rather than capital projects even in lower-risk environments such as the United States (see, e.g., Weinstein 2009). This can be partly explained by the risk approach and its emphasis on donors' discount rate. Furthermore, in economically volatile environments, philanthropic friction resulting from the different priorities of supporters and leaders may help undermine philanthropy, human capital, and social trust in nonprofits. Fovaso, FIVA, Centro, and, to a lesser extent, Pronatura displayed signs of philanthropic friction during the study. Their responses to the crisis contributed to alienating previous supporters and members of staff. Faced with a sudden rise in risk and often steep revenue decline, most nonprofits studied had to undertake profound changes in financing, organization, and work, which led to a profound transformation of their impact. As the economy and organizational resources picked up again, however, many of those changes were never reversed. Many strategic changes were more palatable to staff and supporters during the crisis, because most had few alternative income opportunities and they generally believed that many of the organizational changes adopted during the crisis would be eventually reversed when the economy recovered. As the economy picked up again in 1996, most strategic changes were not reversed, becoming implanted into the organizations' fabric, irretrievably changing their purpose. During an annual meeting of its key supporters, donors repeatedly mentioned how Fovaso had changed, how it was a different organization after the crisis. A different organization may need different donors. It is also telling that, with the exception of FIVA, all of these nonprofits had voluntary staff departures at a time of rapidly rising unemployment. Interviews with some of those who left their organizations invariably revealed discontent with the way leaders were responding to the crisis.

Even when organizations do not change permanently, to the extent that nonprofits adjust with a lag, they may be continuously maladjusted. Adaptation strategies should lead to better environmental fitness and sustainability. When the environment is constantly changing, however, past adaptations often become inappropriate for the current environment, forcing yet further adaptations. This process of continuous adaption drains significant organizational resources, potentially weakening efficiency and eroding the resource base needed for long-term sustainability. By promoting philanthropic friction and eroding the current support base, a continuous adaptation effort to a rapidly changing environment also undermines resource diversification and increases vulnerability to idiosyncratic shocks.

There is some evidence that Mexicans do not generally trust secular nonprofits. Michael Layton and colleagues at the Instituto Tecnológico Autónomo de México, a Mexican university, conducted one of the few surveys on Mexican philanthropy (ITAM 2005). They found that only 22% of participants had "a lot" or "much" trust in nonprofits in general, and 69% did not trust such organizations. Even among those with university education, 61% did not trust nonprofits! This means that in Mexico nonprofits are less trusted than any of the levels of government (federal, state, and local) and even large companies (28% had "a lot" or "much" trust, and 65% did not trust large companies). Interestingly, 76% of participants had "a lot" or "much" trust in the Red Cross fundraising campaign. Mexico is frequently afflicted by natural disasters such as earthquakes, hurricanes, and volcano eruptions. The Red Cross is generally at the forefront of humanitarian relief in such events, a fact that Mexican society has recognized. The low

levels of trust in the nonprofit sector and the exception of an emergency relief organization—the Red Cross—are consistent with the risk perspective.

Aside from limiting the options available for risk management, high-risk environments also regularly lead to common risk-management strategies backfiring and leading
to more, rather than less, risk exposure. The considerable challenges involved in building a dependable philanthropic base in high-risk environments encouraged nonprofit
leaders to find alternative ways to finance the needed capital base. According to survey
and case study data, increasing commercial revenue was the most popular option. This
study, however, suggests that commercial revenue can be a double-edged sword. A lower
beta risk means commercial revenue increases significantly less than philanthropy during good times. Because even the most volatile countries have historically had four good
years for every downturn year, dependence on commercial revenue could lead to significant opportunities being missed in boom years and to a weaker resource base in
the long term. Moreover, in line with previous research, commercial income seemed
to be frequently associated with a strategic reorientation away from the—commonly
loss-making—mission pursuit toward unrelated profit-making activities (see Weisbrod
1998; Young 2007). Commercialization, therefore, may increase nonprofit resilience but
decrease its relevance. In the long term, decreased relevance can compromise social
support for nonprofits' existence and fiscal benefits, as FIVA found out. Commercialization, therefore, can actually contribute to higher vulnerability, especially when it focuses
on services that are unrelated to nonprofits' social mission and when it is not complemented by other types of revenue as part of a diversified portfolio.

Diversification is another common risk-management strategy that can have perverse effects in a high-risk environment. Resource diversification is the commonly
recommended starting point for the reduction of financial risk in any organization.
Diversification is regularly described as "the only free lunch" in financial circles (e.g.,
Appel 2009). Yet, against a background of declining philanthropy and undependable
government funding, it is not surprising that case studies' efforts aimed at increasing resource diversification regularly failed, leaving nonprofits more vulnerable in the
end. This study, therefore, suggests that a *diversification dilemma* commonly plagues
nonprofits. While nonprofits need to diversify their resource base to reduce vulnerability to idiosyncratic shocks, their diversification attempts may absorb valuable
resources and leave them *more* vulnerable to idiosyncratic (and systematic) shocks.
The less correlated the target resource was in relation to existing resources, the greater
the diversification potential and, at the same time, the higher the risk of failure in the
diversification effort. The best example is international funding. Almost all case studies spent significant resources, including considerable leadership time, trying to access
international funding, but only one actually succeeded. Diversification efforts, therefore, must be seen as long-term investments that, if successful, increase the value of
a resource portfolio. Ironically, however, risk-averse supporters in high-risk environments are less likely to support such long-term investments because of their riskiness

and long-term orientation. Yet it is precisely in those environments that diversification is most needed!

The case studies also highlight the unpredictability of government support during high-risk periods. Government support was always erratic, but during the crisis and immediately following it government support became impossible to predict. To the extent that such erratic behavior increases resource predictability in government agencies and increases uncertainty in nonprofits, it constitutes a transfer of risk from the public to the nonprofit sector. The risk theory proposes that the impact of government funding on the risk nonprofits face will depend greatly on whether government agencies behave in a risk-neutral fashion, as some theoretical analyses claim, or risk-averse fashion. In line with several other studies, data on the cases studied here point to a rejection of theoretical claims about government's risk neutrality. Interviews with several government officials reveal that constrained resources during periods of high systematic risk and pressures by the electorate to show that government officials are "doing something" severely limit the incentives to fund nonprofits. Since nonprofits cannot generally enforce government funding contracts, government agencies reneged on their funding commitments with impunity.

Nevertheless, the case studies also point to the critical role of government support in helping to build a reserve fund. All organizations with a reserve fund, Fovaso, FIVA, and Pronatura, were able to build the fund through direct or indirect support from government. In the case of Fovaso and FIVA, the government complemented philanthropy through a matching formula. On the other hand, Pronatura greatly benefited from financing from a debt swap operation, which required high-level government approval and the financial capacity of rich members of the board.[20] Such opportunities, however, emerged from idiosyncratic conditions and personal relationships with government officials, which are not readily available to the majority of nonprofits. With limited access to support for capital expansion, Mexican nonprofits commonly had a very limited financial and physical capital base. For most nonprofits, the only route was the retention of surpluses from commercial revenue.

This analysis does not imply that economic shocks are devoid of opportunities. Case study, survey, and startup data suggest a few organizations are able to thrive in high-risk environments. Consistent with the risk perspective, those organizations tend to focus on programs with immediate, low-risk impact that attract emergency philanthropy or service fees, such as food banks and hospitals. The case of El Barzón suggests, furthermore, that organizations focusing on household risk-lowering impacts can also thrive in high-risk environments (though they may suffer when risk declines).

Lastly, nonprofit leaders' attitudes toward risk are a fundamental influence over how nonprofits respond to risk. Leader attitudes toward risk play a critical role in the ability of nonprofits to reduce their vulnerability by building nonprofits' capital base and investing in attempts to diversify their resource portfolio. Survey evidence suggests that leaders with lower risk-aversion were commonly at the helm of more vulnerable nonprofits. This is not surprising, as entrepreneurs commonly lead younger and smaller organizations, which with a smaller capital base than larger organizations typically are also more vulnerable. However, after controlling for potentially confounding influences such as organizational age and size, analysis of survey evidence found that entrepreneur-led nonprofits generated significantly less surplus revenue than their manager-led counterparts. Since surplus revenue is essential in building financial reserves, entrepreneur-led nonprofits tended to be less able to reduce vulnerability through financial reserves. Case study evidence also suggests that manager-led nonprofits produced a larger surplus than entrepreneur-led ones even when their revenue declined as in the case of Pronatura and FIVA. During the crisis, more risk-averse managers cut spending sharply to increase surpluses because risk expectations were highest at that point. Moreover, manager-led nonprofits were likely to have financial capital protection rules, which effectively tied managers' hands during the crisis. Both Pronatura and FIVA had rules requiring management to maintain the value of their financial reserve fund. Of course, since the board of directors had the power to release financial reserve funds in extreme cases, reserves still helped reduce the risk of bankruptcy during periods of revenue decline, but procyclical spending and countercyclical surpluses contributed to other types of capital erosion such as human and social capital erosion due to staff departures and reduced impact in the community. In the long term, however, conservatism seems to have paid off in Mexico's high-risk environment, as higher risk-aversion leaders helped build less vulnerable organizations.

Comparative evidence on the impact of the Great Depression, the East Asian crisis, and economic instability between 1880 and 2000 equally suggests that macroeconomic crises can have a long-term weakening effect on the nonprofit sector. Together with the Mexican experience, this comparative long-term evidence lends support to the PKC and the economic risk as a mechanism through which economic development impacts the sector.

The fact that exogenously determined economic instability has a powerful depressing impact on the sector in such different settings raises important concerns, especially given the recent increases in global economic volatility. Fortunately, the Chilean nonprofit sector and the Mexican case studies offer vital clues about a possible antidote to rising macroeconomic volatility. It is possible, however, that this "antidote" would be insufficient for the nonprofit sector in countries that, like Mexico, may be trapped by a combination of very high levels of economic risk and a very weak philanthropic base on which to build a nonprofit sector expansion.

The "Risk Trap"

The above discussion on the long-term impacts of risk exposure to economic volatility suggests the ensuing risk increases the costs of entry for new organizations and the resource base "critical mass" that is needed for long-term survival in the nonprofit sector. Nonprofit startup data show both a strong procyclical pattern and a reduction in the long-term startup rate after the Tequila Crisis. This is not surprising since, in line with the risk framework, a startup is generally a long-term investment that is likely to be heavily discounted in high-risk environments. Despite the fact that between 1996 and 2005 Mexico only faced a mild recession, several idiosyncratic shocks eventually led to the collapse of half of the case studies, which were vulnerable by their low capitalization and high resource concentration. A follow-up of the case studies in 2007 revealed that a total of three of six case studies—namely, Biocenosis, Fovaso, and FIVA—had collapsed in the decade following the crisis. In contrast, two of the three surviving case studies prospered after the Tequila Crisis. Centro was able to double the number of teachers it employs. Benefiting from weaker competition, Pronatura continued its spectacular growth. Its annual income grew from N$1.158 million[21] in 1990 to N$82.092 million[22] in 2005 (a nineteen-fold increase when measured in U.S. dollars). Income from international sources continued to play a key role in this expansion, remaining high at 53.4% of total income in 2005. El Barzón remains active, but it is a pale shadow of what it was during its peak immediately after the crisis.

While some organizational mortality should be expected, this ratio vastly exceeds mortality patterns of nonprofit organizations in more stable economies. Wolfgang Bielefeld (1994), for example, found that 20% of the organizations in a panel of nonprofits in the Minneapolis–St. Paul metropolitan area ceased operations between 1980 and 1988. Similarly, using 1989–2003 data on 290,000 public charities in the United States, Harrison and Laincz (2008) found that annual exit rates across different years and sectors oscillated between 1 and 3%. As shown above, the random survey of forty-seven nonprofits is consistent with the large organizational mortality rate experienced by the case studies. The disbanding of Fovaso and FIVA was surprising since before the crisis both organizations had a large reserve fund, and, while Fovaso had a diversified resource base, FIVA benefited from commercial revenue with good operating margins. Careful study of their post-crisis evolution shows how higher systematic risk levels can contribute to higher levels of idiosyncratic risk by increasing philanthropic friction and hindering diversification efforts.

At the macro-level, cross-national evidence presented in chapter 3 pointed toward a potential "risk trap" for the nonprofit sector in countries with high levels of nonprofit exposure to economic risk such as Peru, Romania, Slovakia, and, of course, Mexico. As figure 3.4 (chapter 3) shows, at low levels of economic risk even small rises in risk can cause large declines in philanthropy and nonprofit sector size. At high levels of economic risk, even significant reductions in risk bring about only small increases in nonprofit sector strength. Evidence on nonprofit sector evolution helps to explain this surprising cross-national pattern. A fragile sector in a high-risk environment is in a weak position to make the long-term investments involved in creating new organizations, expanding philanthropy and other nonprofit resources, and building sufficient resilience to ensure sustainability. Economic volatility, an uncooperative government, high risk-aversion attitudes and resource concentration, and low levels of social trust are likely to coincide with political and social instability to limit nonprofit sector growth opportunities and effectively create a risk trap for the sector. This "perfect storm" is more likely in middle-income countries, which are currently undergoing profound economic, political, and social transitions, than in rich or poor countries. On the other hand, nonprofit exposure to economic risk actually has its most powerful impact in low-risk countries. Even marginal increases in risk seem to be associated with steep reductions in nonprofit sector strength. As risk increases, the sector loses vulnerable organizations and keeps resilient ones—through a process akin to "natural selection"—so that further increases in nonprofit risk have progressively smaller depressing effects on the sector.

The risk trap is consistent with the PKC. Economic growth has its weakest marginal impact on nonprofit sector strength around the PKC's nadir, because at middle-range levels of economic development the economic risk faced by the nonprofit sector is near its highest levels. Following the PKC, as economic development passes the curve's nadir it should generate decreases in economic risk and continued increases in prosperity, both of which should promote nonprofit sector development slowly at first and then more sharply as economic development continues. Economic development, therefore, may also bring about the conditions needed for the nonprofit sector to exit the risk trap. However, to the extent that economic development does not fully determine the level of risk faced by the nonprofit sector, risk levels may remain high and the nonprofit sector trapped even as economic development proceeds apace. The story becomes more complex when we introduce the impact of the nonprofit sector on economic development, which this study has shown to be significant (chapter 3). The risk trap may be very persistent, because limiting nonprofit sector development also limits economic development and, in turn, limits reductions in macroeconomic risk. Interrupting this vicious cycle may require policy intervention, as discussed in the next chapter.

This analysis provides a sobering perspective on the prospects for nonprofit sector development in middle-income countries. Nevertheless, counterexamples, namely Centro and Pronatura at the micro-level and Chile at the macro-level, indicate that building nonprofit resilience is possible. The challenges are enormous. But awareness about the challenges is the first step toward overcoming them.

At the micro-level, one conclusion is foregone. Study of Mexican nonprofits during this risky period shows that there are no easy answers to working and surviving in high-risk environments. If there were a simple strategy nonprofits could follow to reduce their vulnerability and, consequently, risk exposure, most of them would have pursued it. Nevertheless, in the conclusion I examine several strategies that enabled nonprofits to overcome some of these challenges and build resilience in a risky environment. I also make the argument that government or international donor support is vital in helping the nonprofit sector exit the risk trap.

6 Nonprofit Sector in Crisis

*Broader Implications and Strategies
for Risk Management*

How and why does nonprofit sector strength vary across nations and over time? This book identified and developed an explanation for the puzzling U-shaped relationship between nonprofit sector strength and economic development—the philanthropic Kuznets curve—which defies nonprofit sector theories proposing a linear relationship between economic development and nonprofit sector strength. Based on the intuition that historically high levels of economic instability could be a main cause of nonprofit sector weakness in middle-income countries, I began an investigation into the relationship between the nonprofit sector and economic risk. In stark contrast with research on business and public sectors, however, research on the influence of risk on the nonprofit sector remains surprisingly limited. This book revisits the relationship, developing a new theoretical framework for the study of the nonprofit sector based on finance and game theory principles. I developed a framework suggesting that the relationship between economic development and nonprofit sector strength is mediated by risk. Simply put, the framework argues that risk generally depresses social support to the nonprofit sector and weakens nonprofit sector capacity by leading to an increase in the rate with which contributors discount future nonprofit impact. The more distant the impact is likely to be, the more heavily it will be discounted. Risk should thus attenuate most incentives for philanthropy, increase "philanthropic friction," and encourage government agencies to shift risk to nonprofit organizations. Risk should also weaken sector capacity by eroding existing financial, human, and social capital and discouraging startups and new capacity development. At the same time, rising risk should stimulate some nonprofit sector activities, most notably in short-term emergency relief, risk-sharing associations, and commercially funded organizations, in addition to providing a competitive advantage to the most resilient nonprofit organizations. Thus, risk should have a profound influence on the nature and size of the nonprofit sector.

Using cross-national and longitudinal evidence, the study examines the level of consistency between the theoretical hypotheses and nonprofit sector data. Tough questions could be raised about each of the types of evidence used in this analysis, but overall, the diverse set of independent quantitative and qualitative measures of both philanthropy and the nonprofit sector in Mexico and other nations suggests strong support for the framework.

The PKC can be explained by a combination of influences. At low levels, economic development commonly leads to increases in systematic risk, risk-aversion in the culture, and nonprofit sector exposure to idiosyncratic risk. At high levels, this process is reversed, so that economic development leads to decreases in systematic risk, risk-aversion, and nonprofit sector idiosyncratic risk. This contradictory influence helps explain why philanthropy and the nonprofit sector are weakest in middle-income countries and why various measures of nonprofit sector strength and economic development display a nonlinear, U-shaped relationship.

Attention to the influence of risk generates a more nuanced understanding of the impact of economic development on the nonprofit sector. Previous research has examined the influence of economic development through changes in household income, welfare provision, and modernization, among others. Attention to risk suggests the need to also include effects of resource volatility, financial vulnerability, and expectations about the future. Risk also has an influence on the nonprofit sector that is independent from economic development: even among countries with similar levels of economic development, riskier environments lead to lower philanthropy and a weaker nonprofit sector.

Thus, theoretical and empirical analyses lend support to the argument that *risk unlocks some of the nonprofit sector's most essential traits: its size, resource composition, relationship with supporters, and even time horizon.* Moreover, risk is an important mechanism through which economic development influences nonprofit sector strength and is a key explanation for the PKC puzzle.

How can we explain why business and government continue to grow at low levels of economic development, while the nonprofit sector actually weakens? Risk, of course, affects all sectors. While a full assessment of the impact of risk on other sectors is beyond the scope of this book, I would argue that differences in the three sectors' access to capital markets offer a plausible explanation. Nonprofits cannot, like government, externalize risk to taxpayers or, like businesses, sell risk to shareholders. With clear ownership rights and the ability to distribute profits, businesses exchange capital investments for "shares" in potential future profits or losses (i.e., risk). Nonprofits' limited access to capital markets, combined in most cases with considerable obstacles to capital accumulation from, for example, supporters' preferences for immediate impacts, makes the nonprofit sector more vulnerable to economic risk than government or business. That is why, as the PKC illustrates, at low levels of economic development, volatility and risk increase, resulting in weakening philanthropy and the nonprofit sector. Meanwhile the less vulnerable government and business are able to expand. At high levels of economic development, volatility and risk decrease, leading to a strengthening of all three sectors. The nonprofit sector, therefore, has a unique relationship with risk, and that relationship helps determine the sector's evolution over time.

Of note, the risk framework also helps explain several puzzles at the micro-level: Why nonprofits often run countercyclical surpluses, even though procyclical surpluses would increase organizational impact. Why supporters commonly refuse to support capital projects during recessions even though the opportunity cost of capital is at its lowest. Why, in the case of Mexico, volunteering was procyclical even though the opportunity of cost of labor is procyclical. Risk helps explain why, even in the United States, government funding to nonprofits tends to be procyclical, even though social needs are countercyclical. Lastly, risk highlights the inadequacy of international donor efforts to help "build civil society" in developing countries, which seem to assume a linear relationship between level of economic development and nonprofit sector strength, phasing out support to nonprofits in middle-income countries just when they are likely to be most financially vulnerable.

Before discussing this study's broader implications, a caveat is necessary. Currently available data limit the empirical test of the PKC in important ways. The first major limitation is that the number of countries for which we have an accurate measure of philanthropy and nonprofit sector size is relatively small (i.e., forty) given the complexity of the statistical tests involved. I addressed this limitation by examining the robustness of the PKC using social trust and civic participation data from a different cross-national dataset, the World Values Survey (WVS), which includes twice as many countries (see figure 1.3). Nevertheless, while analysis of WVS data is broadly consistent with the main analysis, WVS data do not directly measure nonprofit sector weakness. The second major limitation is the absence of cross-national longitudinal data on the nonprofit sector. For the moment, the PKC can only be established using cross-sectional data. In terms of assessing the PKC's causes, cross-sectional tests limit our ability to address potential omitted variable and simultaneity biases. To mitigate the impact of this serious limitation, I employed robust econometric methods designed to minimize potential biases in cross-sectional analysis, namely 2SLS and 3SLS (see chapter 3). However, as a "snapshot," cross-sectional data cannot fully evaluate hypotheses about the impact of dynamic variables, such as the process of economic development. In an effort to further mitigate the limitations from lack of longitudinal data, the book presents a quantitative and qualitative analysis of how the Mexican nonprofit sector changed over time, illustrating the intimate relationship between economic development, risk, and nonprofit sector strength (chapters 4 and 5).

Broader Implications

Following the focus on how economic development and concomitant variation in economic risk influences the nonprofit sector, this section considers broader implications. How do economic development and risk influence the social impact of the nonprofit sector? The theoretical and empirical strands in this book encourage a reassessment of the nonprofit sector's roles in three areas: democratization, social welfare, and economic development.

One of the most important corollaries of the PKC is that the *relationship between the nonprofit sector and other direct correlates of economic development will generally fit a nonlinear, typically U-shaped, curve.* For example, since poor countries are also commonly those with the lowest levels of democracy, the relationship between nonprofit sector and political development is also nonlinear and equally surprising. Indeed, the empirical relationship between nonprofit sector size (measured as total employment) and democracy level (as measured by the Polity IV index) adopts a quadratic, U-shaped curve. This implies that the nonprofit sector may be weaker in countries with intermediate levels of democracy, which are typically middle-income countries, than in autocracies, which are typically poor countries. The same U-shaped relationship can be found in the case of other nonprofit sector correlates such as civic participation and social trust. This study demonstrates that this surprising relationship is partly due to the influence of economic development and risk, suggesting caution before researchers claim that autocracy can strengthen civil society. These rarely studied relationships clearly illustrate the potential value of lessons from the emerging field of cross-national nonprofit sector research.

The consequences for the strength and nature of democracy in developing countries are staggering. The PKC suggests that, as in Mexico, even as middle-income countries democratize they generally have a weak nonprofit sector, which, in turn, is associated with low levels of social trust, citizen participation, and satisfaction with democracy (see Paras and Coleman 2006; Layton 2009). High levels of dissatisfaction and civic malaise may endanger middle-income countries' incipient democratization process and lead many citizens to long for their autocratic past. This has been a common pattern in third-wave democracies in Latin America and Central and Eastern Europe (Seligson and Booth 2009; Sztompka 1999). Even when democratization proceeds unabated, the fact that the nonprofit sector is weakest during a time of great political and economic transition means that emergent political and economic institutions will have little, and potentially biased, nonprofit sector input. This is a major problem if the nonprofit sector is an important vehicle for the participation of socially excluded groups. The relationship between the PKC and other major political and social transformations is, therefore, critical but, unfortunately, cannot be explored here. This is an important area for future research as thus far the vast literature on democratization has neglected the nonlinear relationship between nonprofit sector, civil society, and democracy. Increasing awareness of the PKC should encourage new studies on the implications of a nonlinear relationship between nonprofit sector and economic development for democratization, especially among autocracies and young democracies.

The PKC and its risk explanation also have important implications for social welfare. Given the central role of risk in social welfare, we must ask who should be involved in risk management (Quiggin 2007). Increasing recognition of government's shortfalls and "failures" has encouraged a general trend toward the privatization of social risk, which Hacker (2006) called "the great risk shift." This trend means that the nonprofit sector, and all private agents more generally, has an increasingly central role in social protection. Most research extols the virtues of the nonprofit sector's involvement in the social welfare system both independently and in partnership with the government. It generally advocates that a public-private, mixed or plural, social welfare system should be more efficient, resilient, and democratic than the traditional government-centered system (Salamon 1987; Smith and Lipsky 1993; Clark 1991). In theory, the nonprofit sector can increase efficiency of the social welfare system by helping to alleviate government failures (e.g., Weisbrod 1988; Salamon 1987). For example, by encouraging philanthropy, the nonprofit sector fosters voluntary income transfers between rich and poor without the negative welfare consequences of a taxation system based on coerced extraction and bureaucratized distribution (Tanzi 2000). Philanthropy increases individual utility by generating "warm glow" among givers (Rose-Ackerman 1996; Andreoni 1990), while forced income transfer through taxation reduces utility. Philanthropy also instills a deeper and more active sense of responsibility among donors, who will tend to be more actively involved in helping recipients compared to taxpayers (Shapiro 2007:278). Moreover, less burdened by bureaucracy, nonprofit organizations are typically more adaptable, innovative, and responsive to local needs (Young and Salamon 2002; Dollery and Wallis 2004). As Vito Tanzi (2000:74) argues, "Institutionalized income transfers have obvious negative efficiency implications even in a democratic political system . . . Furthermore institutionalized income transfers often require substantial administrative resources which may introduce a large wedge between what taxpayers give and what the beneficiaries receive." Lastly, free from the electoral cycle, nonprofit organizations can add stability and consistency to the social welfare system (see Salamon 1987; Dollery and Wallis 2004).

This analysis, however, is one-sided. Analysis of the nonprofit sector's role in social protection and risk management must be complemented by an evaluation of how risk itself affects the nonprofit sector. Notwithstanding the static advantages of philanthropy over taxation, this study's empirical analysis of philanthropy dynamics over the macroeconomic cycle in a high-risk country lends support to the argument that countercyclical "free riding" and "philanthropic insufficiency" greatly limit the sector's social protection impact (see Salamon 1987). The efficiency of public-private partnerships depends largely on the ability of private organizations to manage risk transferred from government (OECD 2008). In countries where government spending is procyclical—as is common in developing countries—nonprofit activity tends to be lowest when social needs are highest and resources for social protection are least abundant due to government and market failure, and it tends to be highest when social needs are weakest and resources for social protection are most abundant. By focusing efforts when they are least needed, nonprofit procyclicality significantly reduces efficiency as compared to a more constant or countercyclical pattern. Analysis of Mexican nonprofit sector data presented in this study suggests three reasons why nonprofit spending is procyclical. The first is that nonprofit resources tend to have positive beta risks and some resources, such as philanthropic giving, are several times more volatile than national output. Procyclical revenues encourage procyclical spending. The second reason is that nonprofits generally do not have a reserve fund sufficiently large to finance a sustained deficit spending during recessions. Countercyclical spending requires spending cuts during booms, but, in the face of significant community needs, many nonprofit leaders are reluctant to accumulate reserves at any time. Third, higher risk-aversion among managers means that the largest and richest nonprofits, which tend to be led by managers as opposed to entrepreneurs, typically behave in a risk-averse manner, generating precautionary surpluses during the crisis to boost reserves against future contingencies. In the examples I examined, as the economy improved, they decreased their surpluses. Such countercyclical surpluses are rational from the perspective of organizational survival in a risky environment, but they reduce nonprofit efficiency.

These trends suggest that, during the period of study, nonprofit involvement in the welfare system increased overall system volatility[1] by adding spending during booms and cuts during recessions. The nature of this impact, however, depends on whether government and household welfare spending is procyclical, acyclical, or countercyclical. This analysis does not seek to diminish the valuable contribution of nonprofits during recessions and recoveries. It simply suggests that a temporal rearrangement of nonprofit sector spending would likely produce significant efficiency gains and that policies should be enacted to help offset nonprofit procyclicality in order to build nonprofit risk-coping capabilities.[2] Later in this chapter, I examine candidate policies and strategies that should help reduce the nonprofit sector's procyclicality.

The relationship with economic development is another main reason for the renewed interest in civil society, and the nonprofit sector within it. This book demonstrates that *the relationship between the nonprofit sector and economic development can be interpreted causally, and causation runs both ways*. Variation in level of economic development causes variation in nonprofit sector strength and vice versa. At the same time, however, while economic development may lead to the strengthening or weakening of the nonprofit sector at different levels of economic development (i.e., the PKC), the evidence presented here suggests that nonprofit sector strengthening always leads to economic development. Several reasons may account for the positive impact of nonprofit sector strength on economic development. Aside from the nonprofit sector directly contributing to the economy, so that increased nonprofit sector production directly corresponds to increased national production, there is accumulating evidence that the nonprofit sector contributes to social capital, which, in turn, leads to economic development. For example, Putnam (1993) shows that historically social capital has led to economic development in Italy. Sztompka (1999) associates the economic decline of Poland post-1989 with a generalized decline in social capital and the economic growth in the mid-1990s with rising social capital. Knack and Keefer (1997) examine cross-national evidence and control for potential endogeneity between social capital and economic development. They conclude that social capital is indeed a significant determinant of economic growth in both policy and statistical senses.

Social capital, however, remains a highly elusive policy target (Knack and Keefer 1997; Putnam and Grossman 2002). The evidence presented here supports a direct role for philanthropy and the nonprofit sector in promoting economic development, providing a more concrete option for policy aimed at promoting economic development in the long term. By fostering philanthropic giving, volunteering, and nonprofit sector employment, policymakers should also encourage broader economic development. The reverse, however, is not always true. At low levels, economic development is accompanied by rising economic risk, which weakens the nonprofit sector. While available evidence suggests that high levels of economic development are accompanied by falling risk, it is possible that even in rich countries certain economic development processes increase economic risk, potentially leading to decline in nonprofit sector strength. At a minimum, therefore, policymakers must remain vigilant to ensure that economic development does not hurt philanthropy and the nonprofit sector and to create compensatory measures when it does. If policymakers focus on the economy at the expense of the nonprofit sector, gains in the economic front may be partly offset by losses in the nonprofit sector and its subsequent detrimental effect on the economy and welfare. As the previous two chapters document, this is precisely what appears to have happened in Mexico in the 1990s.

The cross-national evidence presented here suggests that the development of a vibrant nonprofit sector underlies much of rich countries' political and economic success. Yet, this book's most general evidence suggests pessimism for middle-income countries. As economic risk rises, philanthropy and nonprofit sector employment tend to decline. These tendencies, in turn, weaken the prospects for democratization and economic development. At the same time, the PKC also suggests that, in the long term, economic development should lead to nonprofit sector strengthening in part by reducing macroeconomic risk. The recent increase in global macroeconomic risk, however, indicates that economic development does not always lead to macroeconomic risk reductions as is commonly assumed (see, e.g., Acemoglu 2009). If this is the case, and economic risk continues to rise in the future, many middle-income countries such as Mexico may stay stuck in a risk trap caused by the mutually reinforcing relationships between stagnant economic development, high risk, and a weak nonprofit sector. Even in rich countries, the nonprofit sector may continue to experience the pressures it experienced during the last decade. Historical evidence on philanthropic giving in the United States is broadly consistent with this prediction. Following a decline in the 1970s, giving as a proportion of GDP remained constant during the 1980s and recovered in the 1990s, finally surpassing its 1969 level. In the late 2000s, however, philanthropic giving as a proportion of GDP fell again. Combined with the contraction in GDP, the latest decline also corresponded to a decline in absolute terms. Moreover, in line with predictions based on the risk framework, different fields were affected differently: giving to fields with high capital investments and long-term impact, such as health and education, suffered significant declines, while fields with immediate impact, such as social services and international affairs, actually experienced a slight increase during this period (Center on Philanthropy at Indiana University 2010).

The PKC and risk framework, therefore, have important implications for our understanding of the nonprofit sector, nonprofit sector policy, and, consequently, broader political development and economic prosperity. This study shows that, lamentably, government support for the sector is commonly sacrificed in favor of other policy goals and the common efforts to shift program risk from government to the nonprofit sector through public-private contracting. The irony, however, is that since the nonprofit sector may contribute to economic growth, this policy choice can, and often does, backfire. Government needs, therefore, to take a more proactive role and, together with nonprofit leaders and supporters, must pursue appropriate strategies to promote nonprofit sector resilience.

Building Nonprofit Sector Resilience

How can countries avoid their nonprofit sector falling into the risk trap? How can the nonprofit sector exit the risk trap? What can account for the turning point evident in the PKC? That is, how does a pattern of self-reinforcing contraction give way to one of self-reinforcing expansion? The evidence presented here suggests that the process of economic development eventually leads to reductions in macroeconomic instability, which, in turn, should contribute to a reduction in the level of economic risk to which the nonprofit sector is exposed, helping to strengthen it. Theoretically, a sustained reduction in macroeconomic risk and/or a reduction in nonprofit sector economic vulnerability should fuel a self-reinforcing expansionary trend. Broadly consistent with this, the evidence in this book indicates three main processes. One is a structural reduction in macroeconomic volatility, which takes place as an economy moves from transition to a post-transition steady state. Increasing diversification of production and consolidation of new institutions are likely to be key elements in this stabilization trend (Acemoglu 2009). Such a reduction in macroeconomic volatility decreases nonprofit risk and facilitates its development. The fact that, within this study's sample, the turning point of economic volatility precedes that of the different nonprofit sector indicators lends support to this structural explanation. The second process evident in the survey of nonprofits is the "natural" selection of the most resilient organizations and disappearance of the most vulnerable ones. The recovery process is aided by the fact that social demand for the few survivors should be robust, and, based on the principle of diminishing returns, remaining organizations should have considerable social impact. Consequently, the nonprofit sector is unlikely to disappear even in the riskiest environments. The surviving organizations should be able to quickly benefit from greater economic development and macroeconomic stability.

Policymakers and nonprofit leaders can also take steps to promote nonprofit sector resilience and reduce its risk exposure, thus helping to exit the risk trap or avoid it entirely. Successful policies to promote the sector resilience must: (1) reduce overall risk in society, (2) reduce risk in nonprofit organizations' resource environment, or (3) help to increase nonprofit organizations' resilience in the face of economic risk. A discussion of management strategies aimed at increasing nonprofit resilience follows the discussion on policy options.

The risk mechanism identified by the study suggests that some interventions are structural, and difficult to implement, such as reducing macroeconomic risk. Others, such as focusing on risk-reduction strategies on the nonprofit sector's specific resource environment, are more feasible. From a policy perspective, therefore, the PKC points to a tendency rather than an automatic "natural law." International donors and developing country governments could learn from the experiences of middle-income countries by adopting nonprofit sector–friendly development strategies and measures. This would permit them to build a strategic "bridge across" the PKC, as illustrated in figure 1.4 and exemplified by analysis of the Chilean nonprofit sector in chapter 5.

Individual philanthropy is difficult to boost in a context characterized by economic uncertainty, where individual donors have high discount rates, which encourage support only to the most pressing and urgent problems and discourage support to risky, but potentially high-social-return, investments. Commercial revenue produces a more feasible path for resource acquisition. But with nonprofit sectors in middle-income countries already so dependent on this type of revenue, nonprofits need to emphasize other types of revenue to promote greater diversification. Moreover, tradeoffs between social and financial bottom lines typically plague this type of funding. The most likely prospects for effective resource diversification, therefore, come from government and international donor funding as well as local volunteering.

Unfortunately, in an increasingly global economy, policymakers' ability to reduce macroeconomic risk is rather limited, as the case of Europe's current debt crisis demonstrates. Recognizing this constraint, government and other donors can still play an important role in risk reduction of the nonprofit sector's resource environment. Government and donors must proceed with caution since dependence on external funding may rob organizations of an incentive to expand their support base, limiting their ability to strengthen social capital and ultimately increasing their vulnerability to risk. Moreover, international donors' exuberant support for some organizations and apathy toward others raises important questions (Bob 2005). Nevertheless, Pronatura's experience evidences key government and donor policies that may help to reduce the level of risk faced by nonprofit sector organizations.

Since reductions in structural macroeconomic risk are difficult or nearly impossible and survival of the fittest is problematic, the third process focuses on reducing nonprofit sector vulnerability. The comparison between Mexico and Chile is informative in this respect. While in Chile the relationship between government and the nonprofit sector rests on the principles of privatization and genuine partnership, in Mexico the relationship is based on retrenchment and rhetorical partnership. Government's, and likely also international donors', policy toward the nonprofit sector is a main determinant of its financial vulnerability and, therefore, size and sustainability. Like interdependence theory, the risk approach suggests that the relationship with the government is critical for nonprofit sector development. However, unlike interdependence theory, the risk approach suggests that at low levels of economic development, a closer relationship between the sectors weakens the nonprofit sector rather than strengthens it, due to the tendency toward risk-aversion within the population and government officials. In such contexts, government funding is likely to be undependable, potentially increasing non-profit sector risk exposure as government agencies seek to shift as much risk as possible to nonprofit and other private actors.

Furthermore, nonprofit sector strength and institutional quality are mutually constitutive (see Putnam 2000). The supportive role of government in Chile helped non-profit sector development and, at the same time, a stronger nonprofit sector promoted a healthier, more accountable government. Accordingly, weak nonprofit sectors tend to coexist with weak and unaccountable governments. While government can make an important contribution to alleviating nonprofit sector vulnerability, it will probably not do so in the cases of greatest need, where the nonprofit sector is weakest and most vulnerable.

Fortunately, while this book's evidence suggests that the PKC is a general trend, it also suggests possible ways out of it. Firstly, funding from government and international donors can contribute to a reduction in the risk nonprofit sector organizations face, especially if it is countercyclical and provided as scheduled. The Mexican government's procyclical funding and erratic payment schedule added further complexity and risk to its nonprofit sector contractors and grantees. Conversely, Pronatura benefited enormously from international support, which increased in value during the crisis due to the devaluation of the Mexican peso. However, this was an isolated case. The general procyclical pattern of foreign aid to Mexico during the 1990s, marked by a reduction of aid during the crisis, is evidence of the lack of consideration of economic risk in donor support decisions. Despite international donors' stated commitment to "building civil society," I could not find one donor policy directed at helping the nonprofit sector cope with economic crises or economic risk. This is a dangerous position. The international donors' phasing-out plan was premature. Today, even after adjusting for inflation, Mexico receives twice as much foreign assistance annually as it did in the late 1990s. According to the Development Assistance Committee of the OECD, between 1995 and 1999 Mexico received $139.8 million annually. Between 2000 and 2004 the annual average went up to $219.4 million, and between 2005 and 2008, the average went up again to $282 million (all figures in constant 2007 dollars). Mexico's experience during the 1990s suggests that policy makers' neglect of the impact of risk on the nonprofit sector contributed to the erosion of sector capacity, leading to deleterious effects on welfare, democracy, and economic growth. As the roles of the nonprofit sector in social risk management grow, attention to its vulnerability in the face of economic risk must also grow.

Secondly, the conditions attached to funding for nonprofit sector organizations are also important. In high-risk environments, funders should limit or waive typical cost-sharing demands. By increasing the correlation between different funding sources, cost-sharing slashes or eliminates any potential risk reduction from diversification. This was most apparent in the Mexican government's funding agreement with the social services organization, whereby each peso raised by the organization through philanthropy was matched by two pesos from the government. International donors and foundations also required cost-sharing, even during the crisis. Such policies increase the procyclicality of nonprofit sector funding, as matching funding opportunities are desiccated during crises.

Thirdly, tax benefits are important in reducing risk in nonprofit sector organizations' resource environment. Lack of access to tax benefits constrains long-term capitalization, as nonprofit sector surpluses during periods of economic growth must be spent to avoid taxation. Tax deductibility may also help diversification by reducing the cost of philanthropic giving. Moreover, international donors often perceive tax deductibility as a signal of organizational legitimacy. For instance, Pronatura's leaders believed that without tax deductibility, they would have been unable to attract international funding. Interviews with donors confirmed this preference for organizations with tax deductibility. Lack of tax deductibility produces another perverse effect. The prospect of being taxed on investment returns encouraged nonprofit sector organizations to invest in less liquid assets such as equipment and real estate. Low liquidity, however, is a major source of financial vulnerability, especially during credit crunches. While the Mexican government has made significant progress in extending tax benefits to nonprofit sector organizations, only three out of the six case studies had tax deductibility. The study of the Mexican nonprofit sector undertaken by CIVICUS concluded that many organizations dedicated to development, human rights, and other civic pursuits remain excluded from access to tax deductibility (Verduzco and Reveles 2001).

Fourthly, the cases studied suggest that volunteering plays a critical role in times of rapidly shrinking financial resource availability. Policies of state sponsorship of volunteering during crises could provide important countercyclical resources for nonprofit organizations as well as opportunities for individual skill development at a time when the opportunity cost of labor is lowest. From nonprofit sector organizations' perspective, volunteers offer a resource that can be employed toward expanding civic activity at a time of great social need. From the volunteers' perspective, building their skill base through volunteering increases their opportunities, once the economy recovers and employment rises again.

When governments are unable or unwilling to promote nonprofit sector development, international donors must play a leading role. This study shows that even in the least philanthropic society in the world, the nonprofit sector attracts considerable social support. Yet, high levels of economic risk and frequent economic shocks hinder its development. One of the main reasons why economic crises are so destructive is that capacity erosion resulting from liquidity crises is costly to reverse. When a dismissed employee leaves because a nonprofit temporarily lacks sufficient funds to pay his or her salary, there is a subsequent loss in human capital. Rebuilding eroded human capital, if it is indeed possible, may require a considerable investment with large opportunity costs in forgone immediate social impact. Likewise, it is cheaper to pay for regular maintenance of cars and other physical assets than to have to pay to fix them later. Yet, liquidity-starved nonprofits must frequently postpone scheduled asset maintenance.

The nonprofit sector's vital contribution to economic and other types of development, combined with its limited ability to access credit markets during economic downturns, suggests that donors should step in to provide financial liquidity during economic crises. If international donors are genuinely committed to "building civil society" in developing countries, they must play the role of "insurer of last resort," which government is unwilling or incapable of playing. Such systematic risk insurance would be cost-effective by avoiding costly-to-reverse asset erosion in nonprofits and, in countries where the real interest rate is procyclical, providing capital during periods when its opportunity cost (i.e., interest rate) is at its lowest.

To this effect, this study recommends that international donor agencies should create a financial "liquidity facility" similar to the one they are considering for the International Monetary Fund (IMF). The proposed liquidity facility was designed to *prevent* economic collapse by supporting governments facing liquidity crises. Currently, the IMF provides liquidity (i.e., loans) only after countries have experienced a major financial crisis, and the liquidity support aims to prevent further economic collapse.

I anticipate two major objections to such a recommendation. The first is the "slippery slope" objection. If nonprofits were rescued during crises, why should businesses not be rescued as well? And what about consumers? Where do you stop? Clearly, the government cannot rescue everyone. My reply to such objections is twofold. Firstly, nonprofits should be rescued for the same reason that they receive tax benefits: because of their valuable, though not always valued, contribution to society. This study provides evidence that they also have a positive impact on future economic development. Partly because of their contribution to public welfare, nonprofits are unable to sell risk to shareholders in return for capital. Secondly, businesses, and often consumers, have, in fact, been rescued in the past. In the case of the Tequila Crisis, banks received significant cash injections. Consumers were also aided by various debtor programs. Because few nonprofits were in debt, they received nothing. In fact, they received letters saying that the government was suspending its contractually arranged payments. During the most recent crisis in the United States, car manufacturers and dealers received government financial support, alongside banks and insurers. Again, nonprofits received nothing. There's evidence that American nonprofits received a cut in government funding during the previous recession (2001–2002) (see NFF 2008). Several reports in the press suggest government funding also declined in the most recent recession (2008–2009). The current lack of international donor and government policy to support the nonprofit sector during crises leads to wastage of precious public service capacity and reduces the efficiency of taxpayer funds. Support for the nonprofit sector during economic downturns would cost less, due to recessions' deflationary environment, and produce a stronger impact, due to the increase in social demands and the general lack of alternatives. Pro-cyclical government support to the nonprofit sector, which is prevalent even in the case of rich governments such as the United States, reduces the impact of public funding (see chapter 2).

The second major objection is that a liquidity facility may encourage "moral haz-ard." Nonprofits may take excessive risks in the expectation that they will be rescued if the risk materializes in crisis. However, systematic risk insurance is not equivalent to a "bail out" of selected organizations because they find themselves in financial difficulties due to idiosyncratic shocks that could have presumably been averted. Emergency loans would aim at alleviating the impact of *systematic* shocks beyond the nonprofits' control. Rich countries could develop a similar facility to support their own nonprofit sector. As a starting point on this discussion, I recommend that international donor agencies encourage the IMF to extend part of its liquidity lending to the nonprofit sector.

How can nonprofits build resilience to reduce the level of risk they face? There is much that nonprofit leaders can do as well. Increasing division of labor, which typically accompanies economic development, suggests increasing professionalization of non-profit organizations. However, as the case studies illustrate, nonprofit leaders should not turn away from utilizing volunteers as it can be one of the few resources available dur-ing economic crises. Unemployment and lower opportunity cost of labor during down-turns suggest that the supply of volunteers should increase in difficult economic times. Moreover, middle-income countries are still rich in traditional social bonds, which may facilitate volunteer recruitment. However, without previous relationships and an estab-lished network, nonprofits find it hard to tap into this resource only during a crisis. Nonprofit leaders should be aware that an active volunteer base is a major contributor to organizational resilience. Similarly, donors looking for long-term partnerships might consider a demonstrable volunteer base as evidence of social support, which is likely to support the nonprofit partners' long-term survival.

Nevertheless, while volunteers provide precious labor, most nonprofits also need financial resources. Reductions in nonprofit risk can result from environmental changes such as a reduction in macroeconomic instability or more government and donor sup-port. It can also result from better financial management by nonprofits. My observations suggest that there is a lot of room for improvement in this area. Case study observations suggest that many nonprofits lack the financial management capacity needed to oper-ate in a high-risk environment. Inordinate efforts are devoted to raising funds, but the management of available funds receives considerably less attention. This problem was partly related to a second one. Case study and survey data suggest that nonprofit lead-ers are overly optimistic about financial matters and macroeconomic prospects. This is particularly a problem affecting nonprofit entrepreneurs. Before an economic crisis occurred, entrepreneurs generally assigned a lower probability that a contraction would take place sometime during the following twelve months than did managers, staff, and supporters. Furthermore, entrepreneurs tended to expect the crisis to be less severe and to end sooner. This constitutes an important distinction between entrepreneurs and other nonprofit leaders. This optimism stands in sharp contrast to their general pessimism with respect to the future of the organization's central purpose (e.g., environment, social welfare). While vital for the initial impetus to create a new social venture, such optimism hampers their long-term survival in a risky environment. To enhance organizational resilience, nonprofit entrepreneurs must check their financial optimism. Combined with the power imbalance typically present in the relationship with donors and government, financial optimism leads nonprofits to take on most of the risk in contracts in the hope that potential losses will never materialize.

When times are rosy, all appears to be well. However, when the economy dives, or a source of funding dries out, risk materializes and many nonprofits become unviable. The result is a reduction in nonprofit sector vitality, which is negative for society and for government in search of service-delivery partners. My hope is that nonprofits and governments begin an open conversation about the risk implications of different contracting options so that those who can do it most effectively manage the risk.

The above analysis is also relevant for the nonprofit sector in rich countries. Although macroeconomic instability has been low for the past few decades, the last decade witnessed a return to levels of economic instability not seen since the 1930s (Krugman 2008). Many of the lessons from the nonprofit survey are relevant in understanding the medium-and long-term impacts of the recent crisis on the nonprofit sector in rich countries. Moreover, at the organizational level, resource vulnerability remains widespread, particularly among nonprofits making key social contributions by working with the poor and excluded. Risk is ubiquitous.

That is why the nonprofit sector everywhere should also take responsibility for building its own financial resilience. Nonprofit sector organizations can deliberately pursue strategies to do this. The organizations studied here adapted to their high-risk environment by pursuing several risk management strategies, with varying degrees of success. Resource diversification is essential in dealing with idiosyncratic risk, but is ineffective in reducing risk during economic crises, as funding opportunities generally decline during such periods. To deal with systematic risk, nonprofit sector organizations can build financial capital reserves, reduce fixed costs, and develop their social capital base. Adequate capitalization helps to increase long-term survival, but can be ineffective in reducing short-term vulnerability as organizations seek to conserve withering capital. Reducing fixed costs is a sound strategy to promote financial resilience. However, because labor costs are often a main organizational fixed cost, this strategy may limit organizational capacity by limiting professionalization. At any rate, the availability of volunteers may rise during economic crises as the opportunity cost of labor falls. The ability to tap into this countercyclical resource by readily employing volunteers was a distinctive characteristic of countercyclical organizations in this book, which were able to hedge their risk exposure by accepting supporters' contributions of both cash and labor. During tough economic periods, at a time when labor had a low opportunity cost, supporters generally found it more difficult to raise cash and preferred instead to volunteer their labor. Conversely, during times of economic prosperity, when the opportunity cost of labor was high, supporters would often prefer to make cash contributions. It may be difficult to maintain such a high level of resource flexibility in the long term, but the risk-hedging advantages to this strategy are significant. Indeed, this flexibility greatly contributed to lower free-riding rates in organizations employing this strategy.

Doña Mica understood risk and was prepared for the palpable possibility that during the Tequila Crisis things might get worse before they got better. However, stuck between a mercurial economy and a risk-averse set of supporters, she was largely powerless to deal with the impending storm and to save her organization. Risk imposed many intractable tradeoffs. Her organization could seek to build financial reserves but in doing so risk alienating supporters who would prefer to see the money spent on clear, present needs rather than distant ones. Her organization undertook bold programmatic changes in an effort to adapt to a more resource-scarce environment, but economic volatility and the accompanying unpredictability of supporter preferences undermined its efforts. Perhaps most troubling, the incessant resource-diversification efforts were typically unsuccessful, absorbing precious resources and increasing organizational exposure to future risk. This is why nonprofits are unlikely to be able to exit the risk trap by themselves. Survival requires significant investments in the long term. In turn, long-term investments require stability and predictability. The good news is that we do not have to change the macroeconomic environment. Great progress can be achieved by adding greater predictability to the nonprofit sector's resource environment by, for example, establishing countercyclical government and donor support.

By influencing individual and organizational responses, economic development and the risk it engenders shape the nonprofit sector. We need to learn from those courageous and resilient organizations that are able not only to survive, but also to take risks so that they can respond when social needs are greatest. Greater attention by government, practitioners, and donors to the management of risk in nonprofit organizations should increase the proportion of nonprofit organizations that can successfully navigate risky economic environments, to the benefit of society as a whole. Furthering nonprofit sector theory through a risk perspective ultimately helps us to better understand the evolution of the sector, thus enhancing its impact on critical social processes such as democratization, social protection, and economic development. Academics and policy makers are beginning to recognize the broader impacts of the nonprofit sector, and particularly during economic crises. Yet, they have taken the sector's resilience to risk for granted. As this book demonstrates, building nonprofit sector resilience is not easy, but it is critical to the development of civil society and to ensuring that the sector itself does not fall into a crisis.

Notes

1. A Cross-National Philanthropic Puzzle

1. The name of Fovaso's officer was changed in line with my promise of anonymity.

2. As judged by the risk premium on public debt, which denotes market expectations of debt default.

3. Philanthropic giving is only 0.3% of national income, and total volunteered time is equivalent to only 0.1% of the labor force, both of which also correspond to the lowest levels in the world according to comparative nonprofit sector data collected by Salamon et al. (2004).

4. Since Mexico's level of social diversity is also intermediate, nonprofit theories emphasizing the role of social diversity would also predict an intermediate position for Mexico's nonprofit sector size.

5. Research on political participation in Mexico has produced the paradoxical and troubling finding that Mexicans were disappointed with democracy even as the country made steady progress toward increasing political competition, which culminated in the first free congressional election in 1997 and presidential election in 2000. In that year, according to World Values Survey data, the majority (58.9%) of respondents were not happy with the way democracy was developing. Despite steady institutional democratization in the late 1990s and early 2000s, the number of people who never discuss politics increased from 26.1% in 1995 to 45.2% in 2000 (a 73% increase), the number of people who thought that democracy is bad for the economy increased from 47.3% to 55.5% (a 17% increase) in the same period, and the number of people who do not trust the government increased from 24.3% in 1990 to 29.9% in 2000 (a 23% increase). The 2003 midterm elections witnessed the lowest-ever voting participation in Mexico's history, 42% (Paras and Coleman 2006), and more recent elections have generated only marginal increases in participation.

6. Level of economic development is measured by GDP per capita. Also see chapter 2 for a justification.

7. Evidence from the Johns Hopkins CNP except for the last two fields, which is based on data on membership in religious and women's nonprofits from the World Values Survey, Fourth Wave (1999–2002).

8. The graph displays the predicted values of nonprofit expenditure as a proportion of national income, paid employment as a proportion of the labor force, volunteering as a proportion of the labor force, and total employment, which includes both paid and full-time equivalent volunteering, as a proportion of the labor force. While an assumption of linearity produces a familiar direct relationship between nonprofit sector strength and national income, the data actually displays a nonlinear relationship, more closely following a quadratic U-shaped curve. The adjusted R-squared for the quadratic model is 0.24, significantly higher than 0.09 for the linear model.

9. Of course, cross-sectional analyses of the relation between prosperity and the nonprofit sector can be misleading. The cross-section pattern may not have a longitudinal interpretation. The nonprofit sector could be weakening everywhere, even though the nonprofit sector is still stronger in poor and rich countries when compared to middle-income ones. A similar problem has plagued the (original) Kuznets curve. Even though cross-sectional data on social inequality and prosperity commonly support the Kuznets curve, longitudinal data typically don't.

10. Musick and Wilson (2008, ch. 16) looked at service, advocacy, and religious volunteering separately. Only advocacy volunteering was associated with gross national income, and, interestingly, it

was more common in low-income countries. "This is surprising because we associate more developed countries with more vibrant civil societies and less developed countries with restricted political rights and opportunities (gross national income and scores on Freedom House measures of political rights are very highly correlated) and we would expect higher volunteer rates in the high-income countries for this reason. . . . The countries with few political rights are also poor countries. It would seem this negative effect is attributable to low income more than it is having few political rights. Since we are focusing here on advocacy volunteering, in which labor unions and professional associations are included, it would seem that poorer countries encourage more advocacy volunteering because people are trying to improve their economic conditions" (Musick and Wilson 2008:353).

11. These competing views are sometimes reconciled by allusion to the different resource composition of social movements. Accordingly, nonprofits in poor countries should be primarily resourced by labor participation, while its counterparts in rich countries should be primarily resourced by financial contributions (the relative cost of giving decreases as wealth increases).

12. Inglehart (1997) finds a strong positive correlation between a country's score on survival/self-expressive values and its volunteer rate: the more a society values self-expression, the higher the volunteer rate in that country. This is true for all types of volunteer work. A country's score on the traditional/secular-rational dimension is related only to volunteering in church, youth, sports, professional, and cultural organizations. The more secular a society, the fewer people volunteer for these kinds of organizations.

13. This would take place, for example, when a study dismisses prosperity because a linear correlation or coefficient within a multivariate regression was statistically insignificant.

14. The nature of religious values is also important since Protestantism is associated with stronger civic values and lower levels of corruption than other denominations (e.g., Swamy, Knack, Lee and Azfar 2001; Dollar, Fisman, and Gatti 2001).

15. World Values Survey data (1999–2002, N:77) show an inverse correlation ($r = -0.624$, $p < 0.001$) between national income per capita and the national average for respondents' reply to the question "How important is God in your life?" which was ranked from (1) not at all important to (10) very important. Moreover, the relationship was close to linear. The same data also show an inverse correlation ($r = -0.472$, $p < 0.001$) between the national average on a "religiosity scale" and national level of income per capita. Compiled by Inglehart and Norris (2003), the Religiosity Scale is a 0–100 scale composed of six survey questions: (1)"Independently of whether you go to church or not, would you say you are . . . a religious person, not a religious person, or a convinced atheist?" (% who say they are religious); (2) "Apart from weddings, funerals and christenings, about how often do you attend religious services these days?" (% attending once a week or more); (3) "How important is God in your life?" (% who say "very" scaled 6–10); (4) "Do you believe in God?" (% who say "Yes"); (5) "Do you believe in life after death?" (% who say "Yes"); (6) "Do you find that you get comfort and strength from religion?" (% who say "Yes").

16. In this context, the FSB, International Monetary Fund, and Bank for International Settlements have developed a working definition of systemic risk as the risk of a disruption to financial services that is (i) caused by an impairment of all or parts of the financial system, and (ii) has the potential to have serious negative consequences for the real economy (FSB/IMF/BIS 2009).

17. This figure derives from a keyword search on "risk" and "volatility" using the IMF's publically accessible documents at http://www.imf.org/external/pubind.htm (accessed on February 10th, 2011).

18. Based on 1995 nonprofit sector statistics in Verduzco (2000) and 1996 government employment statistics in Hammouya (1999).

2. A Risk Perspective on the Nonprofit Sector

1. I do not, therefore, make a distinction between risk and uncertainty. Frank Knight (1921) proposed a distinction between "risk," which can be estimated using statistical tools and historical data,

and "uncertainty," which can't be estimated a priori. While such a distinction can be useful, I follow the more common terminology used by risk management and financial experts, as well as by social scientists such as Anthony Giddens and Ulrich Beck, which makes no explicit distinction between "risk" and "uncertainty."

2. Here the term *risk* refers to an uncertain outcome, while the terms *shock* and *event* refer to an adverse realization of a stochastic variable. Risk is an ex ante concept while shock and event are ex post concepts. At the same time, however, historical (i.e., ex post) data are commonly used to estimate long-term risk ex ante.

3. Social dilemmas are commonly represented as an n-person Prisoner's Dilemma game.

4. Measured as giving and value of volunteering, including religious giving, as a proportion of GDP from Salamon et al. (2004).

5. The outcome of the PD game is sensitive to whether the players can interact beforehand and potentially coordinate their actions. To be effective, however, such coordination generally requires at least the chance that the players will meet again in the future, after the game. Otherwise talk is cheap. As Robert Axelrod's (1984:12) seminal work shows, "what makes it possible for cooperation to emerge is the fact that the players might meet again. This possibility means that the choices made today not only determine the outcome of this move, but can also influence the later choices of the players."

6. In considering the critical importance of future consequences, Axelrod (1984:11–12) identified a few restrictions to the PD game. First, "there is no mechanism available to the players to make enforceable threats or commitments. Since the players cannot commit themselves to a particular strategy, each must take into account all possible strategies that might be used by the other player. Moreover the players have all possible strategies available to themselves." Second, "there is no way to be sure what the other player will do on a given move. This eliminates the possibility of metagame analysis, which allows such options as 'make the same choice as the other is about to make.' It also eliminates the possibility of reliable reputations such as might be based on watching the other player interact with third parties. Thus the only information available to the players about each other is the history of their interaction so far." Third, "there is no way to eliminate the other player or run away from the interaction. Therefore each player retains the ability to cooperate or defect on each move." Fourth, "there is no way to change the other player's payoffs. The payoffs already include whatever consideration each player has for the interests of the other." With the exception of the fourth restriction, all other restrictions involve the possibility of the future influencing present decisions (e.g., credible commitments, reputation) and, therefore, are consistent with the importance of the "shadow of the future" in eliciting cooperation. In the text, I consider the impact of relaxing all of these restrictions and especially the fourth restriction by considering the impact of selective incentives.

7. According to the authors, in 2001 the majority of contributing households (57.5%) reported being worried about their financial future and gave $1,255 on average, while the 42.5% of contributing households who said they were not worried about their financial security gave $2,306 on average.

8. The beta risk of an income source is calculated by dividing the covariance between the income source and an market index by the variance of the market index.

9. At present, both Yahoo Finance and Bloomberg offer free information on the beta of most securities.

10. The beta risk of a security is calculated by running a simple regression of the periodic variation in the price of the security on the periodic variation in the value of a market-tracking index such as the S&P500. The beta coefficient of the independent variable will be the beta risk value. A main obstacle to calculating the beta risk of a particular funding source is the infrequency with which financial data is collected in the nonprofit sector. It is easy to find data on the daily variation of security prices and market indices. It is difficult to find nonprofit financial data that are more frequent than annual. Few observations increase the standard error of the beta estimate, probably rendering it statistically insignificant within a typical confidence interval. I would argue that accurate beta calculation would be difficult with

less than quarterly data for ten years. Ultimately, of course, the statistical significance of any estimate in a small sample depends on the underlying structure of the sample, that is, its variance. Rather than use a market index, calculations of beta risk in nonprofits would probably make more sense if they employed quarterly GDP data. In any case the correlation between market indices and GDP is very high.

11. A few nonprofits may have countercyclical resource mobilization. In such instances they can reduce vulnerability to systematic risk by spending countercyclically.

3. Economic Development, Risk and the Nonprofit Sector in Cross-National Perspective

1. Multicollinearity was not a significant problem in the different models as variance inflation factors for the independent variables were below 5.

2. The adjusted-R^2 Akaike information criterion (AIC) and Bayesian information criterion (BIC) are all tools for model selection (see Greene 2002). While a higher value of the adjusted-R^2 is preferable to a lower value, the reverse is true for AIC and BIC.

3. In cross-national statistical research, the log of income per capita is commonly used instead of the simple measure because it better approximates a normal distribution and generates proportional change interpretation of effects (see Greene 2002).

4. Following Easterly, Islam, and Stiglitz (1999), I do not detrend the data in cross-national analysis because that would greatly increase the complexity of the analysis, would decrease comparability with the more common variance (or standard deviation) measure of volatility and risk, and would introduce an element of subjectivity about the process that should be used to detrend volatility. Nevertheless, as a robustness assessment I do detrend standard deviation (i.e., volatility) data in the longitudinal analysis of the Mexican nonprofit sector in chapter 5.

5. Hofstede's newest dimension, "long-term orientation," would also seem appropriate in assessing attitudes toward risk. This dimension, however, is inherited from another research (conducted by Michael H. Bond from the Chinese University of Hong Kong) meant to study cultural differences among students in twenty-three different countries. Aside from having a very small sample, its findings do not appear to be consistent with risk-aversion as measured by present bias or long-term discount rate (see Wang et al. 2010).

6. Data on social welfare spending would have been preferable since a large proportion of government consumption may be related to areas unrelated to the nonprofit sector, such as the military (see Salamon and Anheier, 1998). However I could not find cross-national data on social welfare spending for all countries and therefore use final government consumption expenditure as a proxy measure. In any case, I also ran a regression using social welfare spending, available for twenty-four countries, but this did not change the main results presented here.

7. At http://www.urban.org/toolkit/data-methods/instrumental.cfm (accessed on January 16, 2011).

8. Neither the natural log of philanthropy nor the natural log of nonprofit sector size is correlated at the 95% confidence level with either age dependency or the natural log of population size.

4. When Crisis Hits

1. The year 1995 had 443,000 compared to 372,000 in 1994, 332,000 in 1993, and 388,000 and 390,000 in 1996 and 1997, respectively (Homeland Security 2006). Illegal migrants represented almost 50% of total migration (6.2 million of 14 million). In the 1990s jumped to 6.2 million from 4.0 million in 1980s. In the 2000s remained more stable at 6.5 million.

2. CDC, 2001, "Preventing and Controlling Tuberculosis along the U.S.-Mexico Border," at http://www.cdc.gov/mmwr/preview/mmwrhtml/rr5001a1.htm.

3. To ensure consistency with existing literature on nonprofit finance I use the four proxies of financial vulnerability identified by Keating et al. (2005) and Greenlee and Tuckman (2007), namely: insolvency (negative net assets), financial distress (significant decline in net assets), funding distress (significant drop in total revenue), and program distress (significant drop in program expenses).

4. Equivalent to US$16,660, pre-crisis exchange rate. Exchange rate conversions create formidable problems for accountants due to their high variability. Typically, aggregated account conversions are undertaken using an average annual rate or the rate at the end of the year. Unless stated otherwise, in this chapter I use a rounded pre-crisis 1994 rate of US$1 = N$3 (nuevos pesos). Aside from approximating the average annual rate, the advantage of using such a rounded figure is that it better reflects actual mental calculations undertaken by my interviewees.

5. Equivalent to US$600,000 in 1994 dollars.

6. Equivalent to US$474,000 in 1994 dollars.

7. Equivalent to US$61,660 in 1995 dollars. In this chapter I use a rounded 1995 rate of US$1 = N$6 (nuevos pesos).

8. Annual income from donations had averaged N$880,000 (US$293,330 in 1994 dollars) between 1990 and 1993, dropping to N$130,000 in 1994 (US$43,330 in 1994 dollars), and to N$50,000 (US$8,330 in 1995 dollars) in 1995.

9. The state government did make any payments in 1993 or 1994, although according to the agreement it ought to have paid over N$500,000 (US$166,660 in 1994 dollars). The federal government had been even less reliable; it did not pay anything in 1992. During the first three years of the funding deal the federal government owed N$1.82 million (US$606,660 in 1994 dollars), equivalent to about half of the amount agreed in the contract.

10. The federal government paid N$250,000 (US$83,330 in 1994 dollars) in 1994, and both state and federal governments combined paid N$240,000 (US$40,000 in 1995 dollars) in 1995.

11. The video store broke even in 1993, produced a profit of N$50,000 (US$16,660 in 1994 dollars) in 1994, N$70,000 (US$11,660 in 1995 dollars) in 1995, and N$80,000 (US$13,330 in 1995 dollars) in 1996.

12. Equivalent to US$500,000 in 1994 dollars.

13. Equivalent to US$145,000 in 1995 dollars.

14. Approximately N$500,000, that is, US$83,330 in 1995 dollars.

15. Moreover, most nonprofits tend to be perceived as "high risk" by banks, which means that lenders will charge a risk premium on top of the basic interest rate.

16. We would also expect that the power of the department handling fundraising should also rise during a crisis. This did not happen in Fovaso as most fundraising was undertaken by the managing director and the board of directors.

17. Equivalent to US$933,330 in 1994 dollars.

18. Equivalent to US$233,330 in 1995 dollars.

19. Moreover, approximately 97% of the income was derived from reliable sources: interest from investments and lending fees.

20. Equivalent to US$76,660 in 1995 dollars.

21. Equivalent to US$8 million, pre-crisis exchange rate.

22. Equivalent to US$2,603,395 in 1994 dollars.

23. Equivalent to US$1,333,340 in 1995 dollars.

24. Equivalent to US$602,333 in 1995 dollars.

25. Equivalent to US$ 282,330 in 1994 dollars.

26. Equivalent to US$70,830 in 1995 dollars.

27. Peso figures in December 1994 constant pesos, which are equivalent in 1994 to US$514,359 (1994 dollars), and in 1995 to US$416,806 (1995 dollars).

28. One study estimated a universe of 7,885,217 debtors in 1995 (Marchini 2004).

29. Subsidiarity is an organizational principle that states that power should reside in the lowest (or local) organizational units. Higher organizational units (state and federal, for example) are therefore subsidiary to lower levels, performing only those tasks that cannot be performed at the lower levels level; that is, their main purpose is to serve lower units. It represents a reversal of traditional "top-down" bureaucracy (Anheier and Themudo 2002).

30. The exact extent of its social impact is, of course, difficult to measure. With few exceptions, research has focused on examining the nature and workings of El Barzón but not measuring its outcomes. This is not surprising. As a loose confederation, most of its actions were spontaneous and never recorded. El Barzón did not even keep a central registry of members, so any estimates are just approximations based on best guesses.

31. The average between 1995 and 1999 was 88.9%. Before the crisis, the spending was largely equal to income plus or minus any budget variance.

32. These included, for example, construction materials to build fences in natural reserves, vehicles and gasoline, informational technology equipment, and field trips for headquarters staff.

33. FIVA did not demand that collateral assets be included in its lending contracts. Having collateral, however, is a good indicator of lower financial risk of a borrower when compared to a borrower without collateral, who is probably also poorer.

34. Another plausible explanation, which was not derived from actual observation, is that a higher AC ratio may indicate financial inefficiency resulting from weak governance and management. In such cases, management and board may not be interested in cutting administrative costs to protect programs. Ironically, therefore, an organization with a larger financial cushion, in the form of higher administrative costs, may actually be less inclined protect programmatic activity than an organization with lower administrative costs and, therefore, a smaller financial cushion.

5. The Long-Term Impact of Economic Risk on Nonprofit Sector Strength

1. Equivalent to US$53,000 in 1995 dollars.

2. A common misperception about Fovaso is that any success it had was the product of the founder's son's political position as Mexico City's mayor. Philanthropic donations to Fovaso were therefore intended to curry favor among the Espinoza Villareal family, rather than show a commitment to the organization's work. While it is impossible to deny that much of the organization's ability to attract donations was related to the founder's privileged social standing (as it often is elsewhere as well), the founder's son was the mayor in the three-year period between 1994 and 1997, during most of which Fovaso faced terrible financial difficulties. Nevertheless it is possible that Espinosa was instrumental in Fovaso's rapid capitalization when he was the director of Nacional Financiera, a government development bank with considerable assets, between 1991 and 1993.

3. Approximately equivalent to US$21,532 in 1995 dollars

4. Approximately equivalent to US$1.4 million in 2000 dollars.

5. The 990 form must be filed annually with the United States tax authorities by organizations with a formal nonprofit status (however, most religious organizations are exempt from this requirement). The form is very detailed, including key financial, organizational, and personnel data, providing invaluable data for the analysis of the nonprofit sector in the United States.

6. Economic indicators such as funding, paid employment, and volunteers would have greatly enriched this analysis. Unfortunately, I could not find accessible data on those dimensions of the nonprofit sector. The Mexican version of the Johns Hopkins Comparative Research Project (Verduzco 2003) was able to gather data on these indicators for one year (1993) through a painstaking examination of Mexican National Economic Accounts and a complementary survey sent out to nonprofits. This effort

was undertaken by a team of researchers over several months. The longitudinal nature of this study entailed a need for data over several years, which made such a data collection strategy fully unviable with the resources I had available.

7. All interviews were undertaken in Spanish as I am fluent in the language.

8. All survey figures were adjusted to nuevos pesos in the year 2000 using inflation estimates included in the World Bank's World Development Indicators dataset.

9. A better indicator would also include data on nonprofit deaths, to provide a more accurate picture of active nonprofits, but these data are presently unavailable in Mexico and most countries.

10. The log difference method, calculated as Log (period t)—Log (period t-1), provides a more consistent measure of economic growth than percentage change, which is more commonly employed in nonacademic circles. Unlike the log difference method, the percentage change method provides inconsistent assessments between a positive and a negative variation. For example, assume a country has a GDP per capita of $2,000. A 10% rise in GDP per capita would raise it to $2,200. However, if the following year the country experienced a 10% decrease in GDP per capita, its absolute value would fall by $220 to $1,980. In turn, the log difference method would produce the same variation estimate independently from a particular starting point, being therefore a more consistent method.

11. The correlation between cyclical (detrended) changes in economic and nonprofit between 1982 and 2003 is also very high ($r = 0.67$, $p < 0.001$). Cyclical changes in economic activity were measured by calculating the log difference of annual per capita GDP over the period, identifying a trend using the Hodrick-Prescott filter, and establishing the difference between actual economic change and the trend, which is roughly equivalent to annual percent change in per capita GDP. A similar calculation was undertaken to examine the cyclical variation in nonprofit numbers.

12. Cerra and Saxena (2008) used a trend including six years' data on economic growth before the peak and extended it into six years after the peak. I used nine years to maximize available data and to reduce the impact of potential idiosyncratic errors from our much less precise nonprofit capacity measure.

13. Some nonprofits in the dataset had no stated purpose, which is why the number of nonprofits in the different fields may not add up to the total number of nonprofits created that year.

14. The data from the National Climatic Data Center was downloaded from its website at http://www.ncdc.noaa.gov/nacem and refers to the Chapingo station in the State of Mexico, near Mexico City, where a very large proportion of the protests took place. The 90th percentile is calculated using all available data, from 1955 till 1998.

15. Data on political participation were collected in 1990, 1995, and 2000. Unfortunately, data on membership and volunteering were collected only in 1990 and 2000, and do not consequently provide information on the short-term impacts of the 1995 crisis.

16. For example, Williams (2001).

17. This departure from economic volatility measured as the standard deviation of economic growth over a given period was due to the general lack of data since 1880 for the countries of interest. Data on the number of recessions and their intensity are more readily available and, consequently, are used here.

18. For example, all countries were highly democratic, open to trade, and educated. Except for Mexico and its control, Argentina, all countries were also rich and highly modernized.

19. Based on the World Bank's WDI dataset the standard deviation of annual GDP growth between 1960 and 2000 was 4.759 in Chile and 4.606 in Mexico.

20. In this case, a debt swap refers to a financial operation whereby Pronatura buys Mexico's foreign debt in the secondary debt market at a discount and sells it to the Mexican government at face value, generating a valuable financial surplus for the nonprofit. This intermediary role played by Pronatura in a debt swap typically requires the approval of the Mexican government and the original seller of debt before it can be undertaken. It requires, therefore, strong connections with the Mexican government and international donors (original sellers of the debt).

21. About US$386,000 in 1994 dollars.
22. About US$7.463 million, in 2005 dollars.

6. Nonprofit Sector in Crisis

1. A more complete assessment of efficiency entails a comparison of both nonprofit sector and government procyclicality, as well as other potential impacts on efficiency such as the production function. In the case of Mexico, government procyclicality, as measured through social welfare spending, was much less intense than the nonprofit sector's procyclicality, as shown in this book's macro-level data. If this limited data is indicative of the true patterns, then nonprofit procyclicality probably does reduce system efficiency, other factors being equal.

2. Unfortunately, a robust assessment of nonprofit sector's contributions, both positive and negative, requires data on the nonprofit sector that are currently unavailable. As the nonprofit sector becomes a veritable partner in social protection, countries must collect nonprofit sector data, especially over time, for a proper assessment of different policy options.

Bibliography

Acemoglu, Daron. 2009. *Introduction to Modern Economic Growth*. Princeton, N.J.: Princeton University Press.

Acemoglu, Daron, Michael Kremer, and Atif Mian. 2007. "Incentives in Markets, Firms, and Governments." *Journal of Law, Economics, and Organization* 24:273–306.

Acemoglu, Daron, and James A. Robinson. 2006. *Economic Origins of Dictatorship and Democracy*. Cambridge: Cambridge University Press.

Agénor, Pierre-Richard. 2002. "Business Cycles, Economic Crises, and the Poor: Testing for Asymmetric Effects." *Journal of Policy Reform* 5:145–160.

Aiolfi, Marco, Luis Catão, and Allan Timmemann. 2011. "Common Factors in Latin America's Business Cycles." Journal of Development Economics 95:212–228.

Aizenman, Joshua, and Brian Pinto, eds. 2004. *Managing Economic Volatility and Crises: A Handbook*. Cambridge: Cambridge University Press.

Aldrich, Howard. 1999. *Organizations Evolving*. London: Sage Publications.

Alesina, Alberto, Arnaud Devleeschauwer, William Easterly, Sergio Kurlat, and Romain Wacziarg. 2003. "Fractionalization." *Journal of Economic Growth* 8:155–194.

Alesina, Alberto, and Guido Tabellini. 2005. "Why Is Fiscal Policy Often Procyclical?" Harvard Discussion Paper Number 2090. http://post.economics.harvard.edu/hier/2005papers/20051ist.html

Alexander, Jennifer, Renee Nank, and Camilla Stivers. 1999. "Implications of Welfare Reform: Do Nonprofit Survival Strategies Threaten Civil Society?" *Nonprofit and Voluntary Sector Quarterly* 28:452–475.

Alexander, Kern, Rahul Dhumale, and John Eatwell. 2006. *Global Governance of Financial Systems: The International Regulation of Systemic Risk*. Oxford: Oxford University Press.

Almond, Gabriel A., and Sidney Verba. 1963. *The Civic Culture: Political Attitudes and Democracy in Five Nations*. Princeton, N.J.: Princeton University Press.

———, eds. 1980. *The Civic Culture Revisited*. London: Sage Publications.

Andreoni, James. 1990. "Impure Altruism and Donations to Public Goods: A Theory of Warm Glow Giving." *Economic Journal* 100:464–477.

Anheier, Helmut K. 2004. *Civil Society: Measurement, Evaluation, Policy*. London: EarthScan.

———. 2005. *The Nonprofit Sector: Approaches, Management, Policy*. London: Routledge.

Anheier, Helmut K., and A. Ben-Ner, eds. 2003. *The Study of Nonprofit Enterprise: Theories and Approaches*. New York: Plenum/Kluwer.

Anheier, Helmut K., Marlies Glasius, and Mary Kaldor, eds. 2001. *Global Civil Society 2001*. New York: Oxford University Press.

Anheier, Helmut K., and Hagai Katz. 2003. "Mapping Global Civil Society." In *Global Civil Society 2003*, ed. Mary Kaldor, Helmut K. Anheier, and Marlies Glasius, 241–258. Oxford: Oxford University Press.

Anheier, Helmut K., and Regina List. 2000. *Cross-border Philanthropy: An Exploratory Study of International Giving in the United Kingdom, United States, Germany and Japan*. West Malling: Charities Aid Foundation.

Anheier, Helmut K., and Lester M. Salamon. 1998. "Introduction: The Nonprofit Sector in the Developing World." In *The Nonprofit Sector in the Developing World*, ed. Helmut K. Anheier and Lester M. Salamon, 1–53. Manchester: Manchester University Press.

———. 2006. "The Nonprofit Sector in Comparative Perspective." In *The Nonprofit Sector: A Research Handbook*, ed. Walter W. Powell and Richard S. Steinberg, 89–117. New Haven, Conn.: Yale University Press.

Anheier, Helmut K., and Nuno Themudo. 2002. "Organisational Forms of Global Civil Society: Implications of Going Global." In *Global Civil Society 2002*, ed. Marlies Glasius, Mary Kaldor, and Helmut Anheier, 196–216. New York: Oxford University Press.

———. 2004. "The Internationalization of the Nonprofit Sector." In *The Jossey-Bass Handbook of Nonprofit Leadership and Management*, 2nd ed., ed. Robert D. Herman, 102–127. San Francisco: Jossey-Bass.

Appel, Marvin. 2009. *Investing with Exchange-Traded Funds Made Easy*. 2nd ed. Upper Saddle River, N.J.: Pearson.

Archambault, Edith. 2001. "Historical Roots of the Nonprofit Sector in France." *Nonprofit and Voluntary Sector Quarterly* 30:204–220.

Arrow, Kenneth J. 1963. "Uncertainty and the Welfare Economics of Medical Care." *American Economic Review* 53:941–73.

Arrow, Kenneth J., and R. C. Lind. 1970. "Uncertainty and the Evaluation of Public Investment Decisions." *American Economic Review* 60(3):364–378.

———. 1999. "Observations on Social Capital." In *Social Capital: A Multifaceted Perspective*, ed. Partha Dasgupta, and Ismail Serageldin, 3–6. Washington, D.C.: World Bank.

Ascoli, U., and Costanzo Ranci, eds. 2002. *Dilemmas of the Welfare Mix: The New Structure of Welfare in an Era of Privatization*. New York: Kluwer Academic/Plenum.

Ascoli, Ugo, and Ram Cnaan. 1997. "Volunteers for Human Service Provisions: Lessons from Italy and the USA." *Social Indicators Research* 40:299–327.

Axelrod, Robert. 1984. *The Evolution of Cooperation*. New York: Basic Books.

Aydemir, A. Cevdet. 2008. "Risk Sharing and Counter-cyclical Variation in Market Correlations." *Journal of Economic Dynamics and Control* 32:3084–3112.

Baez-Saldana, A. R., J. R. Perez-Padilla, M. A. Salazar-Lezama. 2003. "Discrepancias entre los datos ofrecidos por la Secretaria de Salud y la Organizacion Mundial de la Salud sobre tuberculosis en Mexico, 1981–1998." *Salud Publica en Mexico* 45(2):78–83.

Banfield, Edward C. 1958. *The Moral Basis of a Backward Society*. New York: Free Press.

Barclay, Pat. 2004. "Trustworthiness and Competitive Altruism Can Also Solve the 'Tragedy of the Commons.'" *Evolution and Human Behavior* 25:209–220.

Bardhan, Pranab K. 2000. "Understanding Underdevelopment: Challenges for Institutional Economics from the Point of View of Poor Countries." *Journal of Institutional and Theoretical Economics* 156:216–235.

Barr, Nicholas. 1998. *The Economics of the Welfare State*. Oxford: Oxford University Press.

———. 2001. *The Welfare State as Piggy Bank: Information, Risk, Uncertainty, and the Role of the State*. Oxford: Oxford University Press.

Bates, Robert H. 1990. "Macropolitical Economy in the Field of Development." In *Perspectives on Political Economy*, ed. James E. Alt and Kenneth A. Shepsle, 31–55. Cambridge: Cambridge University Press.

———. 2001. *Prosperity and Violence: The Political Economy of Development*. New York: W. W. Norton.

Baum, Christopher F. 2006. *An Introduction to Modern Econometrics Using Stata*. College Station, Tex.: Stata Press books.

Beck, Ulrich. 1992. *Risk Society: Towards a New Modernity*. London: Sage Publications.

Beito, David T. 2000. *From Mutual Aid to the Welfare State: Fraternal Societies and Social Services, 1890–1967*. Chapel Hill: University of North Carolina Press.

Bekkers, René, and Olaf Crutzen. 2007. "Just Keep It Simple: A Field Experiment on Fundraising Letters." *International Journal of Nonprofit and Voluntary Sector Marketing* 12:371–378.

Bekkers, René, and Pamela Wiepking. 2006. "To Give or Not to Give, That Is the Question: How Methodology Is Destiny in Dutch Giving Data." *Nonprofit and Voluntary Sector Quarterly* 35:533–540.

Bellante, Don, and Albert N. Link. 1981. "Are Public Sector Workers More Risk Averse Than Private Sector Workers?" *Industrial and Labor Relations Review* 34:408–412.

Benjamin, Lehn. 2008. "Account Space: How Accountability Requirements Shape Nonprofit Practice." *Nonprofit and Voluntary Sector Quarterly* 37:201–223.

Ben-Ner, Avner, and Theresa van Hoomissen. 1991. "Nonprofit Organizations in the Mixed Economy: A Demand and Supply Analysis." *Annals of Public and Cooperative Economics* 62:519–50.

———. 1993. "Nonprofit Organizations in the Mixed Economy: A Demand and Supply Analysis." In *The Nonprofit Sector in the Mixed Economy*, ed. Avner Ben-Ner and Benedetto Gui, 27–58. Ann Arbor: University of Michigan Press.

Bergman, U. Michael, Michael D. Bordo, and Lars Jonung. 1998. "Historical Evidence on Business Cycles: The International Experience." Working Paper Series in Economics and Finance 255. Stockholm School of Economics.

Bielefeld, Wolfgang. 1994. "What Affects Nonprofit Survival?" *Nonprofit Management and Leadership* 5:19–36.

Billis, David. 1989. "A Theory of the Voluntary Sector: Implications for Policy and Practice." Working Paper 5. Centre for Voluntary Organisations, London School of Economics.

Binder, Seth, and Eric Neumayer. 2005. "Environmental Pressure Group Strength and Air Pollution: An Empirical Analysis." *Ecological Economics* 55:527–538.Bob, Clifford. 2005. *The Marketing of Rebellion: Insurgents, Media, and International Activism*. New York: Cambridge University Press.

Boli, John, and George Thomas, eds. 1999. *Constructing World Culture: International Nongovernmental Organizations since 1875*. Stanford, Calif.: Stanford University Press.

Boorman, Scott. 1975 "A Combinatorial Optimization Model for Transmission of Job Information through Contact Networks." *Bell Journal of Economics* 6:216–249.

Borge, Dan. 2001. *The Book of Risk*. New York: John Wiley and Sons.

Boris, Elizabeth T., and Eugene Steuerle, eds. 1999. *Nonprofits and Government: Collaboration and Conflict*. Washington, D.C.: Urban Institute Press.

Borzaga, Carlo, and Jacques Defourny, eds. 2001. *The Emergence of Social Enterprise*. London: Routledge.

Boulding, Kenneth E. 1962. "Notes on a Theory of Philanthropy." In *Philanthropy and Public Policy*, ed. Frank G. Dickinson, 57–72. Washington, D.C.: National Bureau of Economic Research.

Bourdieu, Pierre. 1986. "The Forms of Capital." In *Handbook of Theory and Research for the Sociology of Education*, ed. John. G. Richardson, 241–258. New York: Greenwood.

Bowman, Woods. 2002. "The Uniqueness of Nonprofit Finance and the Decision to Borrow." *Nonprofit Management and Leadership* 12:293–311.

———. 2007. "Managing Endowment and Other Assets." In *Financing Nonprofits: Putting Theory into Practice,* ed. Dennis Young, 271–289. Lanham, Md.: Rowman and Littlefield.

Brilliant, Eleanor L. 2001. *Private Charity and Public Inquiry: A History of the Filer and Peterson Commissions.* Bloomington: Indiana University Press.

Brinkerhoff, Derick W. 2002. "Government-Nonprofit Partners for Health Sector Reform in Central Asia: Family Group Practice Associations in Kazakhstan and Kyrgyzstan." *Public Administration and Development* 22:51–61.

Brinkerhoff, Jennifer M. 2002. "Government-Nonprofit Partnership: A Defining Framework." *Public Administration and Development* 22:19–30.

Brinkerhoff, Jennifer M., and Derick W. Brinkerhoff. 2002. "Government-Nonprofit Relations in Comparative Perspective: Evolution, Themes and New Directions." *Public Administration and Development* 22:3–18.

Brody, Evelyn. 2006. "The Legal Framework for Nonprofit Organizations." In *The Nonprofit Sector: A Research Handbook,* ed. Walter Powell and Richard Steinberg, 243–266. New Haven, Conn.: Yale University Press.

Brown, L. David, and Tandon, Rajesh. 1994. "Institutional Development for Strengthening Civil Society." *Institutional Development (Innovations in Civil Society)* 1(1):3–17.

Brumley, Krista M. 2004. "Making a Difference? Social Protest, El Barzón, and Social Change in Monterrey, Mexico." Conference presentation at the 2004 Meeting of the Latin American Studies Association, Las Vegas, Nevada, October 7–9, 2004.

Bryce, Herrington J. 2005. *Players in the Public Policy Process: Nonprofits as Social Capital and Agents.* New York: Palgrave Macmillan.

Buendía, Jorge, and Fernanda Somuano. 2003. "Participación electoral en nuevas democracias: la elección presidencial de 2000 en México." *Política y gobierno* 10(2):289–323.

Burger, Ary, and Vic Veldheer. 2001. "The Growth of the Nonprofit Sector in the Netherlands." *Nonprofit and Voluntary Sector Quarterly* 30:221–246.

Burke, Colin B. 2001. "Nonprofit History's New Numbers and the Need for More." *Nonprofit and Voluntary Sector Quarterly* 30:174–203.

Burlingame, Dwight F. 2001. "Corporate Philanthropy's Future." In *Third Sector Policy at the Crossroads: An International Nonprofit Analysis,* ed. Helmut. K. Anheier and Jeremy Kendall, 91–102. London: Routledge.

———, ed. 2004. *Philanthropy in America: A Comprehensive Historical Encyclopedia.* Santa Barbara, Calif.: ABc–CLIO.

Buurman, Margaretha, Robert Dur, and Seth Van den Bossche. 2009. "Public Sector Employees: Risk Averse and Altruistic?" Discussion Paper 4401. IZA, Bonn.

Cadena Roa, Jorge. 2008. "Evaluación del desempeño de los movimientos sociales." In *Acción colectiva y organización: estudios sobre desempeño asociativo,* ed. Cristina Puga y Matilde Luna. México: Instituto de Investigaciones Sociales—UNAM.

Calhoun, Craig. 1997. "The Public Good as a Social and Cultural Product." In *Private Action and the Public Good,* ed. Walter W. Powell and Elisabeth Clemens, 20–35. New Haven, Conn.: Yale University Press.

Campbell, John Y., and John H. Cochrane. 1999. "By Force of Habit: A Consumption-Based Explanation of Aggregate Stock Market Behavior." *Journal of Political Economy* 107:205–251.

Canuto, Otaviano, and Justin Yifu Lin. 2001. "Introduction." In *The Great Recession in Developing Countries,* ed. Mustapha K. Nabli, 1–11. Washington, D.C.: World Bank.

Capek, Mary Ellen S., and Molly Mead. 2006. *Effective Philanthropy: Organizational Success through Deep Diversity and Gender Equality.* Cambridge, Mass.: MIT.

Carter, Michael R., and John A. Maluccio. 2003. "Social Capital and Coping with Economic Shocks: An Analysis of Stunting of South African Children." *World Development* 31(7):1147–1163.

Castells, Manuel. 1996. *The Rise of Network Society.* Oxford: Blackwells.

Center on Philanthropy at Indiana University. 2002. *Giving USA 2002: The Annual Report on Philanthropy for the Year 2001.* Indianapolis: Giving USA Foundation.

———. 2009. *Giving USA 2009: The Annual Report on Philanthropy for the Year 2008.* Indianapolis: Giving USA Foundation.

———. 2010. *Giving USA 2010: The Annual Report on Philanthropy for the Year 2009.* Indianapolis: Giving USA Foundation.

Cerra, Valerie, and Sweta Chaman Saxena. 2008. "Growth Dynamics: The Myth of Economic Recovery." *American Economic Review* 98(1):439–57.

Chambre, Susan M. 1997. "Civil Society, Differential Resources, and Organizational Development: HIV/AIDS Organizations." *Nonprofit and Voluntary Sector Quarterly* 26:466–488.

Chang, Cyril, and Howard Tuckman. 1996. "The Goods Produced by Nonprofit Organizations." *Public Financial Quarterly* 24:25–43.

Charnovitz, Steve. 1997. "Two Centuries of Participation: NGOs and International Governance." *Michigan Journal of International Law* 18:183–286.

Chatfield, Charles. 1997. "Intergovernmental and Nongovernmental Associations to 1945." In *Transnational Social Movements and World Politics: Solidarity beyond the State,* ed. Jackie Smith, Charles Chatfield, and Ron Pagnucco, 19–41. Syracuse, N.Y.: Syracuse University Press.

Chavas, Jean-Paul. 2004. *Risk Analysis in Theory and Practice.* New York: Elsevier.

Chesterman, Michael. 1979. *Charities, Trusts and Social Welfare.* London: Weidenfeld and Nicholson.

Clark, John. 1991. *Democratizing Development: The Role of Voluntary Agencies.* West Hartford, Conn.: Kumarian Press.

———. 2003. *Worlds Apart: Civil Society and the Battle for Ethical Globalization.* London: Earthscan.

Clark, John, and Nuno Themudo. 2004. "The Age of Protest: Internet Based 'Dot-Causes' and the 'Anti Globalization' Movement." In *Globalizing Civic Engagement: Civil Society and Transnational Action,* ed. John Clark. London: Earthscan.

Clark, Peter, and James Wilson. 1961. "Incentive Systems: A Theory of Organizations." *Administrative Science Quarterly* 6:129–66.

Clarke, Gerad. 1998. "Nongovernmental Organisations and Politics in the Developing World." *Political Studies* 46:36–52.

Clemens, Elisabeth S. 1993. "Organizational Repertories and Institutional Change: Women's Groups and the Transformation of the US Politics 1890–1920." *American Journal of Sociology* 98:755–98.

———. 2006. "The Constitution of Citizens: Political Theories of Nonprofit Organizations." In *The Nonprofit Sector: A Research Handbook,* ed. Walter W. Powell and Richard Steinberg, 207–220. New Haven, Conn.: Yale University Press.

Clotfelter, C. T., and Thomas Ehrlich, eds. 1999. *Philanthropy and the Nonprofit Sector in a Changing America.* Bloomington: Indiana University Press.

Cnaan, Ram A., Femida Handy, and Margaret Wadsworth. 1996. "Defining Who Is a Volunteer: Conceptual and Empirical Considerations." *Nonprofit and Voluntary Sector Quarterly* 25:364–83.

Cnaan, Ram, and Carl Milofsky. 2009. *The Handbook of Community Movements and Local Organizations.* Philadelphia: Springer.

Cohen, Lizabeth. 1990. *Making a New Deal: Industrial Workers in Chicago, 1919–1939.* New York: Cambridge University Press.

Coleman, James S. 1990. *Foundations of Social Theory.* Cambridge, Mass.: Harvard University Press.

Collier, Paul, and Jan Dehn. 2001. "Aid, Shocks and Growth." Policy Research Working Paper 2688. World Bank, Washington, D.C.

Comaroff, John L., and Jean Comaroff. 1999. *Civil Society and the Political Imagination in Africa: Critical Perspectives.* Chicago: University of Chicago Press.

Corbin, John J. 1999. "A Study of Factors Influencing the Growth of Nonprofits in Social Services." *Nonprofit and Voluntary Sector Quarterly* 28:296–314.

Creswell, John W. 2003. *Research Design: Qualitative, Quantitative, and Mixed Method Approaches.* Thousand Oaks, Calif.: Sage.

Crosson, Rachel, Femida Handy, and Jen Shang. 2009. "Keeping Up with the Joneses: The Relationship between Perceived Descriptive Social Norms, Social Information and Charitable Giving." *Nonprofit Management and Leadership* 19:467–489.

Daft, Richard. 1997. *Management.* Fort Worth: Harcourt Brace College.

Dahrendorf, Ralf. 2001. *Goodman Lecture 2001.* London: National Council of Voluntary Organisations.

Dal Bó, Pedro. 2005. "Cooperation under the Shadow of the Future: Experimental Evidence from Infinitely Repeated Games." *American Economic Review* 95(5):1591–1604.

Darcy de Oliveira, Miguel, and Rajesh Tandon. 1994. "An Emerging Global Civil Society." In *Citizens: Strengthening Global Civil Society,* ed. Miguel Darcy de Oliveira and Rajesh Tandon, 1–17. Washington, D.C.: CIVICUS, World Alliance for Citizen Participation.

Dasgupta, Partha, and Ismail Serageldin, eds. 1999. *Social Capital: A Multifaceted Perspective.* Washington, D.C.: World Bank.

Datt, Gaurav, and Hans Hoogeveen. 2003. "El Nino or El Peso? Crisis, Poverty and Income Distribution in the Philippines." *World Development* 31:1103–1124.

Davis, Lance E., and Douglass C. North. 1971. *Institutional Change and American Economic Growth.* New York: Cambridge University Press.

Dawson, Alexander. 2006. *First World Dreams: Mexico since 1989.* New York: Zed Books.

Dawson, Sandra. 1996. *Analysing Organisations.* London: Macmillan.

De Nicolo, Gianni, and Myron L. Kwast. 2002. "Systemic Risk and Financial Consolidation: Are They Related?" *Journal of Banking and Finance* 26:861–880.

Defourny, Jacques. 2001. "Introduction: From Third Sector to Social Enterprise." In *The Emergence of Social Enterprise,* ed. Carlo Borzaga and Jacques Defourny. New York: Routledge.

Dekker, Paul, and Andries van den Broek. 1998. "Civil Society in Comparative Perspective: Involvement in Voluntary Associations in North America and Western Europe." *Voluntas* 8(1):11–38.

Della Porta, Donatella. 2000. "Social Capital, Beliefs in Government, and Political Corruption." In *Disaffected Democracies,* ed. Susan J. Pharr and Robert D. Putnam. Princeton, N.J.: Princeton University Press.De Janvry, Alain, and Elisabeth Sadoulet. 2000. "Growth,

Poverty, and Inequality in Latin America: A Causal Analysis." *Review of Income and Wealth* 46:267–287.

Dechalert, Preecha. 2003. "Managing for Survival?: NGOs and Organisational Change: Case Studies of Four Small Thai NGOs." PhD dissertation, London School of Economics.

Denney, David. 2005. *Risk and Society.* London: Sage Publications.

Diamond, Larry, Marc F. Plattner, Yun-han Chu, and Hung-mao Tien, eds. 1997. *Consolidating the Third Wave Democracies: Themes and Perspectives.* Baltimore: Johns Hopkins University Press.

Diani, Mario, and Doug McAdam, eds. 2003. *Social Movements and Networks.* Oxford: Oxford University Press.

DiMaggio, Paul J., and Helmut Anheier. 1990. "A Sociological Conceptualization of Non-profit Organizations and Sectors." *Annual Review of Sociology* 16:137–59.

Djankov, Simeon, Yingyi Qian, Gerard Roland, and Ekaterina Zhuravskaya. 2007. "What Makes a Successful Entrepreneur? Evidence from Brazil." Working Paper w0104. Center for Economic and Financial Research (CEFIR).

Doherty, Neil A. 2000. *Integrated Risk Management: Techniques and Strategies for Reducing Risk.* New York: McGraw-Hill.

Dollery, Brian E., and Joe L. Wallis. 2004. *The Political Economy of the Voluntary Sector.* Northampton: Edward Elgar Publishing.

Douglas, James. 1987. "Political Theories of Nonprofit Organization." In *The Nonprofit Sector: A Research Handbook,* ed. Walter W. Powell, 43–54. New Haven, Conn.: Yale University Press.

Drucker, Peter F. 1990. *Managing the Non-Profit Organization: Principles and Practices.* New York: HarperCollins.

Durkheim, Émile. 1984. *The Division of Labour in Society.* New York: Free Press. Originally published as *De la Division du Travail Social.* Paris: Presses Universitaires De France, 1893.

Easterly, William, Roumeen Islam, and Joseph Stiglitz. 1999. "Shaken and Stirred: Volatility and Macroeconomic Paradigms for Rich and Poor Countries." Michael Bruno Memorial Lecture, given at the XII World Congress of the IEA, Buenos Aires, August 27.

Ebrahim, Alnoor. 2002. "Information Struggles: The Role of Information in the Reproduction of NGO-Funder Relationships." *Nonprofit and Voluntary Sector Quarterly* 31:84–114.

———. 2003. *NGOs and Organizational Change: Discourse, Reporting and Learning.* Cambridge: Cambridge University Press.

Economist. 1995. "Rescuing the Sombrero: America's Swift Action Has Restored Confidence in Mexico, but Exposed a New Weakness in the World's Ability to Manage a Liquidity Crisis." January 21.

———. 2000. "Special Article: NGOs: Sins of the Secular Missionaries." January 29.

Edwards, Bob, and Michael Foley. 1998. "Civil Society and Social Capital beyond Putnam." *American Behavioral Scientist* 42:124–139.

Edwards, Bob, Michael Foley, and Mario Diani. 2001. *Beyond Tocqueville: Civil Society and the Social Capital Debate in Comparative Perspective.* Hanover, N.H.: University Press of New England.

Edwards, Michael. 2004. *Civil Society.* Malden, Mass.: Polity Press.

Edwards, Michael, and David Hulme, eds. 1995. *Beyond the Magic Bullet: NGO Performance and Accountability in the Post-Cold War World.* London: Macmillan.

———. 1996. "Too Close for Comfort? The Impact of Official Aid on Nongovernmental Organizations." *World Development* 24:961–73.

Eichengreen, Barry, and Michael Bordo. 2001. "Crises Now and Then: What Lessons from the Last Era of Financial Globalization?" Paper prepared for the conference in honor of Charles Goodhart, London, November 15–16. http://www.econ.berkeley.edu/~eichengr/research/goodhartfestschriftjan9.pdf.

Esping-Andersen, Gøsta. 1999. *Social Foundations of Postindustrial Economies.* Oxford: Oxford University Press.

Feinberg, Robert M., and Thomas A. Husted. 1993. "An Experimental Test of Discount-Rate Effects on Collusive Behavior in Duopoly Markets." *Journal of Industrial Economics* 41(2):153–60.

Ferguson, Niall. 2008. *The Ascent of Money: A Financial History of the World.* New York: Penguin.

Fischer, Robert L., Amanda Wilsker, and Dennis R. Young. 2007. "Exploring the Revenue Mix of Nonprofit Organizations—Does It Relate to Publicness?" Working Paper 08–03. Andrew Young School of Policy Studies. Georgia State University, Atlanta.

Fisher, Julie. 1993. *The Road from Rio: Sustainable Development and the Nongovernmental Movement in the Third World.* Westport, Conn.: Praeger.

Florini, Ann, ed. 2000. *The Third Force: The Rise of Transnational Civil Society.* Washington, D.C.: Carnegie Endowment for International Peace.

Flynn, Patrice, and Virginia Hodgkinson, eds. 2001. *Measuring the Impact of the Nonprofit Sector.* New York: Plenum/Kluwer.

Fowler, Alan. 2000. *The Virtuous Spiral: A Guide to Sustainability of NGOs in International Development.* London: Earthscan.

Fox, Jonathan. 1997. "How Does Civil Society Thicken? The Political Construction of Social Capital in Rural Mexico." In *State-Society Synergy: Government and Social Capital in Development,* ed. Peter Evans, 119–149. Berkeley: University of California Press.

Franco, Raquel Campos. 2005. "Defining the Nonprofit Sector: Portugal." Working Papers of the Johns Hopkins Comparative Nonprofit Sector Project 43. Johns Hopkins Center for Civil Society Studies.

Francois, Patrick. 2002. *Social Capital and Economic Development.* New York: Routledge.

Frank, Robert H. 1988. *Passions within Reason: The Strategic Role of the Emotions.* New York: Norton.

Freeman, Richard. 1997. "Working for Nothing: The Supply of Volunteer Labour." *Journal of Labour Economics* 15:140–166.

Frumkin, Peter. 2002. *On Being Nonprofit: A Conceptual and Policy Primer.* Cambridge, Mass.: Harvard University Press.

Frumkin, Peter, and Alice Andre-Clark. 2000. "When Missions, Markets and Politics Collide: Values and Strategies in the Nonprofit Human Services," *Nonprofit and Voluntary Sector Quarterly* 29:141–63.

FSB/IMF/BIS. 2009. "Guidance to Assess the Systemic Importance of Financial Institutions, Markets and Instruments: Initial Considerations." Background Paper. Bank for International Settlement. http://www.bis.org/publ/othp07.htm.

Fukuyama, Francis. 1995. *Trust: Social Virtues and the Creation of Prosperity.* New York: Simon and Schuster.

Gabre-Madhin, Eleni Z. 2001. "Market Institutions, Transaction Costs, and Social Capital in the Ethiopian Grain Market." Research Report 124. International Food Policy Research Institute, Washington, D.C.

Galaskiewicz, Joseph, and Wolfgang Bielefeld. 1998. *Nonprofit Organizations in an Age of Uncertainty: A Study of Organizational Change.* New York: A. de Gruyter.

Galtung, Johan. 1992. "Theory Formation in Social Research: A Plea for Pluralism." In *Comparative Methodology: Theory and Practice in International Social Research,* ed. Else Oyen, 96–112. London: Sage Publications.

Ganz, Marshall. 2000. "Resources and Resourcefulness: Strategic Capacity in the Unionization of California Agriculture, 1959–1966." *American Journal of Sociology* 105:1003–1062.

Gaskin, Katharine, and Justin Smith. 1997. *A New Civic Europe? A Study of the Extent and Role of Volunteering.* London: National Centre for Volunteering.

Gazley, Beth. 2008. "Beyond the Contract: The Scope and Nature of Informal Government-Nonprofit Partnerships." *Public Administration Review* 68:141–154.

Gazley, Beth, and Jeffrey Brudney. 2007. "The Purpose and Perils of Government-Nonprofit Partnership." *Nonprofit and Voluntary Sector Quarterly* 36:389–415.

Gibelman, Margie, and Sheldon Gelman. 2001. "Very Public Scandals: Nongovernmental Organizations in Trouble." *Voluntas: International Journal of Voluntary and Nonprofit Organizations International Journal of Voluntary and Nonprofit Organization* 12:49–66.

Giddens, Anthony. 1999. "Runaway World." *BBC Reith Lectures 1999.* http://news.bbc.co.uk/hi/english/static/events/reith_99/week2/week2.htm.

Gidron, Benjamin, Michael Bar, and Hagai Katz. 2003. *The Israeli Third Sector: Between Welfare State and Civil Society.* New York: Kluwer Academic/Plenum.

Gidron, Benjamin, Stanley Katz, and Yeheskel Hasenfeld, eds. 2002. *Mobilizing for Peace: Conflict Resolution in Northern Ireland, Israel/Palestine and South Africa.* Oxford: Oxford University Press.

Glaeser, Edward L., David Laibson, and Bruce Sacerdote. 2000. "The Economic Approach to Social Capital." National Bureau of Economic Research Working Paper 7728. Harvard Institute of Economic Research. post.economics.harvard.edu/hier/2001papers/2001iist.html.

———. 2001. "The Economic Approach to Social Capital." Harvard Institute of Economic Research Discussion Paper 1916. http://www.economics.harvard.edu/pub/hier/2001/HIER 1916.pdf

Glasgall, William. 1995. "Welcome to the New World Order of Finance." *Business Week,* February 13, 1995.

Glasius, Marlies, Mary Kaldor, and Helmut Anheier, eds. 2002. *Global Civil Society Yearbook 2002.* Oxford: Oxford University Press.

Glasius, Marlies, David Lewis, and Hakan Seckinelgin, eds. 2004. *Exploring Civil Society: Political and Cultural Contexts.* London: Routledge.

Gourevitch, Peter. 1986. *Politics in Hard Times: Comparative Responses to International Economic Crises.* Ithaca, N.Y.: Cornell University Press.

Graf, Pablo. 1999. "Policy Responses to the Banking Crisis in Mexico." Bank for International Settlements Policy Papers 6, 164–184. http://www.bis.org/publ/plcy06f.pdf.

Graham, Carol, and Sandip Sukhtankar. 2003. "Economic Crisis, Markets, and Democracy in Latin America: Some Evidence from the Economics of Happiness." *Brookings Review* 21:36–40.

Grammont, Hubert C. 2001. *El Barzón: Clase media, ciudadanía y democracia.* Madrid, Spain: Plaza y Valdés.

Granovetter, Mark S. 1974. *Getting a Job: A Study of Contacts and Careers.* Cambridge, Mass.: Harvard University Press.

———. 1983. "The Strength of Weak Ties: A Network Theory Revisited." *Sociological Theory* 1:201–233.

Greene, William H. 2002. *Econometric Analysis*. 5th ed. New York: Prentice Hall.

Greenlee, Janet S., and Howard Tuckman. 2007. "Financial Health." In *Financing Nonprofits: Putting Theory into Practice*, ed. Dennis R. Young. Lanham, Md.: Rowman-Alta Mira Publishing.

Grønbjerg, Kirsten A. 1993. *Understanding Nonprofit Funding: Managing Revenues in Social Services and Community Development Organizations*. San Francisco: Jossey-Bass.

———. 2001. "The U.S. Nonprofit Human Service Sector: A Creeping Revolution." *Nonprofit and Voluntary Sector Quarterly* 30(2):276–297.

Guo, Baorong. 2006. "Charity for Profit? Exploring Factors Associated with the Commercialization of Human Service Nonprofits." *Nonprofit and Voluntary Sector Quarterly* 35:123–138.

Gutmann, Amy. 1998. "Freedom of Association: An Introductory Essay." In *Freedom of Association*, ed. Amy Gutmann, 3–32. Princeton, N.J.: Princeton University Press.

Haber, Stephen, Herbert S. Klein, Noel Maurer, and Kevin J. Middlebrook. 2008. *Mexico since 1980*. New York: Cambridge University Press.

Hacker, Jacob S. 2004. "Privatizing Risk without Privatizing the Welfare State: The Hidden Politics of Social Policy Retrenchment in the United States." *American Political Science Review* 98:243–260.

———. 2006. *The Great Risk Shift: The Assault on American Jobs, Families, Health Care, and Retirement*. Oxford: Oxford University Press.

Hadenius, Axel, and Fredrik Uggla. 1996. "Making Civil Society Work, Promoting Democratic Development: What States and Donors Can Do." *World Development* 24(10):621–639.

Halac, Marina, and Sergio L. Schmukler. 2004. "Distributional Effects of Crises: The Financial Channel." *Economia* 5:1–67.

Hall, Peter D. 1992. *Inventing the Nonprofit Sector and Other Essays on Philanthropy, Voluntarism, and Nonprofit Organizations*. Baltimore: Johns Hopkins University Press.

———. 2003. *A Historical Overview of Philanthropy, Voluntary Associations, and Nonprofit Organizations in the United States, 1600–2000*. Boston: Hauser Center for Nonprofit Organizations, John F. Kennedy School of Government, Harvard University.

Hammack, David C., ed. 1998. *Making the Nonprofit Sector in the United States*. Bloomington: Indiana University Press.

———. 2001. "Introduction: Growth, Transformation, and Quiet Revolution in the Nonprofit Sector over Two Centuries." *Nonprofit and Voluntary Sector Quarterly* 30:157–173.

———. 2002. "Nonprofit Organizations in American History: Research Opportunities and Sources." *American Behavioral Scientist* 45:1638–1674.

———. 2003. "Failure and Resistance: Pushing the Limits in Depression and Wartime." In *Charity, Philanthropy, and Civility in American History*, ed. Lawrence Friedman and Mark McGarvie, 263–280. New York: Cambridge University Press.

Hammack, David C., and Steven Heydemann, eds. 2009. *Globalization, Philanthropy, and Civil Society: Projecting Institutional Logics Abroad*. Bloomington: Indiana University Press.

Hammack, David C., and Dennis R. Young. 1993. *Nonprofit Organizations in a Market Economy: Understanding New Roles, Issues, and Trends*. San Francisco: Jossey-Bass.

Hammouya, Messaoud. 1999. "Statistics on Public Sector Employment." ILO Working Papers WP.144. International Labor Office, Geneva.

Handy, Femida. 1995. "Reputation as Collateral: An Economic Analysis of the Role of Trustees in Nonprofits." *Nonprofit and Voluntary Sector Quarterly* 24:293–305.

Handy, Femida, and Meenaz Kassam, 2006. "Practice What You Preach? The Role of Rural NGOs in Women's Empowerment." *Journal of Community Practice* 14:69–91.

Handy, Femida, Meenaz Kassam, and Shree Ranade. 2003. "Factors Influencing Women Entrepreneurs of NGOs in India." *Nonprofit Management and Leadership* 13:139–154.

Handy, Femida, Laurie Mook, and Jack Quarter. 2008. "The Interchangeability of Paid Staff and Volunteers in Nonprofit Organizations." *Nonprofit and Voluntary Sector Quarterly* 37:76–92.

Hann, Chris, and Elizabeth Dunn, eds. 1996. *Civil Society: Challenging Western Models.* London: Routledge.

Hannan, Michael T., and John Freeman. 1977. "The Population Ecology of Organizations." *American Journal of Sociology* 82:929–64.

Hansmann, Henry. 1987. "Economic Theories of Non-profit Organisations." In *The Nonprofit Sector: A Research Handbook,* ed. Walter W. Powell, 117–139. New Haven, Conn.: Yale University Press.

———. 1996. *The Ownership of Enterprise.* Cambridge, Mass.: Harvard University Press.

Harris, Margaret. 1999. *Organizing God's Work: Challenges for Churches and Synagogues.* Hampshire: Macmillan.

Harrison, Teresa D., and Christopher A. Laincz. 2008. "Entry and Exit in the Nonprofit Sector." *B.E. Journal of Economic Analysis and Policy* 8:1–40.

Harvey, David. 2005. *A Brief History of Neoliberalism.* Oxford: Oxford University Press.

Havens, John J., and Paul Schervish. 2001. "The Methods and Metrics of the Boston Area Diary Study." *Nonprofit and Voluntary Sector Quarterly* 30:527–50.

Havens, John J., Mary A. O'Herlihy, and Paul G. Schervish. 2006. "Charitable Giving: How Much, By Whom, To What, and Why." In *The Nonprofit Sector: A Research Handbook,* 2nd ed., ed. Walter W. Powell and Richard Steinberg. New Haven, Conn.: Yale University Press.

Herman, Robert, ed. 1994. *The Jossey-Bass Handbook of Nonprofit Management and Leadership.* San Francisco: Jossey-Bass.

Herreros, Francisco. 2004. *The Problem of Forming Social Capital: Why Trust?* New York: Palgrave Macmillan

Heston, Alan, Robert Summers, and Bettina Aten. 2002. *Penn World Table* version 6.1. Center for International Comparisons of Production, Income and Prices at the University of Pennsylvania.

Hirschman, Alfred O. 1982. *Shifting Involvements: Private Interest and Public Action.* Princeton, N.J.: Princeton University Press.

Hodgkinson, Virginia A., and Michael Foley, eds. 2003. *The Civil Society Reader.* Hanover, N.H.: University Press of New England.

Hodgkinson, Virginia A., K. E. Nelson, and E. D. Sivak Jr. 2002. "Individual Giving and Volunteering." In *The State of Nonprofit America,* ed. Lester M. Salamon, 387–420. Washington, D.C.: Brookings Institution.

Hoffman, Abraham. 1974. *Unwanted Mexican Americans in the Great Depression: Repatriation Pressures, 1929–1939.* Tucson: University of Arizona Press.

Hofstede, Geert. 1991. *Cultures and Organisations, Software of the Mind.* New York: McGraw-Hill.

Hofstede, Geert. 2001. *Culture's Consequences.* 2nd ed. Thousand Oaks, Calif.: Sage.

Homeland Security. 2006. *Yearbook of Immigration Statistics 2004.* Washington D.C.: U.S. Department of Homeland Security, Office of Immigration Statistics.

Honohan, Patrick, and Daniela Klingebiel. 2003. "The Fiscal Cost Implications of an Accommodating Approach to Banking Crises." *Journal of Banking and Finance* 27:1539–60.

Hooghe, Marc. 2003. "Participation in Voluntary Associations and Value Indicators: The Effect of Current and Previous Participation Experiences." *Nonprofit and Voluntary Sector Quarterly* 32:47–69.

Horton, Susan, and Dipak Mazumdar. 2001. "Vulnerable Groups and the Labor Market: The Aftermath of the Asian Financial Crisis." In *East Asian Labor Markets and the Economic Crisis,* ed. G. Betcherman and R. Islam, 379–422. Washington, D.C.: World Bank.

Howell, Jude, and Jenny Pearce. 2001. *Civil Society and Development: A Critical Exploration.* Denver, Colo.: Lynne Rienner.

Hulme, David, and Michael Edwards. 1997. *NGOs, States, and Donors: Too Close for Comfort?* London: Macmillan in association with Save the Children.

Ilchman, Warren F., and Dwight F. Burlingame.1999. "Accountability in a Changing Philanthropic Environment: Trustees and Self-Government at the End of the Century." In *Philanthropy and the Nonprofit Sector,* ed. Charles T. Clotfelter and Thomas Erlich, 198–211. Bloomington: Indiana University Press.

Ilchman, Warren F., Stanley Katz, and Edward L. Queen II, eds. 1998. *Philanthropy in the World's Traditions.* Bloomington: Indiana University Press.

Inglehart, Ronald. 1997. *Modernization and Postmodernization: Cultural, Economic, and Political Change in 43 Societies.* Princeton, N.J.: Princeton University Press.

Inglehart, Ronald, and Wayne Baker. 2000. "Modernization, Cultural Change, and the Persistence of Traditional Values." *American Sociological Review* 65:19–51.

Instituto Tecnológico Autónomo de México (ITAM). 2005. "Encuesta Nacional sobre Filantropía y Sociedad Civil (ENAFI)." Proyecto sobre Filantropía y Sociedad Civil, March 2005. Instituto Tecnológico Autónomo de México, Mexico City.

International Monetary Fund (IMF). 2002. *World Economic Outlook.* Washington, D.C.: International Monetary Fund.

———. 2010. *Global Financial Stability Report: Meeting New Challenges to Stability and Building a Safer System.* Washington, D.C.: International Monetary Fund.

Irarrázaval, Ignacio, Eileen M. H. Hairel, S. Wojciech Sokolowski, and Lester M. Salamon. 2006. *The Chilean Nonprofit Sector in Comparative Perspective Santiago.* Santiago, Chile: PNUD-FOCUS and the Johns Hopkins Center for Civil Society Studies.

James, Estelle. 1987. "The Nonprofit Sector in Comparative Perspective." In *The Nonprofit Sector: A Research Handbook,* ed. Walter W. Powell, 397–415. New Haven, Conn.: Yale University Press.

———. 1989. *The Nonprofit Sector in International Perspective.* New York: Oxford University Press.

James, Estelle, and Dennis R. Young. 2007. "Fee Income and Commercial Ventures." In *Financing Nonprofits: Bridging Theory and Practice,* ed. Dennis R. Young, 93–120. Lanham, Md.: Alta Mira Press.

Jenkins, Craig. 2006. "Nonprofit Organizations and Political Advocacy." In *The Nonprofit Sector: A Research Handbook,* ed. Walter W. Powell and Richard S. Steinberg, 307–332. 2nd ed. New Haven, Conn.: Yale University Press.

Karlstrom, Mikael. 1999. "Civil Society and Its Presuppositions: Lessons from Uganda." In *Civil Society and the Critical Imagination in Africa: Critical Perspectives,* ed. John Comaroff and Jean Comaroff, 104–123. Chicago: University of Chicago Press.

Kearns, Kevin P. 1994. "The Strategic Management of Accountability in Nonprofit Organizations." *Public Administration Review* 54:185–192.

———. 2007. "Income Portfolios in Nonprofit Organizations: Theory, Practice, and Research Questions." In *Financing Nonprofits: Bridging Theory and Practice*, ed. Dennis Young, 291–314. Lanham, Md.: Alta Mira Press.

Keating, Elizabeth K., Mary Fischer, Teresa P. Gordon, and Janet Greenlee January. 2005. "Assessing Financial Vulnerability in the Nonprofit Sector." Hauser Center for Nonprofit Organizations Paper 27.

Keefer, Philip, and Stephen Knack. 2005. "Social Capital, Social Norms and the New Institutional Economics." In *Handbook Of New Institutional Economics*, ed. Claude Menard and Mary M. Shirley.701–725. Dordrecht, the Netherlands: Springer.

Kendall, Jeremy. 2003. *The Voluntary Sector: Comparative Perspectives in the UK*. London: Routledge.

Kennedy, Peter. 2003. *A Guide to Econometrics*. Cambridge, Mass.: MIT Press.

Kessler, Timothy P. 1999. *Global Capital and National Politics: Reforming Mexico's Financial System*. Westport: Praeger.

Kimball, Miles S., Claudia R. Sahm, and Matthew D. Shapiro. 2009. "Risk Preferences in the PSID: Individual Imputations and Family Covariation." *American Economic Review Papers and Proceedings* 99:363–368.

Knack, Stephen, and Philip Keefer. 1997. "Does Social Capital Have an Economic Payoff? A Cross-Country Investigation." *Quarterly Journal of Economics* 112(4):1251–1288.

Knoke, David. 1981. "Commitment and Detachment in Voluntary Associations." *American Sociological Review* 46:141–58.

Kovach, Hetty, Caroline Neligan, and Simon Burall. 2003. "The Global Accountability Report: Power without Accountability?" London: One World Trust. http://www.wto.org/english/news_e/news03_e/gar2003_e.pdf.

Knight, Frank H. 1921. *Risk, Uncertainty and Profit*. New York: Houghton Mifflin.

Kramer, Ralph. 2000. "A Third Sector in the Third Millennium?" *Voluntas: International Journal of Voluntary and Nonprofit Organizations* 11:1–23.

Kreimer, Alcira, Margaret Arnold, and Anne Carlin, eds. 2003. *Building Safer Cities: The Future of Disaster Risk*. Washington, D.C.: World Bank.

Kreps, David M. 1990. *A Course in Microeconomic Theory*. Princeton, N.J.: Princeton University Press.

Krugman, Paul. 2008. *The Return of Depression Economics and the Crisis of 2008*. New York: W. W. Norton.

Kumar, Sarabajaya, and Kevin Nunan. 2002. *A Lighter Touch: An Evaluation of the Governance Project*. York: Voluntary Action Camden.

Kuznets, Simon. 1955. "Economic Growth and Income Inequality." *American Economic Review* 49:1–28.

———. 1973. "Modern Economic Growth: Findings and Reflections." *American Economic Review* 63(3):247–258.

La Porta, Rafael, Florencio Lopez-De-Silanes, Andrei Shleifer, and Robert W. Vishny. 1999. "The Quality of Government." *Journal of Law, Economics and Organization* 15(1):222–279.

Landim, Leila. 1998. "The Nonprofit Sector in Brazil." In *The Nonprofit Sector in the Developing World*, ed. Helmut K. Anheier and Lester M. Salamon, 53–121. Manchester: Manchester University Press.

Layton, Michael D. 2009. "Philanthropy and the Third Sector in Mexico: The Enabling Environment and Its Limitations." *Norteamérica* 4(1):87–120.

Lecy, Jesse. 2010. "Sector Density, Donor Policy, and Organizational Demise: A Population Ecology of International Nonprofits." Dissertation essay #2, Maxwell School, Syracuse, N.Y.

Lederman, Daniel, Ana María Menéndez, Guillermo Perry, and Joseph Stiglitz. 2000. "Mexico: Five Years after the Crisis." Presentation at the ABCDE Conference of the World Bank, April 18–19, 2000.

Lewis, David, ed. 1998. *International Perspectives on Voluntary Action: Rethinking the Third Sector.* London: Earthscan.

———. 2007. *The Management of Non-governmental Development Organisations: An Introduction.* London: Routledge.

Light, Paul C. 2002. *Pathways to Nonprofit Excellence.* Washington, D.C.: Brookings Institution.

Lindenberg, Mark, and Coralie Bryant. 2001. *Going Global: Transforming Relief and Development NGOs.* Bloomfield, Conn.: Kumerian Press.

Lohmann, Roger A. 1992. *The Commons: New Perspectives on Nonprofit Organization and Voluntary Action.* San Francisco: Jossey-Bass.

———. 2007. "Charity, Philanthropy, Public Service, or Enterprise: What Are the Big Questions of Nonprofit Management Today?" *Public Administration Review* 67:437–444.

Lomnitz, Larissa. 1977. *Networks and Marginality.* New York: Academic Press.

Lune, Howard. 2009. *Urban Action Networks: HIV/AIDS and Community Organizing in New York City.* Boulder, Colo.: Rowman and Littlefield.

Lustig, Nora, ed. 1995. *Coping with Austerity: Poverty and Inequality in Latin America.* Washington, D.C.: Brookings Institution.

———. 1999. "Crises and the Poor: Socially Responsible Macroeconomics." Presidential Address at the Fourth Annual Meeting of the Latin American and Caribbean Economic Association. LACEA, Santiago, Chile, October 22.

Maluccio, John, Lawrence Haddad, and Julian May. 2000. "Social Capital and Household Welfare in South Africa, 1993–98." *Journal of Development Studies* 36:54–81.

Marchini, Geneviève. 2004. "Financial Liberalisation, the Banking Crisis and the Debtors' Movement in Mexico." *Portal* 1:1–27.

Marshall, Monty G., Keith Jaggers, and Ted Robert Gurr. 2011. *Polity IV Project: Dataset Users' Manual.* Vienna, Va.: Center for Systemic Peace—Polity IV Project.

McAdam, Doug, John McCarthy, and Mayer Zald, eds. 1996. *Opportunities, Mobilization Structures and Framing Processes.* Cambridge: Cambridge University Press.

McAdam, Doug, Sidney Tarrow, and Charles Tilly. 2001. *Dynamics of Contention.* Cambridge: Cambridge University Press.

McCarthy, Kathleen D. 1993. *Women's Culture: American Philanthropy and Art, 1830–1930.* Chicago: University of Chicago Press.

———. 2001. *Women, Philanthropy, and Civil Society.* Bloomington: Indiana University Press.

———. 2003. *American Creed: Philanthropy and the Rise of Civil Society 1700–1865.* Chicago: University of Chicago Press.

MacKinnon, David P., Chondra M. Lockwood, Jeanne M. Hoffman, Stephen G. West, and Virgil Sheets. 2002. "A Comparison of Methods to Test Mediation and Other Intervening Variable Effects." *Psychological Methods* 7(1):83–104.

MacKinnon, David P., G. Warsi, and J. H. Dwyer. 1995. "A Simulation Study of Mediated Effect Measures." *Multivariate Behavioral Research* 30:41–62.

McKenzie, David J. 2003. "How Do Households Cope with Aggregate Shocks? Evidence from the Mexican Peso Crisis." *World Development* 31(7):1179–1199.

Maloney, William F., Wendy Cunningham, and Mariano Bosch. 2004. "Who Suffers Income Falls during Crises?: An Application of Quantile Analysis to Mexico, 1992–95." *World Bank Economic Review* 18(2):155–174.

Menard, Claude, and Mary M. Shirley, eds. 2005. *Handbook of New Institutional Economics.* Dordrecht, the Netherlands: Springer.

Milgrom, P., and J. Roberts. 1992. *Economics, Organization and Management.* Englewood Cliffs, N.J.: Prentice Hall International.

Minkoff, Debra. 1997. "Producing Social Capital: National Social Movements and Civil Society." *American Behavioral Scientist* 40:606–19.

Mintzberg, Henry. 1979. *The Structuring of Organizations.* Englewood Cliffs, N.J.: Prentice Hall.

Moore, Mark H. 2000. "Managing for Value." *Nonprofit and Voluntary Sector Quarterly* 29:183–204.

Morris, Andrew J. F. 2009. *The Limits of Voluntarism: Charity and Welfare from the New Deal through the Great Society.* Cambridge: Cambridge University Press.

Morsink, James, et al. 2002. "Recessions and Recoveries." In *World Economic Outlook 2002: Recessions and Recoveries,* ed. International Monetary Fund Research Department, 104–137. Washington D.C.: International Monetary Fund.

Moss, David A. 2002. *When All Else Fails: Government as the Ultimate Risk Manager.* Cambridge, Mass.: Harvard University Press.

Moulton, Lynn, and Helmut Anheier. 2000. "Public-Private Partnerships in the United States: Historical Patterns and Current Trends." In *Public-Private Partnerships: Theory and Practice in International Perspective,* ed. Stephen Osborne, 105–119. London: Routledge.

Musick, Marc A., and John Wilson. 2008. *Volunteers: A Social Profile.* Bloomington: Indiana University Press.

Naidoo, Kumi, and Rajesh Tandon. 1999. "The Promise of Civil Society." In *Civil Society at the Millennium,* ed. K. Naidoo and B. Knight, 1–16. West Hartford, Conn.: Kumarian Press.

Najam, Adil. 2000. "The Four-C's of Third Sector–Government Relations: Cooperation, Confrontation, Complementarity, and Co-optation." *Nonprofit Management and Leadership* 10:375–97.

Narayan, Deepa. 1999. "Bonds and Bridges: Social Capital and Poverty." Policy Research Working Paper 2167. World Bank, Poverty Reduction and Economic Management Network, Washington, D.C.

National Bureau of Economic Research. "Business Cycle Dating Committee, National Bureau of Economic Research." http://www.nber.org/cycles/sept2010.html.

Nonprofit Finance Fund (NFF). 2008. "Nonprofit Trends: The 2001 Economic Slowdown and Its Aftermath." http://nonprofitfinancefund.org/files/docs/2008/nff_downturn_dataFINAL_02_08.pdf.

Norris, Pippa. 2003. *Democratic Phoenix Reinventing Political Activism.* Cambridge: Cambridge University Press.

North, Douglass C. 1990. *Institutions, Institutional Change and Economic Performance* Cambridge: Cambridge University Press.

Odendahl, Teresa. 1990. *Charity Begins at Home.* New York: Basic Books.

Odendahl, Teresa, and Michael O'Neill, eds. 1994. *Women and Power in the Nonprofit Sector.* San Francisco: JosseyBass.

Organization for Economic Cooperation and Development (OECD). 2008. *Public-Private Partnerships: In Pursuit of Risk Sharing and Value for Money.* Paris, France: OECD.

Olson, Mancur. 1965. *The Logic of Collective Action.* Cambridge, Mass.: Harvard University Press.

—. 1982. *The Rise and Decline of Nations: Economic Growth,. Stagflation, and Economic Rigidities.* New Haven, Conn.: Yale University Press.

Olsson, Carl. 2002. *Risk Management in Emerging Markets: How to Survive and Prosper.* New York: Pearson.

O'Neill, Michael. 2001. "Research on Giving and Volunteering: Methodological Considerations." *Nonprofit and Voluntary Sector Quarterly* 30:505–14.

—. 2002. *Nonprofit Nation: A New Look at the Third America.* San Francisco: Jossey-Bass.

Osborne, Stephen. 1998. "Organizational Structure and Innovation in U.K. Voluntary Social Welfare Organizations: Applying the Aston Measures." *Voluntas: International Journal of Voluntary and Nonprofit Organizations* 9:345–62.

Oster, Sharon. 1995. *Strategic Management for Nonprofit Organizations.* New York: Oxford University Press.

Ostrander, Susan, and Paul G. Schervish. 1990. "Giving and Getting: Philanthropy as a Social Relation." In *Critical Issues in American Philanthropy: Strengthening Theory and Practice,* ed. Jon Van Til, 67–98. San Francisco: Jossey-Bass.

—. 2004. "Giving and Getting: Philanthropy as a Social Relation." In *Philanthropy in America: A Comprehensive Historical Encyclopedia,* ed. Dwight F. Burlingame, 798–813. Santa Barbara, Calif.: ABc–CLIO.

Ostrom, Elinor. 1990. *Governing the Commons: The Evolution of Institutions for Collective Action.* New York: Cambridge University Press.

Ostrower, Francie. 1995. *Strategic Management of Nonprofit Organizations.* New York: Oxford University Press.

—. 1997. *Why the Wealthy Give.* Princeton, N.J.: Princeton University Press.

Otero, Gerardo. 2004. *Mexico in Transition: Neoliberal Globalism, the State and Civil Society. Globalization and the Semi-Periphery: Impacts, Opposition, Alternatives.* London: Zedbooks.

Ott, Steven J., ed. 2001. *The Nature of the Nonprofit Sector.* Boulder, Colo.: Westview Press.

Pallage, Stéphane, Michel A. Robe, and Catherine Bérubé. 2004. "On the Potential of Foreign Aid as Insurance." Cahier de recherche/Working Paper 04–04. Centre interuniversitaire sur le risque, les politiques économiques et l'emploi.

Panchanathan, Karthik, and Robert Boyd. 2004. "Indirect Reciprocity Can Stabilize Cooperation without the Second-Order Free Rider Problem." *Nature* 432:499–502.

Paras Garcia, Pablo, and Ken Coleman. 2006. "The Political Culture of Democracy in Mexico 2006." Vanderbilt University. http://www.vanderbilt.edu/lapop/mexico.php.

Pareto, Vilfredo. 1935. *The Mind and Society.* New York: Harcourt.

Pastor, Manuel, and Carol Wise. 2004. "Picking Up the Pieces: Comparing the Social Impact of Financial Crisis in Mexico and Argentina." 2003–2004. CIS Working Papers. Center for International Studies, University of Southern California.

Paton, Rob C. 1998. "The Trouble with Values." In *International Perspectives on Voluntary Action: Rethinking the Third Sector,* ed. David Lewis, 132–141. London: Earthscan.

Perkins, Dwight H., Steven Radelet, and David L. Lindauer. 2006. *Economics of Development.* 6th ed. New York: W. W. Norton.

Perrow, Charles. 2001. "The Rise of Nonprofits and the Decline of Civil Society." In *Organisational Theory and the Non-profit Form,* ed. Helmut Anheier, 33–44. Centre for Civil Society Report 2. London School of Economics.

Perry, Guillermo. 2009. *Beyond Lending: How Multilateral Banks Can Help Developing Countries Manage Volatility Center for Global Development.* Baltimore: Brookings Institution Press.

Pfeffer, Jeffrey, and Gerald Salancik. 1978. *The External Control of Organizations: A Resource Dependence Perspective.* New York: Harper and Row.

Pieck Gochicoa, Enrique. 2000. "La capacitación para jóvenes en situación de pobreza. El caso de México." In *Formación, pobreza y exclusión: los programas para jóvenes,* ed. Maria Antonia Gallart, 313–365. Montevideo: Organización International del Trabajo.

Pinter, Frances. 2001. "Funding Global Civil Society Organisations." In *Global Civil Society 2001,* ed. Helmut K. Anheier, Marlies Glasius, and Mary Kaldor, 195–218. Oxford: Oxford University Press.

Platteau, Jean-Philippe. 2000. *Institutions, Social Norms, and Economic Development.* Reading, UK: Harwood Academic.

Pongsapich, Amara. 1997. *Thailand Nonprofit Sector and Social Development.* Bangkok: Chulalongkorn University Printing House.

Porter, Michael E., and Mark Kramer. 1999. "Philanthropy's New Agenda: Creating Value." *Harvard Business Review* 77:121–30.

Powell, Walter W., ed. 1987. *The Nonprofit Sector: A Research Handbook.* New Haven, Conn.: Yale University Press.

———. 1990. "Neither Market nor Hierarchy: Network Forms of Organization." *Research in Organizational Behavior* 12:295–336.

Powell, Walter W., and Paul DiMaggio, eds.1991. *The New Institutionalism in Organizational Analysis.* Chicago: University of Chicago Press.

Powell, Walter W., and Elisabeth Clemens, eds. 1998. *Private Action and the Public Good.* New Haven, Conn.: Yale University Press.

Powell, Walter W., and Richard Steinberg, eds. 2006. *The Nonprofit Sector: A Research Handbook.* New Haven, Conn.: Yale University Press.

Preacher, Kristopher J., Derek D. Rucker, and Andrew F. Hayes. 2007. "Addressing Moderated Mediation Hypotheses: Theory, Methods, and Prescriptions." *Multivariate Behavioral Research* 42:185–227.

Princen, Thomas, and Mathias Finger. 1994. *Environmental NGOs in World Politics: Linking the Global and the Local.* London: Routledge.

Putnam, Robert D. 1993. *Making Democracy Work: Civic Traditions in Modern Italy.* Princeton, N.J.: Princeton University Press.

———. 2000. *Bowling Alone: The Collapse and Revival of American Community.* New York: Simon and Schuster.

———, ed. 2002. *Democracies in Flux.* New York: Oxford University Press.

Putnam, Robert D., and Kirstin Goss. 2002. "Introduction." In *Democracies in Flux,* ed. R. Putnam, 3–19. New York: Oxford University Press.

Quiggin, John. 2007. "The Risk Society: Social Democracy in an Uncertain World." Occasional Paper Number 2. Centre for Policy Development, Sydney, Australia.

Raddatz, Claudio. 2005. "Are External Shocks Responsible for the Instability of Output in Low-Income Countries?" World Bank Policy Research Working Paper 3680.

Radelet, Steven, and Jeffrey Sachs. 1998. "Economic Growth and the Income of the Poor." Harvard Institute for International Development (November), NBER Working Paper 6680. www.nber.org/papers/w6680.pdf.

Ragin, Charles. 1998. "Comments on 'Social Origins of Civil Society.'" *Voluntas: International Journal of Voluntary and Nonprofit Organizations* 9:261–70.

Ramos-Cortes, Victor M. 1997. *Mexican Foundation for Rural Development: The Synergos Institute Voluntary Sector Financing Program Case Studies of Foundation-Building in Africa,*

Asia and Latin America. Synergos Institute. http://www.synergos.org/knowledge/97/fmdrcasestudy.pdf

Rauchway, Eric. 2008. *The Great Depression and the New Deal: A Very Short Introduction.* New York: Oxford University Press.

Ravallion, Martin. 2002. "Are the Poor Protected from Budget Cuts? Evidence for Argentina." *Journal of Applied Economics* 5:95–121.

Roberts, Gilbert. 1998. "Competitive Altruism: From Reciprocity to the Handicap Principle." *Proceedings of the Royal Society of London* B 265:427–431.

Rodrik, Dani. 2009. "Growth after the Crisis." CEPR Discussion Paper No. DP7480. http://ssrn.com/abstract=1507477.

Roett, Riordan, ed. 1996. *The Mexican Peso Crisis: International Perspectives.* Boulder, Colo.: Lynne Rienner.

Rose-Ackerman, Susan. 1996. "Altruism, Nonprofits and Economic Theory." *Journal of Economic Literature* 34:701–28.

Rothstein, Bo. 2005. *Social Traps and the Problem of Trust.* New York: Cambridge University Press.

Rousseau, Denise M., Sim B. Sitkin, Ronald S. Burt, and Colin Camerer. 1998. "Not So Different after All: A Cross-Discipline View of Trust." *Academy of Management Review* 23:393–404.

Salamon, Lester M. 1987. "Partners in Public Service: The Scope and Theory of Government-Nonprofit Sector Relations." In *The Nonprofit Sector: A Research Handbook,* ed. Walter Powell. New Haven, Conn.: Yale University Press.

———. 1993. "The Marketization of Welfare: Changing Nonprofit and For-Profit Roles in the American Welfare State." *Social Service Review* 67(1):16–39.

Salamon, Lester M., and Helmut Anheier. 1998. "Social Origins of Civil Society: Explaining the Nonprofit Sector Cross-nationally." *Voluntas: International Journal of Voluntary and Nonprofit Organizations* 9:213–248.

Salamon, Lester. M., Helmut Anheier, Regina List, Stefan Toepler, and Wojciech Sokolowski, eds. 1999. *Global Civil Society: Dimensions of the Nonprofit Sector.* Baltimore: Johns Hopkins Center for Civil Society Studies.

Salamon, Lester M., Helmut Anheier, Regina List, Stefan Toepler, and Wojciech Sokolowski, eds. 2004. *Global Civil Society: Dimensions of the Nonprofit Sector, Volume 2.* Baltimore: Johns Hopkins Center for Civil Society Studies.

Salamon, Lester. M., Regina List, and Wojciech Sokolowski, eds. 2003. *Global Civil Society: An Overview.* Baltimore: Johns Hopkins Center for Civil Society Studies.

Salamon, Lester M., and Stefan Toepler. 2000. "The Influence of the Legal Environment on the Development of the Nonprofit Sector." Working Paper 17. Johns Hopkins Center for Civil Society Studies.

Samuelson, Paul A. 1964. "Principles of Efficiency: Discussion." *American Economic Review Proceedings* 54:93–96.

Sargent, Adrian, and Jürgen Kähler. 1999. "Returns on Fundraising Expenditures in the Voluntary Sector." *Nonprofit Management and Leadership* 10:5–19.

Schneewind, Jerome B. 1996. *Giving: Western Ideas of Philanthropy.* Bloomington: Indiana University Press.

Schwert, G. William. 1989. "Why Does Stock Market Volatility Change over Time?" *Journal of Finance* 44:1115–1153.

Seibel, Wolfgang. 1996. "Successful Failures: An Alternative View of Organizational Coping." *American Behavioral Scientist* 39:1011–24.

Seligson, Mitchell A., and John Booth. 2009. *The Legitimacy Puzzle in Latin America: Political Support and Democracy in Eight Nations*. Cambridge: Cambridge University Press.

Selle, Per, and Kristin Strømsnes. 1998. "Organised Environmentalists: Democracy as a Key Value." *Voluntas: International Journal of Voluntary and Nonprofit Organizations* 9:319–43.

Sen, Amartya. 1997. "Rational Fools: A Critique of the Behavioural Foundations of Economic Theory." *Philosophy and Public Affairs* 6:317–332.

———. 1999. *Development as Freedom*. New York: Anchor Books.

Shiller, Robert J. 2003. "From Efficient Markets Theory to Behavioral Finance." *Journal of Economic Perspectives* 17(1):83–104.

Shirley, Mary M. 2005."Institutions and Development." In *Handbook Of New Institutional Economics*, ed. Claude Menard and Mary M. Shirley, 611–638. Dordrecht, the Netherlands: Springer.

Shlaes, Amity. 2007. *The Forgotten Man: A New History of the Great Depression*. New York: Harper.

Shrout, P. E., and N. Bolger. 2002. "Mediation in Experimental and Nonexperimental Studies: New Procedures and Recommendations." *Psychological Methods* 7(4):422–445.

Singer, Amy. 2009. *Charity in Islamic Society*. Cambridge: Cambridge University Press.

Sirianni, Carmen, and Lewis Friedland. 2001. *Civic Innovation in America: Community Empowerment, Public Policy, and the Movement for Civic Renewal*. Berkeley: University of California Press.

Skocpol, Theda. 1992. *Protecting Soldiers and Mothers: The Political Origins of Social Policy in the United States*. Cambridge, Mass.: Belknap Press of Harvard University Press.

———. 2002. "From Membership to Advocacy." In *Democracies in Flux*, ed. Robert Putnam, 103–136. Oxford: Oxford University Press.

———. 2003. *Diminished Democracy: From Membership to Management in American Civic Life*. Norman: University of Oklahoma Press.

Skocpol, Theda, Marshall Ganz, and Ziad Munson. 2000. "A Nation of Organizers: The Institutional Origins of Civic Volunteerism in the United States." *American Political Science Review* 94:527–546.

Smillie, Ian, and John Hailey. 2001. *Managing for Change: Leadership, Strategy and Management in Asian NGOs*. London: Earthscan.

Smith, Davis. 1998. *The 1997 National Survey of Volunteering*. London: Institute of Volunteering Research.

Smith, Steven R., and Michael Lipsky. 1993. *Nonprofits for Hire: The Welfare State in the Age of Contracting*. Cambridge, Mass.: Harvard University Press.

Stack, Carol. 1974. *All Our Kin*. New York: Harper and Row.

Steinberg, Richard. 1993. "Public Policy and the Performance of Nonprofit Organizations: A General Framework." *Nonprofit and Voluntary Sector Quarterly* 22:13–31.

Steinberg, Richard. 2003. "Economic Theories of Nonprofit Organizations: An Evaluation." In *The Study of the Nonprofit Enterprise*, ed. Helmut Anheier and Avner Ben-Ner, 272–308. New York: Kluwer Academic/Plenum.

Steinberg, Richard. 2006. "Economic Theories of Nonprofit Organizations." In *The Nonprofit Sector: A Research Handbook*, 2nd ed., ed. W. Powell and R. Steinberg, 117–139. New Haven, Conn.: Yale University Press.

Stinchcombe, Arthur L. 1965. "Social Structure and Organizations." In *Handbook of Organizations*, ed. James G. March, 142–193. New York: Rand McNally.

Sunderland, David. 2007. *Social Capital, Trust and the Industrial Revolution, 1780–1880.* New York: Routledge.

Suwannarat, Gary. 2003. *Unfinished Business: ODA-Civil Society Partnerships in Thailand.* New York: Synergos Institute.

Székely, Miguel, and Nora Lustig. 1997. "Mexico: Evolución económica, pobreza y desigualdad." Trabajo presentado para la Conferencia CEPAL, BID, PNUD Los determinantes de la pobreza en América Latina, Washington, D.C., December.

Sztompka, Piotr. 1999. *Trust: A Sociological Theory.* Cambridge: Cambridge University Press.

Tanzi, Vito. 2000. *Policies, Institutions and the Dark Side of Economics.* Cheltenham, UK: Edward Elgar.

Tarrow, Sidney. 1994. *Power in Movement: Collective Action, Social Movements and Politics.* New York: Cambridge University Press.

Teorell, Jan, Sören Holmberg, and Bo Rothstein. 2008. *The Quality of Government Dataset,* version 1 July 08. Göteborg: Göteborg University, Quality of Government Institute.

Terrazas, Ireri Ablanedo. 2006. "De sociedad a sociedad civil Análisis de las causas del déficit de participación ciudadana en México." VI Seminario Anual de Investigación sobre el Tercer Sector en México, Centro Mexicano para la Filantropia, Mexico City, September 12–13, 2006. http://www.filantropia.itam.mx/documentos/documentos.html.

Terrazas, Ireri Ablanedo, Michael D. Layton, Alejandro Moreno Mayo. 2008. "Encuesta Nacional sobre Filantropía y Sociedad Civil (ENAFI): Capital Social en México." CEPI Working Paper 17. Instituto Tecnológico Autónomo de México.

Themudo, Nuno S. 2009. "Gender and the Nonprofit Sector." *Nonprofit and Voluntary Sector Quarterly* 38:663–683.

———. 2013. "Reassessing the Impact of Civil Society: Nonprofit Sector, Press Freedom, and Corruption." *Governance: An International Journal of Policy, Administration, and Institution* 26(1):63–89.

Thomas, Adam, ed. 2004. *Philanthropy, Patronage, and Civil Society: Experiences from Germany, Great Britain, and North America.* Bloomington: Indiana University Press.

Titmuss, Richard. 1973. *The Gift Relationship: From Human Blood to Social Policy.* London: Penguin.

Tocqueville, Alexis de. 1969 [1835]. *Democracy in America,* New York: Vintage Books.

Toepler, Stefan, and Helmut Anheier. 2004. "Organizational Theory and Nonprofit Management: An Overview." In *Future of Civil Society: Making Central European Nonprofit-Organizations Work,* ed. Annette Zimmer and Eckhard Priller, 253–270. Wiesbaden: Verlag für Sozialwissenschaften.

Tornell, Aaron, Frank Westermann, and Lorenza Martínez. 2003. "Liberalization, Growth, and Financial Crises: Lessons from Mexico and the Developing World." Brookings Papers on Economic Activity, 2:1–112.

Tuckman, Howard P. 1998. "Competition, Commercialization, and the Evolution of Nonprofit Organizational Structures." *Journal of Policy Analysis and Management* 17:175–194.

Tuckman, Howard P., and Cyril F. Chang. 1991. "A Methodology for Measuring the Financial Vulnerability of Charitable Nonprofit Organizations." *Nonprofit and Voluntary Sector Quarterly* 20:445–460.

Uslaner, Eric M. 2002. *The Moral Foundation of Trust.* New York: Cambridge University Press.

———. 2008. *Corruption, Inequality, and the Rule of Law: The Bulging Pocket Makes the Easy Life.* New York: Cambridge University Press.

Van Slyke, David M. 2007. "Agents or Stewards: Using Theory to Understand the Government: Nonprofit Social Services Contracting Relationship." *Journal of Public Administration Research and Theory* 17:157–187.

Van Till, Jon. 1978. *Mapping the Third Sector.* New York: Foundation Center.

———. 2000. *Growing Civil Society: From Nonprofit Sector to Third Space.* Bloomington: Indiana University Press.

Varian, Hal. 2004. *Intermediate Microeconomics: A Modern Approach.* New York: W. W. Norton.

Vázquez Mota, Josefina. 2005. Conferencia magisterial presentada en el foro Hacia la corresponsabilidad: Encuentro sociedad civil-gobierno federal, realizado del 18 al 20 de junio de 2005, en la Ciudad de México. Verduzco, M. I., and A. Reveles A. 2001. "The CIVICUS Index of Civil Society Project in Mexico: Preliminary Report." Civicus Index on Civil Society Occasional Paper Series vol. 1, issue 7.

Verduzco Igartúa, Gustavo. 2003. "*Organizaciones no lucrativas: visión de su trayectoria en México.*" Mexico City: El Colegio de México.

Verschuur, M., Philip Spinhoven, Arnold van Emmerik, and Frits Rosendaal. 2007. "Making a Bad Thing Worse: Effects of Communication of Results of an Epidemiological Study after an Aviation Disaster." *Social Science and Medicine* 65:1430–1441.

Vesterlund, Lise. 2006. "Why Do People Give?" In *The Nonprofit Sector: A Research Handbook,* ed. Walter W. Powell and Richard S. Steinberg, 568–589. New Haven, Conn.: Yale Press.

Vickrey, William. 1964. "Principles of Efficiency: Discussion." *American Economic Review* 54:88–92.

Villalobos, Jorge. 2005. "Los retos de la sociedad civil en México." Ponencia presentada en el foro Hacia la corresponsabilidad: Encuentro sociedad civil-gobierno federal, realizado del 18 al 20 de junio de 2005, en la Ciudad de México.

Walsh, Edward J., and Rex H. Warland. 1983. "Social Movement Involvement in the Wake of a Nuclear Accident: Activists and Free Riders in the TMI Area." *American Sociological Review* 48:764–780.

Wang, Mei, Marc Oliver Rieger, and Thorsten Hens. 2010. "How Time Preferences Differ: Evidence from 45 Countries." Swiss Finance Institute Research Paper No. 09–47.

Wedekind, Claus, and Manfred Milinski. 2000. "Cooperation through Image Scoring in Humans." *Science* 288:850–852.

Wedig, Gerard J. 1994. "Risk, Leverage, Donations, and Dividends-in-Kind: A Theory of Nonprofit Financial Behavior." *International Review of Economics and Statistics* 3:257–278.

Weinstein, Stanley. 2009. *The Complete Guide to Fundraising Management.* New York: Wiley.

Weisbrod, Burton. 1977. *The Voluntary Nonprofit Sector.* Lexington, Mass.: Lexington Books.

———. 1988. *The Nonprofit Economy.* Cambridge, Mass.: Harvard University Press.

———. 1998. "The Nonprofit Mission and Its Financing: Growing Links between Nonprofits and the Rest of the Economy." In *To Profit or Not to Profit: The Commercial Transformation of the Nonprofit Sector,* ed. Burton A. Weisbrod, 1–24. New York: Cambridge University Press.

Wellman, Barry. 1979. "The Community Question: The Intimate Networks of East Yorkers." *American Journal of Sociology* 84:1201–1231.

Willer, Robb. 2009. "A Status Theory of Collective Action." In *Advances in Group Processes,* vol. 26, ed. Shane R. Thye and Edward J. Lawler, 133–163. London: Emerald.

Williams, Heather L. 2001. *Social Movements and Economic Transition: Markets and Distributive Conflict in Mexico.* New York: Cambridge University Press.

Williams, Rhys H., and Jeffrey Blackburn. 1996. "Many Are Called but Few Obey: Ideological Commitment and Activism in Operation Rescue.'" In *Disruptive Religion: The Force of Faith in Social Movement Activism,* ed. Christian Smith, 167–185. New York: Routledge.

Wilson, James Q. 1995. *Political Organizations.* Princeton, N.J.: Princeton University Press.

Wilson, John, and Mark Musick. 1997. "Who Cares? Toward an Integrated Theory of Volunteer Work." *American Sociological Review* 62:694–713.

Wolf, Holger. 2005. "Volatility: Definition and Consequences." In *Managing Economic Volatility and Crises: A Practitioner's Guide,* ed. Joshua Aizenman and Brian Pinto, 45–64. New York: Cambridge University Press.

Wollebaek, Dag, and Per Selle. 2002."Does Participation in Voluntary Associations Contribute to Social Capital? The Impact of Intensity, Scope, and Type." *Nonprofit and Voluntary Sector Quarterly* 31:32–61.

Woolcock, Michael. 2001. "The place of Social Capital in Understanding Social and Economic Outcomes." *Canadian Journal of Policy Research* 2:1–17.

Woolley, Frances. 2003. "Social Cohesion and Voluntary Activity: Making Connections" In *Economic Implications of Social Cohesion,* ed. L. Osberg, 150–182. Toronto: University of Toronto Press.

World Bank. 2005. *Mexico: An Overview of Social Protection.* Mexico City: Imprime Tus Ideas.

World Values Survey Association. 2006. *European and World Values Surveys Four-Wave Integrated Data File, 1981–2004,* v.20060423. http://www.icpsr.umich.edu/icpsrweb/ICPSR/studies/4531.

Wuthnow, Robert. 1988. *The Restructuring of American Religion: Society and Faith since World War II.* Princeton, N.J.: Princeton University Press.

———. 2002. "Bridging the Privileged and the Marginalized." In *Democracies in Flux,* ed. Robert Putnam, 59–102. Oxford: Oxford University Press.

Young, Dennis R. 1983. *If Not for Profit, for What? A Behavioral Theory of the Nonprofit Sector Based on Entrepreneurship.* Lexington, Mass.: Lexington Books.

———. 2000. "Alternative Models of Government-Nonprofit Relations: Theoretical and International Perspectives." *Nonprofit and Voluntary Sector Quarterly* 29:149–72.

———. 2006. "How Nonprofit Organizations Manage Risk." Paper presented at the bi-annual conference of the International Society for Third Sector Research, Bangkok, Thailand, July 11.

———, ed. 2007. *Financing Nonprofits: Putting Theory into Practice.* Lanham, Md.: Alta Mira Press.

Young, Dennis R., and Lester Salamon. 2002. "Commercialization, Social Ventures, and For-Profit Competition." In *The State of Nonprofit America,* ed. Lester Salamon, 423–446. Harrisonburg: R. R. Donnelley and Sons.

Young, Dennis R., and Richard Steinberg. 1995. *Economics for Nonprofit Managers.* New York: Foundation Center.

Zahavi, Amotz, and Avishag Zahavi. 1997. *The Handicap Principle: The Missing Piece of Darwin's Puzzle.* New York: Oxford University Press.

Zietlow, John, Jo Ann Hankin, and Alan G. Seidner. 2007. *Financial Management for Nonprofit Organizations: Policies and Practices.* Hoboken, N.J.: Wiley.

Index

accountability, 33, 141, 161. *See also* philanthropic friction
accounting, financial, 46, 104
administration costs, 48, 90, 104, 107–108
advocacy, 96–97, 100, 106, 133–136
Anheier, Helmut K., 2, 3, 7, 8, 9, 13, 14–15, 24–25, 27, 73, 76, 96, 133
Argentina, 15, 17, 64, 141–144, 146. *See also* cross-national: analysis of nonprofit sector
Arrow, Kenneth J., 31, 39, 43, 61
arts organizations, 139
assets, 30, 43, 47, 50, 90–95, 106, 114, 167–168
associations, 4, 9, 32, 39, 42, 138, 145, 157
asymmetric information, 8, 12

basic needs approach, 102–104
Ben-Ner, Avner, 8
beta risk. *See* risk: beta risk
Bielefeld, Wolfgang, 8
board of directors, 14, 31, 33, 91–93, 101–102, 106, 113–114, 127, 153–154
Bryce, Herrington J., 33, 44–45, 48
budget, 89–94, 111, 124–127
bureaucratization, 90–91, 105, 111

Canada, 2, 141–144. *See also* cross-national: analysis of nonprofit sector
capital, financial. *See* insurance; reserve fund, case studies, 86–117
CEMEFI (Centro Mexicano para la Filantropia), 117, 130–133, 136
Center on Philanthropy at Indiana University, 23, 127, 137–139, 163
charity, 9, 36–37, 102, 139. *See also* giving, philanthropy, volunteering
chief executive officers (CEOs). *See* leaders
Chile, 15, 144–145, 154, 156, 165–166. *See also* cross-national: analysis of nonprofit sector
churches. *See* religion
civic participation. *See* civic engagement
civic engagement, 3–9, 61, 133–136
CIVICUS, 73, 167
civil society, 8, 13, 21–25, 98, 144, 159–162, 166, 168, 171. *See also* nonprofit sector

CNP. *See* Johns Hopkins Comparative Nonprofit Sector Project
collective action, 10–11, 33–42, 61–64, 72
collective goods, 9, 33–39
commercial income, 20, 27, 43, 46, 48, 50–51, 61, 85–86, 92, 98, 103, 106–107, 112, 114, 118–123, 127, 140, 145–149, 152–153, 157, 165
commercialization, 24, 33, 114, 148, 152
community development, 90, 92, 101, 104–106, 112
competition, 35, 51, 95, 106, 115, 121, 155, 157; religious, 8, 52, 75
complexity, 166
constituencies, multiple. *See* accountability; philanthropic friction
contract costs. *See* public–private partnership
cooperation, 26, 34, 37–38, 61, 74, 91
cost sharing. *See* leverage
costs: cutting, 33, 41, 48, 87, 89–92, 94, 98–101, 104–105, 107–108, 111, 146, 150, 154, 162; fixed vs. variable, 48, 99
crisis. *See* economic volatility; Great Depression; "Great Recession"; procyclicality; "Tequila Crisis"
cross-national: analysis of nonprofit sector, 53–73, 141–144; datasets, 27, 73–78; research, 3, 5, 9–16, 27, 56. *See also* philanthropic Kuznets curve
culture, 2, 4, 9, 37, 50, 74, 133; effects on nonprofit sector, 15; organizational, 91. *See also* Hofstede, Geert

decentralization/centralization of nonprofit organizations, 90, 105
demand heterogeneity, 12, 56, 75, 77
democracy, 3, 4, 18, 75, 77, 80, 85, 137, 166; democratization, 3, 8, 21, 25, 98, 144, 159–161, 163, 171; influence on the nonprofit sector, ix, 13, 52, 54, 56–57
demographics, 77
development: definition of, 27; indicator of, 74; empirical impact on the sector, 53–78; theoretical impact on the sector, 9–11;. *See also* middle-income countries
discounting, 19–20, 26, 29–30, 37–42, 46, 49–50, 65, 67, 74, 107, 118, 148, 150, 155, 157, 165

PHILANTHROPIC AND NONPROFIT STUDIES

Dwight F. Burlingame and David C. Hammack, editors

Thomas Adam. *Buying Respectability: Philanthropy and Urban Society in Transnational Perspective, 1840s to 1930s*

Thomas Adam, editor. *Philanthropy, Patronage, and Civil Society: Experiences from Germany, Great Britain, and North America*

Albert B. Anderson. *Ethics for Fundraisers*

Peter M. Ascoli. *Julius Rosenwald: The Man Who Built Sears, Roebuck and Advanced the Cause of Black Education in the American South*

Karen J. Blair. *The Torchbearers: Women and Their Amateur Arts Associations in America, 1890–1930*

Eleanor Brilliant. *Private Charity and Public Inquiry: A History of the Filer and Peterson Commissions*

Dwight F. Burlingame, editor. *The Responsibilities of Wealth*

Dwight F. Burlingame and Dennis Young, editors. *Corporate Philanthropy at the Crossroads*

Charles T. Clotfelter and Thomas Ehrlich, editors. *Philanthropy and the Nonprofit Sector in a Changing America*

Ruth Crocker. *Mrs. Russell Sage: Women's Activism and Philanthropy in Gilded Age and Progressive Era America*

Marcos Cueto, editor. *Missionaries of Science: The Rockefeller Foundation and Latin America*

William Damon and Susan Verducci, editors. *Taking Philanthropy Seriously: Beyond Noble Intentions to Responsible Giving*

Angela Eikenberry. *Giving Circles: Philanthropy, Voluntary Association, and Democracy*

Gregory Eiselein. *Literature and Humanitarian Reform in the Civil War Era*

Helen Gilbert and Chris Tiffin, editors. *Burden or Benefit?: Imperial Benevolence and Its Legacies*

Richard B. Gunderman. *We Make a Life by What We Give*

David C. Hammack, editor. *Making the Nonprofit Sector in the United States: A Reader*

David C. Hammack and Steven Heydemann, editors. *Globalization, Philanthropy, and Civil Society: Projecting Institutional Logics Abroad*

Jerome L. Himmelstein. *Looking Good and Doing Good: Corporate Philanthropy and Corporate Power*

Warren F. Ilchman, Stanley N. Katz, and Edward L. Queen II, editors. *Philanthropy in the World's Traditions*

Warren F. Ilchman, Alice Stone Ilchman, and Mary Hale Tolar, editors. *The Lucky Few and the Worthy Many: Scholarship Competitions and the World's Future Leaders*

Thomas H. Jeavons. *When the Bottom Line Is Faithfulness: Management of Christian Service Organizations*

Amy A. Kass, editor. *The Perfect Gift*

Amy A. Kass, editor. *Giving Well, Doing Good: Readings for Thoughtful Philanthropists*

Ellen Condliffe Lagemann, editor. *Philanthropic Foundations: New Scholarship, New Possibilities*

Daniel C. Levy. *To Export Progress: The Golden Age of University Assistance in the Americas*

Mike W. Martin. *Virtuous Giving: Philanthropy, Voluntary Service, and Caring*

Kathleen D. McCarthy, editor. *Women, Philanthropy, and Civil Society*

Marc A. Musick and John Wilson, editors. *Volunteers: A Social Profile*

Mary J. Oates. *The Catholic Philanthropic Tradition in America*

Robert S. Ogilvie. *Voluntarism, Community Life, and the American Ethic*

Robert L. Payton and Michael P. Moody. *Understanding Philanthropy: Its Meaning and Mission*

Alfred Perkins. *Edwin Rogers Embree: The Julius Rosenwald Fund, Foundation Philanthropy, and American Race Relations*

Brent Ruswick. *Almost Worthy: The Poor, Paupers, and the Science of Charity in America, 1877–1917*

Paul G. Schervish and Keith Whitaker. *Wealth and the Will of God: Discerning the Use of Riches in the Service of Ultimate Purpose*

J. B. Schneewind, editor. *Giving: Western Ideas of Philanthropy*

William H. Schneider, editor. *Rockefeller Philanthropy and Modern Biomedicine: International Initiatives from World War I to the Cold War*

Bradford Smith, Sylvia Shue, Jennifer Lisa Vest, and Joseph Villarreal. *Philanthropy in Communities of Color*

NUNO S. THEMUDO is Associate Professor at the Graduate School of Public and International Affairs, University of Pittsburgh. His research focuses on public administration, civil society and international development. Before joining the University of Pittsburgh, he taught at the London School of Economics and was visiting professor at El Colegio Mexiquense, Mexico.